16

ISLAMIC
EXCEPTIONALISM

ALSO BY SHADI HAMID

Temptations of Power

ISLAMIC EXCEPTIONALISM

HOW THE STRUGGLE OVER ISLAM IS RESHAPING THE WORLD

SHADI HAMID

St. Martin's Press
New York

www.stmartins.com

Designed by Michelle McMillian

Library of Congress Cataloging-in-Publication Data

Names: Hamid, Shadi, 1983–
Title: Islamic exceptionalism : how the struggle over Islam is reshaping the world / Shadi Hamid.
Description: New York, NY : St. Martin's Press, 2016.
Identifiers: LCCN 2015049286 | ISBN 978-1-250-06101-0 (hardback) | ISBN 978-1-4668-6672-0 (e-book)
Subjects: LCSH: Islam and politics. | Middle East—Politics and government— 20th century. | Middle East—Politics and government—21st century. | Arab countries—Politics and government—20th century. | Arab countries—Politics and government—21st century. | BISAC: SOCIAL SCIENCE / Islamic Studies.
Classification: LCC BP173.7 .H3554 2016 | DDC 320.55/7—dc23
LC record available at http://lccn.loc.gov/2015049286

Our books may be purchased in bulk for promotional, educational, or business use. Please contact your local bookseller or the Macmillan Corporate and Premium Sales Department at 1-800-221-7945, extension 5442, or by e-mail at MacmillanSpecialMarkets@macmillan.com.

First Edition: June 2016

10 9 8 7 6 5 4 3 2 1

CONTENTS

299

trying to make sense of a complex region—question our own assumptions as well, and God knows that we come with quite a few.

It is bittersweet to be writing this now, just a few months before publication. I'm almost afraid of letting it go. I am also deeply grateful. So many people believed in this project, however provocative and unwieldy it may have first seemed. The Brookings Institution provided the ideal environment to read, research, to question myself, and to think about what I really wanted to do with this book. I have never been a part of an institution like Brookings that puts such a premium on ideas and letting them guide us, rather than the other way around. I was fortunate enough to have the constant support and encouragement of my colleagues. Many thanks are owed to Martin Indyk, Bruce Jones, and Tamara Wittes for nurturing such a supportive environment for the kind of serious, in-depth research that requires disappearing (or traveling in the Middle East) for significant stretches of time.

Michael O'Hanlon, Andrew Exum, Will McCants, Chris Meserole, Jennifer Williams, and Ken Pollack generously reviewed the full manuscript and offered extremely helpful suggestions, challenging me to further refine my ideas. Entire sections were rethought and rewritten due to Ken's characteristically wise, thoughtful, and sharp comments. I thank Ken for pushing and challenging me during every step of the process, but most of all for believing in me.

In addition, Mara Revkin, who has quickly become one of the leading experts on ISIS governance; the young, rising Christian theologian Joshua Ralston; the great Princeton historian Michael Cook; and my friend and colleague Will McCants were all major influences. I can't thank them enough, even if they didn't realize what an important part of this book they ended up becoming. I am grateful to Norm Eisen for reviewing sections of the manuscript and being a ready and enthusiastic sparring partner on questions of religion and the power it holds

CONTENTS

299

ACKNOWLEDGMENTS

I have been living with this book for longer than I know. It is, in some ways, a very personal book. I have been changed by the events that I try my best to document in these pages.

I was moved. I was sad. I was hopeful. Sometimes, I read the newspaper (or my Twitter feed) and wanted to disappear, away from all of it. I joked with friends that I now had a darker view of human nature. Except it probably wasn't a joke. The Middle East has a way of changing you.

That's part of what makes my work both so exciting and so disorienting. One of the most thrilling things as a researcher is to start a project not knowing where it will end and to be changed in the process. In this respect, writing this book was a fascinating experience of absorbing and learning and opening myself up to the possibilities of seeing things—whether Islam, Islamic law, democracy, or the "state"—in new ways. Many of those who call the Middle East home are "rethinking" their assumptions, so it's only natural that we—as outside researchers trying to make sense of a complex region—question our own assumptions as well, and God knows that we come with quite a few.

It is bittersweet to be writing this now, just a few months before publication. I'm almost afraid of letting it go. I am also deeply grateful. So many people believed in this project, however provocative and unwieldy it may have first seemed. The Brookings Institution provided the ideal environment to read, research, to question myself, and to think about what I really wanted to do with this book. I have never been a part of an institution like Brookings that puts such a premium on ideas and letting them guide us, rather than the other way around. I was fortunate enough to have the constant support and encouragement of my colleagues. Many thanks are owed to Martin Indyk, Bruce Jones, and Tamara Wittes for nurturing such a supportive environment for the kind of serious, in-depth research that requires disappearing (or traveling in the Middle East) for significant stretches of time.

Michael O'Hanlon, Andrew Exum, Will McCants, Chris Meserole, Jennifer Williams, and Ken Pollack generously reviewed the full manuscript and offered extremely helpful suggestions, challenging me to further refine my ideas. Entire sections were rethought and rewritten due to Ken's characteristically wise, thoughtful, and sharp comments. I thank Ken for pushing and challenging me during every step of the process, but most of all for believing in me.

In addition, Mara Revkin, who has quickly become one of the leading experts on ISIS governance; the young, rising Christian theologian Joshua Ralston; the great Princeton historian Michael Cook; and my friend and colleague Will McCants were all major influences. I can't thank them enough, even if they didn't realize what an important part of this book they ended up becoming. I am grateful to Norm Eisen for reviewing sections of the manuscript and being a ready and enthusiastic sparring partner on questions of religion and the power it holds over adherents in various faith traditions. Natan Sachs was kind enough to read the second chapter and helped guide me through questions of "fundamentalism"—or the lack thereof—within both Jewish religious practice and modern Israeli politics. I also thank my colleagues Suzanne Maloney, Natan Sachs, Khaled Elgindy, Kemal Kirisci, Dan Byman, and Rob Keane for offering their thoughtful comments and suggestions at various stages of the project.

I hope my research assistants didn't get sick of me, because they certainly put up with a lot. I wish I had more space to thank them not once, but many, many times. The idea for this book existed in my head, as early as the summer of 2013, long before I started writing. I thank Andrew Leber and Meredith Wheeler, who helped me refine the original book proposal when I was still at the Brookings Doha Center. Their enthusiasm played no small part in encouraging me to move ahead with the project. Here in Washington, D.C., Sarah Collins helped tremendously with the book's first chapter and conclusion, tracking down piles of books and becoming, in short order, an expert on consociational democracy and power-sharing arrangements. Meanwhile, Kristine Anderson worked tirelessly to read early drafts of the first several chapters. She immersed herself in the intricacies of Islamist movements and, perhaps most important, told me when she thought I was wrong. Elizabeth Parker-Magyar provided additional research assistance in those scary, last few months before I submitted the first draft of the manuscript. I'm happy to have had the opportunity to work with her. Sloane Speakman read and reviewed the entire manuscript probably several times (I'm not sure I want to know *exactly* how many times). I remember telling her just a few days before a major deadline that I wouldn't have been able to do this without her. And I wouldn't have. Lastly, I thank Rashid Dar for taking a final look at the manuscript and helping me have everything in order for submission.

Acknowledgments

There are so many people in Egypt, Tunisia, and Turkey who were generous with their time and attention that I cannot begin to list them all. Without them, I probably would have been quite lost. Special thanks are owed to Mustafa Akyol, Abdelrahman Ayyash, Sayida Ounissi, Kadir Ustun, Joost Lagendijk, Mehmet Bayraktar, Sarah Feuer, Jihed Mabrouk, and Monica Marks. I would also like to thank the friends, scholars, and teachers who have, in so many different ways, influenced my research and writing, including Michael Willis, Laurence Whitehead, Michael McFaul, Stephen McInerney, Avi Spiegel, Steven Brooke, Stephane Lacroix, Courtney Freer, Charles Lister, Jacob Olidort, Peter Mandaville, Andrew March, Emad Shahin, John Voll, Mohamed Okda, Khalil al-Anani, Omar Ashour, Seth Anziska, Marc Grinberg, Thomas Carothers, and Eugene Rogan.

And, now, words are never enough for this part of it, but I will try. My parents found it somewhat confusing that I was working on another book. They would have preferred I take a break, because, well, writing can be stressful. I suppose it's a bit of a cliché, but it really does make a difference when your parents have your back. They've believed in me from the very first moment when it seemed like I might not become an engineer or a doctor and instead devote my life to studying, of all things, Islamist movements. I love them dearly and I really hope they like the book, after everything. My brother, Sherif, has been one of my biggest supporters, especially now that we're back to living not too far apart from each other. He seemingly reads everything I write and has probably attended more of my talks than anyone else in the world. More important, he's always there for me, and I know I can give him a call whenever I want to get his thoughts on anything, whether it's about the Middle East or not.

Portions of Chapter 7 draw on materials previously published as "Radicalization after the Arab Spring: Lessons from

Tunisia and Egypt," in *Blind Spot: America's Response to Radicalism in the Middle East,* edited by Nicholas Burns and Jonathon Price. I thank them, as well as Brent Scrowcroft and Joseph Nye, for the opportunity to present my ideas in early form at the Aspen Strategy Group.

This book would never have happened without my wonderful agent, Bridget Matzie, who was a font of guidance and good advice from the very beginning. George Witte, my editor at St. Martin's Press, was incredibly patient and supportive every step of the way. I thank him for believing in this project. Thanks are also due to Sara Thwaite and the rest of the team at St. Martin's Press who helped move the book through production. They, and so many others, made this process as painless as I possibly could have hoped.

(1)

TO TAKE JOY
IN A MASSACRE

Something went wrong, but what was it? I was standing in Tahrir Square on February 11, 2011. Around me, hundreds of thousands of Egyptians filled the streets of downtown Cairo. On this, the eighteenth night of the revolution, the crowd buzzed with the news that President Hosni Mubarak was stepping down after nearly thirty years of autocratic rule. The murmurs erupted into deafening cheers. This, whatever *this* was, was what they were waiting for. One of the revolution's young activists, a Muslim Brotherhood blogger named Abdelrahman Ayyash, sent me a simple text message: "We did it." But the euphoria was short-lived; the intervening four years featured a military coup, a succession of mass killings, and the return of dictatorship. Today, Abdelrahman, like so many others, bides his time in exile, longing for an Egypt that may never come back.

If this new phase of the "Arab Spring" was really about anything, it was about a collective loss of faith in politics. I remember how, before the uprisings began in 2011, Egyptians would take pride in the fact that they, unlike some of their neighbors, had little history of political violence. The July 3, 2013 military coup that ousted the country's first democratically elected president would irrevocably change that. The most populous Arab country, long a bellwether for the region, had willfully aborted its democratic process, however flawed it may have been. A military coup, though, is one thing; a massacre is another.

In the weeks that followed the overthrow of President Mohamed Morsi, a longtime Muslim Brotherhood figure, tens of thousands of his supporters gathered by Cairo's Rabaa al-Adawiya mosque in a massive sit-in. The Egyptian military announced that it was ready to use force. The country was on edge. No one quite knew when the army would make its move. There were false alarms nearly daily, sometimes hourly.

It is an odd thing to wait for a massacre. As American and European diplomats scurried in a last-ditch effort to persuade the Egyptians to back down, I spent some time in Rabaa, meeting with Brotherhood activists and leaders. One of those leaders was Essam el-Erian, then the vice chairman of the Freedom and Justice Party, the Brotherhood's political arm. As we sat down in early August, the last of our many meetings spanning nearly a decade, he refused to give any ground. Peppering his Arabic with English for emphasis, he insisted that Brotherhood members were prepared for the ultimate sacrifice. Another Brotherhood official, Gehad El-Haddad, who had given up a successful business career in England to return to Egypt after the revolution, recounted the story of a friend who had just been gunned down by security forces. In his final moments, the young man could barely speak, but he managed to utter the Islamic profession of faith: *There is no god but God and Mohamed is his messenger.* "Don't let my blood go to waste," the man told those gathered around him. They, too, were ready to die, and many of them did. Just days later, on August 14, 2013, over eight hundred Egyptians perished as security forces made good on their threat. Foot soldiers, bulldozers, and armored personnel carriers moved in at dawn with teargas, pellet guns, and live ammunition, forcibly clearing the encampment in what Human Rights Watch called "the worst mass killing in [Egypt's] modern history."[1]

Less than three years earlier, Egypt had shown the world what was possible. Tunisia, the birthplace of the Arab uprisings, was a strategically and geographically remote nation of ten million. It was blessed with higher levels of economic growth and educational attainment than most other Arab countries. If the uprisings had begun and ended there, then the possibility of peaceful protest and regime change could have easily been dismissed. Egypt changed the calculus, trumping the narrative that Tunisia was the region's exception. Buoyed by Mubarak's fall, mass protests soon spread to two other countries, Syria and Libya, which were seen as unlikely candidates for political upheaval. On August 14, 2013, Egypt was once again leading the way, but this time Egyptians—turning against one another—showed us something much darker but just as real.

THERE WAS A TIME when only a few Americans had heard of the Islamic State of Iraq and Syria, or ISIS, soon to be rechristened as simply the Islamic State. That changed in the summer of 2014, first with the fall of Iraq's second largest city of Mosul—when a first wave of around a thousand fighters overtook an Iraqi force that was some thirty thousand strong. The horrifying beheadings of American journalists and the November 2015 killings of 130 civilians in Paris—the worst such attack in France since World War II—anchored the Islamic State's reputation for ostentatious acts of savagery. Seemingly overnight, the Sunni extremist group had emerged as a terrifying new enemy.

It was easy to condemn the Islamic State as evil, because it was. The indifference to death and the eagerness to kill permeated so much of what the group did. But what made the post–Arab Spring era so disturbing was that a more banal kind of evil seemed to be just about everywhere: The evil of otherwise good people turning against one another, sometimes not only accepting bloodshed as the inevitable price of conflict but also embracing it and even taking pleasure in it.

This is the story of a region's descent into madness. There is a temptation to see it as inexplicable, to look the other way as Arabs and Muslims fight and kill each other. Some of it, though, can be explained. Or at least we have to try. The impulse to understand what might appear beyond comprehension is a vital one, especially now. "The peculiar necessity of imagining what is, in fact, real" is how the journalist Philip Gourevitch memorably put it.[2]

This book—based on over a decade of research, including more than six years living, traveling, and studying in the Middle East—is an attempt to make sense not just of sad, terrifying events but of the power of ideas and their role in the existential battles that have shaken the foundations of the Middle Eastern order.

Over the course of this book, I will return to a number of recurring themes and questions which I have made my best effort to grapple with. For instance, when trying to understand the wars of the Middle East, the rise of the Islamic State, and cultural divides over something as seemingly trivial as cartoons of the Prophet Mohamed, how much does Islam really matter? Is it about "religion" or "politics"? And can we even separate the two, when they have become so intertwined in the minds, and hearts, of believers?

TO UNDERSTAND TODAY'S SEEMINGLY INTRACTABLE conflicts, we need to go back to at least 1924, the year the last caliphate was formally abolished. Animating the caliphate—the historical political entity governed by Islamic law and tradition—was the idea that the "spiritual unity of the Muslim community requires political expression."[3] Since the caliphate's dissolution, the struggle to establish a legitimate political order has raged on, with varying levels of intensity. At the center of the struggle is the problem of religion and its role in politics. In this sense, the turmoil of the Arab Spring and its aftermath is the latest iteration of the inability to resolve the most basic questions over what it means to be a citizen and what it means to be a state.

The year 1924 might seem like ancient history, but I'll have to go back even further—to the founding of Islam in the seventh century. Two related arguments form the core of the first half of this book. The first is that Islam is, in fact, distinctive in how it relates to politics. Islam is *different*. This difference has profound implications for the future of the Middle East and, by extension, for the world in which we all live. This admittedly is a controversial, even troubling claim, especially in the context of rising anti-Muslim sentiment in the United States and Europe. "Islamic exceptionalism," however, is neither good nor bad. It just is, and we need to understand it and respect it, even if it runs counter to our own hopes and preferences.

Second, because the relationship between Islam and politics is distinctive, a replay of the Western model—Protestant Reformation followed by an enlightenment in which religion is gradually pushed into the private realm—is unlikely. That Islam—a completely different religion with a completely different founding and evolution—should follow a similar course as Christianity is itself an odd presumption. We aren't all the same, but, more important, why should we be?

If Muslims, and particularly Islamists, take scripture more "seriously" than their Christian counterparts, then how does this manifest itself in everyday politics? When observers discuss the root causes of Middle East conflict, they often speak of a crisis of governance or legitimacy, or both. But if we go down the causal chain, the question remains unanswered: *Why* exactly does the Middle East suffer from a lack of legitimate order? This legitimacy defeat, I argue, is tied to a continued inability to reckon with Islam's relationship to the state.

This is not for a lack of trying. The second half of this book is about the different, contrasting models of how to resolve the dilemma of the once and future Islamic state. I have chosen the word "exceptionalism" in part to avoid casting judgment. Exceptionalism, as I see it, has no intrinsic value in and of itself. It depends on how the problem of Islam and the state actually plays out in practice. In searching for solutions, *mainstream* Islamist movements, adopting a wide variety of approaches and strategies, may have seemed promising, but they all, in their own ways, fell short.

Mainstream Islamists are defined here as the affiliates or descendants of the Muslim Brotherhood, the mother of all Islamist movements, founded in Egypt in 1928 by a schoolteacher named Hassan al-Banna. They hoped to blend the premodern with the modern and East with West. In this sense, contrary to popular imagination, Islamists do not necessarily harken back to seventh-century Arabia. As we will see, they are distinctly modern, perhaps *too* modern. Their distinguishing features are their gradualism (historically eschewing revolution), embrace of parliamentary politics, and willingness to work within existing state structures, even secular ones. Islamist movements are those that believe Islam or Islamic law should play a central role in political life and explicitly organize around those goals in the public arena. Though they now find themselves eclipsed by radicals, the most politically influential Islamist groups have generally been of the mainstream and nonviolent variety, so it's worth focusing considerable attention on them, even if they may not be the ones who, today, attract the most headlines.

I first consider the foundational Brotherhood model, relevant to dozens of countries throughout the world that have their own Muslim Brotherhood–inspired organizations. I then focus on the more localized approaches of Islamists in secularized contexts, namely those in Turkey and Tunisia who have had to contend with decades of forced secularization. These two countries have been touted as models of reconciling Islam and democracy. Interestingly, despite their secularized contexts, they are also two of the only Middle Eastern countries where Islamist parties have come to power. For a variety of reasons, however, these "mild," more secular-friendly Islamists have failed to advance a successful Islamic synthesis. They have even, at times, exacerbated the very tensions they hoped to address. I will consider these fascinating cases in detail, focusing attention on some of the most interesting and important figures shaping internal debates over Islam and politics.

The Arab Spring's failure to produce a legitimate, stable political order opened up space for more radical approaches, forged in violence and absolutism. The "countermodel" of the Islamic State, or ISIS, is the focus of chapter 7. The extremist group's rapid rise in the summer of 2014 may have caught observers off guard, but that something like the Islamic State could thrive in this century, as history's arc was supposedly bending toward justice, was surprisingly appropriate. There had never been a serious, sustained attempt to reestablish the caliphate since its demise in 1924. Now the Islamic State—with its far-flung operational branches, or "provinces"—could claim to have been the first. Not only that, the Islamic State was one of the most successful examples of recognizably Islamist governance in recent decades (even if the bar here was relatively low). The Islamic State took governance and institution building relatively seriously and was better at it than one might expect. Rather than terrorism, this was perhaps the defining characteristic of the group, making it a worthier—and more dangerous—foe. Its governance model might have been horrifying in any number of ways, but it was a distinctive model nonetheless. The Islamic State, in stark contrast to the Brotherhood and other mainstream Islamist movements, had little interest in the Middle East's existing state structures.

For Islamic State partisans, the last caliphate was the Ottoman caliphate, but the last *model* caliphate was that of the Prophet Mohamed's four righteously guided companions, each of whom would briefly reign as caliph of an ever-expanding empire (three of the four were assassinated). That, however, didn't keep the Islamic State from viewing the breakup of the Ottoman caliphate and its portioning off into artificial, arbitrary states as the modern era's original sin. To the extent that modern states depended on some secular notion of citizenship and on parliaments that legislated law other than God's, they were anathema to the Islamic State's totalizing view of God's sovereignty. God, and no one else, was the sole lawgiver. Where the Brotherhood and its compatriots in countries as diverse as Turkey, Tunisia, and Jordan sought to reconcile premodern Islamic law with modern notions of pluralism and democracy, the Islamic State ostentatiously basked in its rejection of them, with results that could be both terrifying and effective. Sometimes they were effective *because* they were terrifying.

Amid all the brutality and chaos, Muslims and non-Muslims alike are trying to understand the role that Islam plays—and the role that it should play. In discussing models and countermodels of Islam in the democratic process, I hope to offer a framework for thinking about Islam and Islamism and their relationship to politics and, perhaps most controversially, the modern nation-state.

If Islam is likely to play an outsized role in Middle East politics for the foreseeable future—and it is my contention that it will—then this has significant implications. It means that, instead of hoping for a reformation that will likely never come, we have to address Islamic exceptionalism and, to the extent we are able and willing, come to terms with it. This is no easy task. As Mark Lilla writes, "Though we have our own fundamentalists, we find it incomprehensible that theological ideas still stir up messianic passions, leaving societies in ruin. We had assumed this was no longer possible."[4] It is more than possible.

The language that Islam has used throughout its history to relate to and give meaning to politics—and the language that hundreds of millions still hold to—may, at first, sound foreign, but that only means that outsiders must make an extra effort to understand it. And that, in some ways, is the most challenging, and ultimately rewarding, aspect of my work: to be exposed to something fundamentally *different*.

Religion Matters

Political scientists, myself included, have tended to see religion, ideology, and identity as "epiphenomenal"—products of a given set of material factors. These factors are the things we can touch, grasp, and measure. For example, when explaining the motivations of suicide bombers, we assume that these young men (and sometimes women) are depressed about their accumulated failures, frustrated with a dire economic situation, or humiliated by domestic repression and foreign occupation. While these are all undoubtedly factors, they are not—and cannot be—the whole story.

In a September 2014 statement, the Islamic State's spokesman Abu Mohamed al-Adnani expounded on the group's inherent advantages: "Being killed . . . is a victory," he said. "You fight a people who can never be defeated. They either gain victory or are killed."[5] In this sense, religion matters, and it matters a great deal. As individuals, most (although not necessarily all) Islamic State fighters on the front line are not only willing to die in a blaze of religious ecstasy, they welcome it. It doesn't particularly matter if this sounds absurd to us. It's what *they* believe. But this basic point about intention and motivation applies not only to extremist groups but also to mainstream Islamist movements like the Muslim Brotherhood that, in stark contrast to the Islamic State, contest elections and work within the democratic process. As one Brotherhood official would often remind me, many join the movement so they can "get into heaven." Discussing his own reasons for joining, he told me, "I was far from religion and this was unsettling. Islamists resolved it for me."[6]

We might be tempted to dismiss such pronouncements as irrational bouts of fancy. But, if you look at it another way, what could be more rational than wanting eternal salvation?

It would be a mistake, then, to view Islamist groups as traditional political parties. Muslim Brotherhood branches and affiliates are acting both for this world and for the next. They aim to strengthen the religious character of individuals through a multitiered membership system and an extensive educational process with a structured curriculum. Each brother is part of a "family," usually consisting of five to ten members, which meets on a weekly basis to read and discuss religious texts. For many members, it is simple and straightforward. Being a part of the Brotherhood helps them obey God and become better Muslims, which, in turn, increases their likelihood of entry into paradise. More spiritually focused members still care about politics, but they may see political action—whether running for a municipal council seat or joining a mass protest—as just another way of serving God and seeking his pleasure.

The tendency to see religion through the prism of politics or economics (rather than the other way around) isn't necessarily incorrect, but it can sometimes obscure the independent power of ideas that seem, to much of the Western world, quaint and archaic. For those who no longer experience the power and relevance of religion in everyday life, it can be difficult to understand why people do seemingly irrational things in the service of seemingly irrational ends. The forces of reason and rationality, if they hadn't already prevailed, were, after all, supposed to prevail *eventually*. As Robert Kagan writes, "For a quarter-century, Americans have been told that at the end of history lies boredom rather than great conflict."[7] Francis Fukuyama, the very scholar who first proclaimed the "end of history" in 1989, seemed almost wistful by that famous essay's final paragraph. "I have the most ambivalent feelings for the civilization that has been created in Europe since 1945," he wrote. "Perhaps this very prospect of centuries of boredom at the end of history will serve to get history started once again."[8] The increasingly apparent influence of religion on politics suggests that Fukuyama was more prescient than his critics give him credit for.

The dramatic rise of the Islamic State is only the most striking example of how liberal determinism—the notion that history moves with intent toward a more reasonable, secular future—has failed to explain Middle East realities. Of course, the overwhelming majority of Muslims do not share the Islamic State's interpretation of religion, but that's not the most interesting or relevant question. The Islamic State, after all, draws on, and draws strength from, ideas that have a broad resonance among Muslim-majority populations. They may not agree with the group's interpretation of the caliphate, but the notion of *a* caliphate is a powerful one, even among more secular-minded Muslims. One of the few surveys on attitudes toward a caliphate found that an average of 65 percent of respondents in Egypt, Morocco, Pakistan, and Indonesia agreed with the objective of "unify[ing] all Islamic countries into a single Islamic state or caliphate."[9] This transcended ideology, with even a majority of nationalists saying they supported the idea of a caliphate.[10]

Even in 2015, well after the Islamic State's murderous methods became impossible to deny, the anthropologist Scott Atran and a team of researchers found qualified support for what the extremist group had managed to do even among those who otherwise detested it. Atran cites a Barcelona imam involved in interfaith work with Jews and Christians. "I am against the violence of al-Qaeda and ISIS, but they have put our predicament in Europe and elsewhere on the map," the imam says. "And the Caliphate . . . We dream of it like the Jews long dreamed of Zion. Maybe it can be a federation, like the European Union, of Muslim peoples. The Caliphate is here, in our hearts, even if we don't know what real form it will finally take."[11]

The caliphate—dissolved unceremoniously only last century—is a reminder of how one of the world's great civilizations endured one of the most precipitous declines in human history. The gap between what Muslims once were and where they now find themselves is at the center of the anger and humiliation driving political violence across the Middle East. There is a sense of loss and longing for an organic legal and political order that flourished for centuries before its slow but decisive dismantling. Since then, Muslims, and particularly Arab Muslims, have been struggling to define the contours of the post-caliphate order. The Islamic State is only the latest but perhaps the most frightening manifestation of this ongoing struggle.

Because of the role that religion has played in the Middle East, trying to draw parallels with other regions has its limitations. For instance, some try to compare the role of Islam in the Arab world today to the role Christianity played in medieval Europe. But here the differences, drawn out over centuries, make themselves apparent. As the historian of religions Michael Cook notes in his groundbreaking book *Ancient Religions, Modern Politics*, the early Christian community "lacked a conception of an intrinsically Christian state" and was willing to coexist with and recognize Roman law.[12] For this reason, among others, the equivalent of the Islamic State simply couldn't exist in Christian-majority societies. Neither would the pragmatic, mainstream Islamist movements that *oppose* the Islamic State and its idiosyncratic, totalitarian take on the Islamic polity. While it has little in common with Islamist extremists, in either means or ends, the Muslim Brotherhood does have a particular vision for society that puts Islam and Islamic law at the center of public life. The vast majority of Christians in the West—including committed conservatives—cannot conceive of a comprehensive legal order anchored in religion. However, the vast majority of Egyptians and Jordanians, for example, can and do. This is not to say that most Arabs or Muslims are Islamists. Most are not. However, one can sympathize with or support Islamist policies without being an Islamist—the phenomenon of *Islamism without Islamists*.

This is why the well-intentioned discourse of "they bleed just like us; they want to eat sandwiches and raise their children just like we do" is a red herring.* After all, one can like sandwiches and want peace, or whatever else, while also supporting the death penalty for apostasy, as 88 percent of Egyptian Muslims and 83 percent of Jordanian Muslims did in a 2011 Pew poll.[13] In the same survey, 80 percent of Egyptian respondents said they favored stoning adulterers, while 70 percent supported cutting off the hands of thieves. Polling is an inexact science, particularly in the Arab world. But even if we assume that these results significantly overstate support for religiously derived criminal punishments—let's say support was closer to 65 or even 45 percent instead—that number would still probably give us pause.

It is worth noting that the Brotherhood and other mainstream Islamist movements in the Arab world no longer include the so-called *hudud* punishments for theft, adultery, and apostasy in their political platforms and rarely discuss them in public. In this respect, the median Egyptian or Jordanian voter is to the right of the main Islamist parties in their respective countries. (Many Muslims say they believe in the *hudud* because the punishments are in the Quran or in the sayings of the Prophet, known as *hadith*; whether they would actually be comfortable with the state—a state they may not like much—cutting off someone's hand for stealing is a rather different question. It's also easy to forget that the application of these punishments

---

*In a debate with television host Bill Maher and author Sam Harris, actor Ben Affleck, referring to the vast majority of Muslims, asked: "How about more than a billion people who are not fanatical, who don't punish women, who just want to go to school, have some sandwiches . . . It's stereotyping." See *Real Time with Bill Maher*, October 6, 2014, https://www.youtube.com/watch?v=vln9D81eO60.

was historically rare, requiring numerous preconditions and often prohibitively high evidentiary standards to be met. The primary purpose of the *hudud* was to deter rather than to punish.[14])

These are only, in any case, the most extreme examples, and it would be problematic to take the *hudud* as somehow emblematic of the sharia, or Islamic law. The sharia has much to say beyond punishments. How, then, do Arabs view the relevance of sharia, including on such issues as gender equality, minority rights, and the role of clerics in drafting national legislation? Why, for example, do only 24 percent of Egyptian women, according to an April 2011 YouGov poll, say they would support a female president?[15] What some might call "culture," and not necessarily Islam, is a major factor, but it would be difficult to pretend that religion has nothing to do with these attitudes. And, presumably, Islam has at least something to do with why 51 percent of Jordanians, according to the 2010 Arab Barometer, say that "a parliamentary system that allows for free competition, but only between Islamic parties" is somewhat appropriate, appropriate, or very appropriate.[16]

It has become unfashionable to suggest that Islam is in any way unique, and understandably so. This slippery slope of overgeneralization can all too easily lead to the demonization of more than 1.6 billion Muslims. At the same time, the fear of being tarred with the brush of cultural essentialism prevents us from fully appreciating the role that religion plays in the politics of the Middle East. We need to take ideas seriously, especially when they're not our own. It is time to "bring religion back," but with care and caution, taking into account the historical richness and diversity that have long been a staple of the Islamic tradition.

Foundational Divides

It is difficult to imagine anyone today writing what the British scholar Elie Kedouri wrote in 1992:

To hold simultaneously ideas which are not easily reconcilable argues, then, a deep confusion in the Arab public mind, at least about the meaning of democracy. The confusion is, however, understandable since the idea of democracy is quite alien to the mindset of Islam.[17]

A new kind of universalism took the place of Kedouri's mindset in the early 2000s, drawing from the energy and promise of the first (and forgotten) Arab spring. That Arab spring was buoyed by President George W. Bush and the neoconservatives' "freedom agenda," which affirmed that democracy was for all peoples and for all times.

In the tense buildup to the 2011 uprisings, an endless barrage of books and articles argued that Arabs were "just like us." Such sentiments, however well-intentioned, suggested their own kind of exceptionalism, that others would come to follow the path the West had apparently settled on decades or even centuries prior. Poll after poll showed that more Egyptians, Jordanians, and Moroccans believed democracy was the best form of government than did Americans or, say, Poles. But "democracy," in the abstract, could mean just about anything, as long it was positive. It is one thing to believe in democracy and another to practice it.

As it turns out, we were spoiled by democratic transitions in Eastern Europe and Latin America. It was easy to think back to "roundtable talks" of enlightened leaders and dissident playwrights becoming presidents. Why should the Middle East be any different? A whirlwind eighteen days of protest pushed Mubarak out of power and showed, or at least seemed to show, that the Arab world could follow a similar path. Here, after all, were young, tech-savvy activists, speaking fluent English and saying all the right things. President Barack Obama captured the feelings of millions of Americans who watched in rapt attention. "What I want is for the kids on the street to win and for the Google guy to become president," Obama told his aides, referring to Wael Ghonim, a Google executive and one of the young, charismatic faces of the Egyptian revolution.[18]

The things that didn't fit the Western-friendly narrative garnered less attention. The Muslim Brotherhood, with its committed following and organizational discipline, played a pivotal role in Tahrir Square, providing food and medical services and protecting protesters from regime thugs. Fearing a backlash, the Brotherhood played it carefully, downplaying their participation in the court of public opinion and prohibiting their members from raising the banner of sharia. Meanwhile, in the final days of the uprising, the number of ultraconservative Salafis—with their distinctive full beards—surged. In a remarkably diverse movement, liberals, socialists, Muslim Brotherhood members, Salafis, and even hardcore soccer fans were drawn together by what they opposed. But if this was the opposition's most impressive moment of unity, it would also prove to be one of its last. This wasn't the end of ideology but the beginning of a protracted cold—and sometimes hot—war, with questions of religion and identity at its center.

More than five decades of dictatorship had kept the lid on the most vexing questions facing Egypt. That was sort of the point, after all. The region's autocrats were fond of reminding America that despite their brutality—or perhaps because of it—they were the ones keeping the peace and ensuring stability. As Mubarak said in a televised address just ten days before he was ousted, "The events of the last few days require us all as a people and as a leadership to choose between chaos and stability."[19] In a sense, he and his fellow autocrats were right—there was, indeed, a trade-off. These were brittle states, divided by religion, sect, or clan. With little warning, the 2011 uprisings pushed these tensions and conflicts, always simmering in the background, to the fore. Arab strongmen had governed unwieldy countries with arbitrary borders and uncertain identities. What they promised was stability at the expense of liberty. Now, without an iron fist holding them together, they were falling apart.

• • •

BRITTLE STATES AND DEEPLY divided societies aren't necessarily unique to the Middle East. There had to be something else. How, after all, could those who claimed to support democracy so quickly turn against it? How could so-called liberals embrace not just a military coup but the mass killings that followed as well? This part of it made less sense. Of course, "liberals" have backed the overthrow of democratically elected leaders in Latin America, Asia, and elsewhere. But, even in the most polarized contexts, liberals have been divided. In Chile, for example, many backed the 1973 coup against socialist president Salvador Allende, but many didn't. Even those who initially backed the army's move, such as the Christian Democrats, quickly grasped the gravity of their error and recanted, joining the ranks of the opposition against the dictatorship of General Augusto Pinochet. Yet in Egypt, the near unanimity of liberal enthusiasm for the military's intervention was remarkable, as is the fact that so few, even at the time of writing, have admitted fault with their original decision to back the coup. Egypt, in this respect, was exceptional.

When observers imply that Arabs or Muslims are prone to violence, they're usually thinking of groups like the Islamic State or al-Qaeda. But the preponderance of Arab violence has come at the hands of ostensibly secular regimes that claim to be reacting *against* Islamist movements. This, though, does not absolve religion or ideology. To be sure, secular autocrats are guarding privilege and power, but the liberal elites upon whose support they depend are well aware that there is more at stake. It is only in such a context that the near unanimous embrace of the overthrow of a democratically elected president—one who was unabashedly Islamist—begins to make sense. The anti-Islamists who lined up behind the military in Egypt and those in Tunisia who threatened to dissolve the democratically elected government and constituent assembly had decided that some things took precedence over any presumed commitment to democracy. They feared that Islamist rule, however "democratic" it might be, would alter the very nature of their countries beyond recognition. And it wouldn't just affect their governments or their laws—though that would be bad enough—but also how they lived, what they wore, how they raised their sons and daughters, maybe even what they could and couldn't drink. This was *personal*.

Islamists Are Islamists for a Reason

When I would talk to friends and colleagues in the region about the importance of respecting democratic outcomes even if you disagreed with them, there was a gap. As a Tunisian journalist once told me, "This is something you study; this is something we live." They were the ones who had to live with the consequences of elections. They were the ones who were protagonists in a raw, existential struggle over the very meaning, nature, and purpose of the modern nation-state. In conservative societies such as Egypt, even liberals believe (or feel compelled to say they believe) that Islam has a role to play in public life. But what kind of role and to what end? This is where the various sides diverged considerably.

In those early days of the Arab Spring, the endless, obsessive public debate over identity and religion struck some as odd. Why did anyone have to tell Egyptians, Tunisians, or Libyans what they already knew—that they were, and always had been, Muslim? The battle over religion and state might have seemed removed from the more prosaic concerns and needs of ordinary citizens, and in a way it was. With the fall of Mubarak and Zine al-Abidine Ben Ali—dictators who were excoriated for heartless economic policies, corruption, and cronyism—Egypt and Tunisia seemed ripe for economic, class-based appeals. But it was not to be. Western countries are, by now, used to a politics consumed by, in Fukuyama's words, "economic calculation, the endless solving of technical problems, environmental concerns, and the satisfaction of sophisticated consumer demands."[20] To arrive, though, at such a utopian state of economic tinkering, it helps to get the fundamental questions answered first.

Islamists are Islamists for a reason. They have a distinctive ideological project, even if they themselves struggle to articulate what exactly it entails. Some Islamist parties, as in Tunisia, are more willing to come to terms with liberal democracy than others. But all Islamist parties, by definition, are at least somewhat illiberal, something that I discuss at length in my previous book, *Temptations of Power.*[21] There has long been a presumption that, over time, mainstream Islamists—embracing a pragmatic politics—will continue moderating and adapting, just as Christian Democrats and Socialists in Western Europe and Latin America did before them. Perhaps, one day, they will cease to be what they are and become "post-Islamists" or even proper liberals. But if they became liberals, then what would be the point exactly?

Another possibility is that Islamist parties might be "forced" into giving up their Islamism as a kind of concession. This was more or less what happened in Tunisia, the lone bright spot of a now-faded Arab Spring. Ennahda, the country's main Islamist party, deserves credit for voluntarily stepping down from power in the face of opposition protests. But what if Ennahda, at some later point, recovered support, won a string of electoral contests, and became emboldened to pursue the Islamist agenda its conservative base wants it to?

Tunisia's 2014 parliamentary and presidential elections were rightly hailed as a success. Here were free elections resulting in the peaceful transfer of power with the losers, in this case Ennahda, accepting an unfavorable electoral verdict. But there were darker undercurrents for those willing to look. During the campaign, Ennahda had very consciously deemphasized its ideological distinctiveness and portrayed itself as the party of national consensus. But this "big trip to the center," as Ennahda leader Rached Ghannouchi described it to me, does not appear to have worked, with Ennahda losing to the secular Nidaa Tounes party, a coalition of liberal, leftist, and old regime elements.[22] Nidaa Tounes ran an ideologically driven campaign arguing that the Islamists were an existential threat and that "state prestige" and "state authority" needed to be restored, an unsubtle nod to the continuing appeal of strongman politics. In a society that remained as polarized as Tunisia's, there simply weren't enough voters to be found in the center. Playing nice might have been the right, honorable thing to do, but it didn't necessarily pay, at least not electorally.

Then there are normative considerations. If Islamist parties, once elected, have to give up their Islamism (even though one of the reasons people presumably vote for them is their Islamism), then this runs counter to the essence of democracy— the notion that governments should be responsive to, or at least accommodate, public preferences. More practically, asking Islamists to concede who they are and what they believe is unsustainable. This was essentially the bargain struck in Turkey: The Islamist-rooted Justice and Development Party (AKP) would concede its Islamism in return for full participation and even the opportunity to govern. The bargain, however, did not hold. Once the threat of military intervention—a predecessor Islamist party was ousted from power and banned as recently as 1997—is removed, Islamists have little incentive to stick to an unfair, undemocratic deal struck under duress. Their most ardent supporters are patient, understanding the limitations of politics in a militantly secular state, but, at some point, they expect their leaders to reflect their ideological preferences. The case of Turkey is especially striking: Turkey, unlike Tunisia, can claim more than sixty years of off-and-on democratic experience. But, sixty years later, a strong center has failed to materialize and, if anything, the center has grown weaker in the post–Arab Spring era. While economic, class, and ethnic cleavages all factor in Turkey, the primary divide remains an Islamist-secular one.

Can Liberalism Still Prevail in the Middle East?

Too often, we look at conflicts abroad and assume that they are, at their core, about politics, power, and the distribution of resources—things that are easily relatable to our own American experience. Religion, to the extent that it matters, is the garb in which to dress the more base human impulses of money, ego, power, and domination. Accordingly, religion is a mode and a means—to be used, abused, and manipulated—but it is not the (or even *a*) prime mover. Even when faith is expressed with seeming sincerity, the individuals who express it may be under the grip of false consciousness, thinking that they are doing things for the noble cause of religion when what's *really* driving them is something altogether more simple and considerably less romantic. Or so the thinking goes.

When religion is less relevant in our own lives, it can be difficult to make that jump, to not just understand—but to relate to—its meaning and power for believers, and for those, in particular, who believe they have a cause beyond this life. Over the past decade, I have tried to immerse myself in the world of political Islam, and the Muslim Brotherhood in particular, in an attempt to understand what inspires its adherents as individuals and what animates them as a movement. Despite my best efforts, however, the one element I continue to struggle with is what might be called *the willingness to die*.

If I had joined a protest in a not-so-democratic country and the army was moving in with live fire, there would be little debate: I'd run for the hills. And that's why my time interviewing Brotherhood activists in Rabaa—just days before the massacre took place—was, at once, fascinating and frightening. It forced me to at least try to transcend my own limitations as an analyst. Gehad El-Haddad, the young Brotherhood spokesman, told me that he was "very much at peace."[23] He was ready to die, and I knew that he, and so many others, weren't just saying it. Because many of them—more than eight hundred—did, in fact, die.

Where does this willingness to die come from? One Brotherhood activist, now unable to return to Egypt, told me the story of an activist who was standing on the front lines when the military began "dispersing" the Rabaa sit-in. A bullet grazed his shoulder. Behind him, a young man fell to the ground. The man had been shot to death. The activist looked over to see what had happened and began to cry. *He* could have died a martyr. He knew the man behind him had gone to heaven in God's glory. This is what he longed for, and it had been denied him. Aspects of the story were, I assume, apocryphal, but the basic point is an important one. This wasn't politics in the normal sense of the word. This was the language of purity and absolution. Just as it was for the secularists who insisted on bringing them down at any cost, the battle, for the Islamists, was existential.

THE *NEW YORK TIMES* columnist David Brooks once defined a moderate as "someone who sees politics as a competition between two partial truths."[24] Political society doesn't necessarily need moderates; citizens can believe in absolute truths as long as they agree to pursue them through politics rather than violence. But the difficult question—one that the Middle East has so far failed to answer—is how exactly to do this when there is much, perhaps too much, at stake.

This book is, admittedly, colored by a post–Arab Spring pessimism and a basic recognition that, at their core, people are neither the same nor do they necessarily want the same things. Faith that better, more reasonable minds will prevail is a hope that the region simply can't afford. Every society must grapple with the question of violence. As the philosopher Alasdair MacIntyre once remarked, "Modern politics is civil war carried on by other means."[25] He was referring to Western societies lacking in a common conception of public morality and ethics, something that he more succinctly calls "virtue." MacIntyre argues that, with the rise of relativism and hyperpluralism, our societies lack "genuine moral consensus."[26] This is true of the West, particularly Europe, but it is no accident: There are simply fewer people willing to fight for and, for that matter, believe in a state entrusted with the promotion of virtue. In this sense, the secularization that has consumed Western societies has been a blessing, but at a price.

The temptation, then, is to assume that a similar process will take hold in the Muslim world—and if it won't take hold, that it *should*. These assumptions about history's inexorable movement toward a more liberal future aren't necessarily made explicit, but they color much of our discourse about the Middle East. We believe, or want to believe, that things have to get better. Drawing on our experiences as Americans, we find it difficult to envision social progress, or even democracy, without liberalism. In our own context, good things went together, so why shouldn't they for everyone else?

Even those, like the political scientist Sheri Berman, who acknowledge liberalism and democracy often don't go together, still hold to the idea of a general historical trajectory. Berman argues that there is nothing exceptional about the Middle East and that the turmoil and violence of the region are "not a bug in political development but a feature of it" and, more generally, that "history shows that illiberal democracy is often a precursor to liberal democracy."[27] The implication is that if this is the way progress happens, then let's not get too worried about it.

Similarly, with the terrifying rise of the Islamic State and the attendant collapse of regional order, a growing number of analysts have envisioned a process of violence and ideological conflict followed by the triumph of something resembling liberalism. The Egyptian author Tarek Osman envisions a decades-long "cathartic period" and a "tortuous journey" that will reach its conclusion with "the secular current overpower[ing] the religious."[28] The former Belgian official and EU representative Koert Debeuf argues that the failure of political Islam, in its various guises, has undermined the religious certainty of more and more young Arabs.[29] This, too, is presented as the prelude to a liberal sensibility. Even Egypt's Dar al-Ifta, the official government body entrusted with issuing fatwas, or religious edicts, has made a similar argument, albeit with rather different intent. According to Dar al-Ifta, the apparent increase in "atheists"—whom it defines not only as actual atheists but also as converts to other religions and Egyptians who support a "secular" state—is due to extremists pushing people away from religion.[30]

Not surprisingly, many of these accounts of how Islam might evolve sound awfully similar to the narrative of how Europe came to shed its religious demons. A period of intense religious passion and religiously inspired violence gave way to a slow but relentless process of secularization. Europe by the early twentieth century had secularized considerably, with its insistence on pushing religion as far outside everyday politics as possible. Yet the most precipitous decline in individual religious practice took place, interestingly, after the Second World War, during the 1960s. It was a deepening, and in some ways a final, consolidation of what had been building over centuries. This was, in Henry Kissinger's words, "a practical accommodation to reality, not a unique moral insight."[31] There had been too much blood shed for idealistic dreams or profound moral insights. According to this reading, violence unleashes the possibilities for a secular political order. Violence on such a scale hastens history's end.

This standard narrative of European enlightenment is convenient not just for the West but also for Muslim liberals, who, understandably from their vantage point, see Islamists and Islamism as a problem, sometimes *the* problem, to be solved. For the still relatively small minority of liberals in the Middle East, believing that liberal ideas will eventually win out offers purpose and, more important, hope. With the exception of the short-lived "liberal" era during the 1930s and '40s, liberals have simply been incapable of winning national elections in the Arab world. Their failures aside, liberals, by definition, believe that liberalism is the best foundation for political order and an especially appropriate response for deeply divided, violence-ridden societies. Liberalism, in the classical (rather than the American political) sense of the word, does something very simple: It allows each individual to pursue his or her own conception of the good as long as no one is harmed in the process.

But believing that liberalism is the best way to manage society and believing that it will inevitably come to be are two different things. There is no particular reason why Islamic "reform" should lead to liberalism in the way that the Protestant Reformation paved the way for the Enlightenment and, eventually, modern liberalism. The Reformation was a response to the Catholic Church's clerical stranglehold over Christian doctrine and practice. What would become Protestantism was inextricably linked to the advent of mass literacy, as a growing number of believers were no longer dependent on the intercession of the church. With the New Testament translated for the first time into German and other European languages, the faithful could directly access the text on their own.

The historical sequencing in the Middle East, as we shall see, has differed in a number of fundamental ways. For starters, Islam has *already* had a "reformation" of sorts. Late-nineteenth-century "Islamic modernism" was an attempt to make Islam, and premodern Islamic law, safe for modernity (and to make modernity safe for Islam). Islamic modernism, rather than a response to clerical domination, was an attempt to rise to the challenges of secularization, European colonialism, and the creeping authoritarianism of the late Ottoman era.

As for the clerics, they had already been weakened considerably. Co-opted by the state, they fell into disrepute. The sidelining of the clerical class, as it turned out, was not necessarily a positive development. Scholars of Islam such as Noah Feldman, Wael Hallaq, and Mohammad Fadel have documented how a self-regulating clerical class provided a crucial check on the sultan's executive power and authority. As keepers of

God-given law, the clerics ensured that the caliph was bound by something beyond himself.* They were granted at least some degree of autonomy, and, in return, they were to grant legitimacy to leaders who they may have otherwise disagreed with or even opposed. As Feldman notes in *The Fall and Rise of the Islamic State*, "To see the [sharia-based system] as containing the balance of powers so necessary for a functioning, sustainable legal state is to emphasize not why it failed but why it succeeded so spectacularly for as long as it did."[32]

If the Reformation was specific to Christianity's experience with clerical despotism—something with no real corollary in the Islamic context—then it would be odd to expect something similar to take hold in the Muslim world. There are more intangible considerations as well: Islam, because of its fundamentally different relationship to politics, was simply more resistant to secularization.

OF COURSE, ISLAM, LIKE anything else, can become something other than what it is and what it was. But the point here is not

---

*The sultan, of course, could use his appointment powers and try to manipulate the law for his own ends. But the limits he faced were considerable. States, in the premodern period, were significantly weaker than they are today. Without massive bureaucracies, modern armies, and the technology to closely monitor citizens, far-flung empires were decentralized and depended on the buy in of local notables, including clerics who were held in high regard. As Knut Vikør writes, "Political changes [in classical Muslim society] have fairly little effect on trade or economy, nor do they greatly affect the community of the learned, the ulama. Both tend to continue their activities within their own networks where towns, trade routes and centers of learning are crucial, but the identity of the ruler of the borders between the states matter relatively little" (Vikør, *Between God and the Sultan: A History of Islamic Law*, Oxford: Oxford University Press, 2005, pp. 186–87). Even if they weren't always observed, important norms had developed around the scholarly community and its distance from political power. The content of the law was theirs to protect and propagate, even though its implementation might depend on the sultan. Clerics were known to anguish over judicial appointments, concerned that their credibility could be compromised within the community of scholars, a community to which they would one day have to return.

that such a scenario is impossible, but that it is unlikely. Analysts and policy makers can continue to hope for unlikely outcomes, but they should not base their long-term assessments of the region on an improbable succession of events. Even if I am wrong and a secular-liberal order does in fact win out, it will take such a long time, dependent on so many "ifs," that it makes little sense to incorporate these expectations into our analysis of the region or the making of policy. Even the relative optimists, like Tarek Osman, emphasize that the journey toward liberalism will be "tortuous." Osman writes, for instance, that the Arab world "will likely disintegrate. Some countries will drift away from the Arab system; others will be divided along tribal, sectarian, and entrenched loyalties." And that's just the first phase. This period of collapse will then produce competing Islamist and secular trends. "A war of ideas will ensue," Osman writes, but "both will fail to ascend to their envisaged ideals."[33] And that's just the second phase.

A deterministic view of history doesn't just lead us to hope in the improbable; it can sap the will to act as well. If we believe that history moves with intent—that the forces of reason and modernity will inevitably prevail—then there is a limited role for outside actors. Why do "more" when there's a risk that Western intervention could backfire and undermine what would otherwise be a natural, evolutionary process? If Arabs are to become exhausted by violence, it is something that *they* must become exhausted by.

While it isn't always obvious, perhaps not even to those who imply it, this liberal faith in natural, historical progress pops up repeatedly in the statements of Western officials. This isn't surprising: It is part of our American faith. The Obama administration seemed to take refuge in the notion that the Islamic State and its ilk would ultimately "be defeated"—in the passive tense—because they didn't "have a vision that appeals to ordinary people."[34] It was almost as if the arc of history would intervene against them, even if we couldn't be bothered to muster

the effort. In a speech responding to the beheading of the journalist James Foley, Obama said that "one thing we can all agree
on is that a group like ISIL has no place in the twenty-first
century."[35] Except it would be nearly impossible to imagine a
group like the Islamic State in any century but the twenty-
first. The group is a distinctly modern product of a struggle
that began in earnest with the decline of the Ottoman caliphate
and intensified with the rise of the nation-state. The Islamic
State is providing an answer to a question, just as others, like
the Muslim Brotherhood, Ennahda in Tunisia, and the AKP in
Turkey, are offering their own answers. To the extent that religion figures prominently in any debate over the regional order,
each of these groups is making an argument about the role of
religion in public life, arguments that I will explore in greater
detail in the coming chapters.

Religion and State Building

The issues I discuss throughout this book deal not only with
how people practice politics today but also with who they are
and what comes "naturally" to them. These are age-old debates.
In the near entirety of recorded history, humans, animated by
biological imperatives and the will to survive, inclined toward
family, tribe, and clan. Yet to establish a state, or something
like it, was to ask subjects to transcend these narrow loyalties
and believe in something greater. The city-states of ancient
Greece, the political community that the Prophet Mohamed
established in the seventh century, and the great empires of the
medieval era all grappled with this tension. What did it mean
to forge a well-ordered state? Was it even possible?

As Plato records in *The Republic*, Socrates took such concerns
to their logical extreme, advocating communal ownership of all
property, including women and children. In sharing women
and children, says Socrates, the guardians "will not tear the city
in pieces by differing about 'mine' and 'not mine'."[36] Socrates is

arguing not that his proposals are ideal but, rather, that they're necessary for the survival and success of the state. Here, we hear early echoes of authoritarian statecraft: *The state above all else, whatever the cost.* In Socrates's modest proposal, the cost, apparently, is the dehumanization of the populace. If man naturally inclines toward family, then the solution was, in effect, to make the state into a kind of larger, all-encompassing family.

To prioritize one's tribe or "family" to the exclusion of others, even if that meant to kill, is—or at least was—our universal condition. As Atran notes: "Across most of human history and cultures, violence against other groups was considered a moral virtue, a classification necessary for killing masses of people innocent of harming others."[37] Today, it may seem like the West has moved well beyond such sentiments through a successful (though often violent) centuries-long process of state building. All states require some unifying set of norms and ideas that bind citizens together. In our own Western context, liberalism and nationalism, or more likely some combination of the two, have provided this societal glue. "That individualism seems today like a solid core of our economic and political behavior," writes Fukuyama, "is only because we have developed institutions that override our more naturally communal instincts."[38] A predominantly secular nationalism, however, isn't the only solution to the dilemmas of state building. As events in the Middle East have demonstrated, liberalism and secular nationalism are unlikely candidates for the provision of stable, legitimate order in the region.

In the broader sweep of history, the heyday of Arab nationalism, peaking in the 1960s, stands as an aberration.[39] Nationalism entered into decline when it couldn't deliver on Arab unity or real economic development. As an ideology, it had little intrinsic value beyond its ability to offer something temporal. After the trials of colonialism, it could offer pride and self-esteem, but those sentiments would erode under the weight of accumulated failure. While Islamism is not immune to some of these same concerns, it is more resilient. Islamists might fail, but Islamism, broadly understood, is an argument about the centrality of religion in public life, an argument that is difficult to discredit. As Fukuyama writes in *The Origins of Political Order*, "Religious beliefs are never held by their adherents to be simple theories that can be discarded if proved wrong; they are held to be unconditionally true, and there are usually heavy social and psychological penalties attached to asserting their falsehood."[40] This, I will argue, is even more so the case for Islam.

States need *asabiyah*, to use the fourteenth-century historian Ibn Khaldun's term, to bind together. *Asabiyah*, roughly translated as social solidarity or group consciousness, provides cohesion and shared purpose.[41] It can take many forms, but the form that has proved most powerful and lasting in the Muslim world is intimately tied to and shaped by Islam. This does not mean that Islam has to be the overarching raison d'être of the modern state. My proposition is more modest: Islam will need to play a significant role in the forging of political community, particularly where political community is weak. Given Islam's inherent flexibility—scholars and ideologues alike have proposed "Islamic socialism," "Islamic capitalism," "Islamic democracy"— the faith can, perhaps counterintuitively, accommodate much that is "modern." For the religious, religion can offer both meaning and legitimacy to ideas that might otherwise seem temporal and temporary. But to exclude Islam or to hope for—or, worse, impose—a top-down secularism requires yet more violence. Excluding religion undermines the social fabric of conservative societies, as in Egypt, and more secular ones, as in Turkey, because it forces those who do believe that Islam should play a central role in political life—and there are many—to make a choice. And it's not a choice one can reasonably expect millions of people to make without provoking considerable disaffection, a disaffection that can often provoke a spiraling of political violence.

Is There an Arab Problem?

A book that claims to make an argument about Islam cannot ignore examples outside the Arab world. The Islamic Republic of Iran, the product of the Iranian revolution of 1979, is one of the longest-running experiments in fusing religion with the constitutional and democratic trappings of the modern state. Iran, however, is outside the scope of this study, since its theological orientation—one based on the innovative and relatively new Shiite doctrine of "guardianship of the clerics"—has not been seriously attempted anywhere else and is anathema to the Sunni Islamists who are the focus of this book. Sunni Islam simply has no comparable notion of clerical rule.

More relevant for our purposes are the South and Southeast Asian nations that together comprise hundreds of millions of the world's approximately 1.6 billion Muslims. Here, too, as in the Arab world, Islam plays an outsized role in political life. Hailed as "models" of pluralism and democratic success, Indonesia and Malaysia feature significantly more sharia ordinances than Egypt, Tunisia, Turkey, Algeria, Morocco, or Lebanon, to name only a few. What's perhaps most interesting about these two cases, however, is how demands for sharia legislation have spread well beyond the usual Islamist suspects, enjoying the sanction and support of ostensibly secular ruling parties. As Joseph Liow, the leading scholar of Islamism in Southeast Asia, notes, most Malaysian states have laws on the books regarding sharia criminal offenses, backed by government-sanctioned religious bodies. In some cases, he writes, "a large segment" of the secular ruling party has been "actively involved in agitating for the implementation of sharia."[42] This is all the more striking considering that Malaysia is more religiously diverse than most Arab countries, with Muslims representing only around 60 percent of the population.

Unlike Malaysia, which still has authoritarian features, Indonesia is a thriving pluralistic democracy. Democratization has gone hand in hand with decentralization, which has allowed more conservative provinces and localities to experiment with religiously inspired legislation. In one article, the Indonesia scholar Robin Bush documents sharia bylaws implemented in South Sulawesi, West Java, and other regions. They include requiring civil servants and students to wear "Muslim clothing," requiring women to wear the head scarf to receive local government services, and requiring demonstrations of Quranic reading ability for admission to university or receipt of a marriage license.[43] But there's a catch. According to a study by the Jakarta-based Wahid Institute, most of these regulations have come from officials of *secular* parties like Golkar.[44] How is this possible? The implementation of sharia law is part of a mainstream discourse that cuts across ideological and party lines, again suggesting that Islamism is not necessarily about Islamists but is about a broader population that is open to Islam playing a central role in law and governance. As Liow writes, "the piecemeal implementation of sharia by-laws across Indonesia has not elicited widespread opposition from local populations."[45] It is very difficult to have liberalism without liberals. Islamism, on the other hand, doesn't necessarily require Islamists.

Democracy is about respecting and reflecting popular sentiment, and Malaysia and Indonesia are still conservative countries, in some ways deeply so. According to Pew surveys conducted in 2011–12, 93 percent of both Malaysian and Indonesian Muslims say religion is "very important" in their lives, easily surpassing the percentage who say so in Egypt, Turkey, and Tunisia.[46] Religiosity, of course, does not necessarily translate into support for Islamic legislation, but in Southeast Asia it apparently does: 86 percent of Malaysian Muslims and 72 percent of Indonesian Muslims favor making Islamic law the official law of the land in their countries.[47]

In sum, it wasn't that religion was less of a "problem" in Malaysia and Indonesia; it's that solutions were more readily available. Islam might have been exceptional, but the political system in both countries was more interested in accommodating this reality than in suppressing it. There wasn't an entrenched secular elite in the same way there was in many Arab countries. Meanwhile, Islamist parties were not as strong, so polarization wasn't as deep and destabilizing. Islamism was the province not of one party but of most. In a sense, Islamists need secularists and secularists need Islamists. But in Malaysia and Indonesia, there was a stronger "middle," and that middle had settled around a relatively uncontroversial conservative consensus.

As we can see, in such a diverse range of countries, Islam has proved remarkably resilient despite the decades-long pressures of modernization and secularization. This popular desire for Islam to be at the center of public life expresses itself in different and complex ways—either as support for Islamist parties, support for Islam, support for Islamic law, or all of the above. My point here, though, is simple enough: Islam's distinctive relationship to politics goes well beyond the Arab world or the Middle East. In the chapters that follow, however, I have chosen to focus on several cases, which are representative of the problems of religion and state in contexts where the role of Islam has not yet been "normalized." Two countries in particular, Turkey and Tunisia, are "hard cases" for my argument. They experienced some of the most vigorous and long-lasting suppression of religious expression, to the extent that societies were permanently rerendered. These were, are, and will remain secularized societies, at least compared with their neighbors. Yet even here—particularly here—Islamist parties have enjoyed unusual success, rising to the halls of government.

The fact that the most democratic countries mentioned here—Tunisia, Turkey, Indonesia, and Malaysia—are the ones where Islamism or Islamists, or both, have fared better is no accident. Democracy went hand in hand with Islamization. To put it differently, where many assume that democracy *can't* exist with Islamism, the opposite is more likely true. What distinguishes Indonesia and Malaysia, or their electorates, isn't some readiness to embrace liberalism or secularism. The difference is that their brand of Islamic politics garners much less attention in the West, in part because these two countries aren't seen as strategically vital and, perhaps more important, because the passage of Islamic legislation is simply less controversial domestically. In Indonesia and Malaysia, there has been a coming to terms with Islam's role in public life, whereas in much of the Middle East, there hasn't—at least not yet.

A Way Out?

A handful of European countries grappled with similar, though perhaps less existential, questions as recently as the 1950s. As centralized, cohesive states such as Germany and France coalesced around them, countries like Belgium, Switzerland, Austria, and the Netherlands struggled to address deep divisions among subcultures in their own societies. These countries soon became models of "consensual democracy," where the subcultures agreed to creative power-sharing arrangements. For example, in Austria a "coalition committee," in which socialist and Catholic leaders were equally represented, made the most sensitive decisions, while in Switzerland the four largest parties were guaranteed representation in the executive branch.

But the Middle East's divides are of a different nature. Countries like Egypt or Tunisia may seem homogenous—the vast majority of the population, after all, belong to one ethnicity, one sect, and one religion—but in some ways this makes the problem all the more vexing. Consensual democracy works best when there are multiple centers of power in society, none of which is strong enough to dominate on its own. In much of the Middle East, however, both Islamists and non-Islamists believe they represent the "true" majority of citizens. Unlike in Belgium, where there are distinct groups of Flemish and Walloon that can be clearly identified, Islamists and non-Islamists are different, but not different enough.

With Shia and Sunni or Muslims and Christians, there is little doubt about who is what. The lines are drawn quite clearly for those who wish to see them. But what about when the enemy is a brother, daughter, sister, or son? An optimist might see this as proof that it can only get so bad: It's within the family, after all. But friends and family can turn on each other, and in Egypt they have. As Egypt's former minister of interior Osama Heikal put it, "The enemy can be our own neighbor. The enemy is in our own homes."[48] In this sense, both sides in the Egyptian conflict, Islamists and their opponents, are historical determinists of a sort. They each think they can persuade their countrymen to join their side and win the war of ideas—if only the conditions are right and they have enough time.

As Arend Lijphart, the leading scholar of consensual democracy, wrote in a classic 1969 article, competing subcultures in countries like the Netherlands and Switzerland were minority groups that had little, if any hope, of becoming majorities. Rather than imposing their will on the nation, they were more interested in autonomy and promoting their own communal interests. Each subculture had its own schools, institutions, hospitals, and businesses and was, to an extent, geographically segmented. It helped that Catholics could, for the most part, avoid interacting with Socialists. According to Lijphart, "subcultures with widely divergent outlooks and interests may coexist without necessarily being in conflict. Conflict arises only when they are in contact with each other."[49] Lijphart refers to this as "a kind of voluntary apartheid policy."[50] But separation, voluntary or forced, requires separate parts. And those separate parts simply do not exist in, for example, the Egyptian context.

This not particularly inspiring idea—that the more people interact, the more they dislike each other—undermines a core tenet of the liberal faith: If only opposing sides talked to each other in good faith, then reason would prevail. This idea inspires our rounds of diplomacy and our educational-exchange programs. This faith in our better angels is commendable (and probably a good way to lead a happier life), but that doesn't necessarily make it an accurate reflection of life as it's lived and politics as it's practiced. Sometimes, reducing contact between opposing sides and allowing for autonomous communities are ways of accepting that some differences cannot be bridged. The best that can be done is to manage them. This is more difficult in mixed communities. But, even here, recognizing foundational divides and taking that as a starting point is probably a more fruitful approach to perhaps one day transcending them. To put it a little bit differently, people can hate each other all they want—as long as they agree to hate each other within the political process, rather than outside it.

HOW DOES ONE SHARE power or, at least, make the battle over it less totalizing? Lessons from successful consensual democracies, even if they don't fit perfectly, offer crucial insights on modifying the winner-takes-all nature of Middle East politics. The basic principles are simple enough: do as much as possible to share, disperse, restrain, and decentralize power. Extra care must be given to ensure electoral minorities have a stake in the system so that, when they lose, they have less incentive to renege on the democratic process.

Where the role of religion proves too divisive, opposing parties, at the start of a transition, could agree to "postpone" debates on divisive ideological issues—such as on Islamizing the legal or educational systems—for a set period of time. Such an interim period would regularize democratic competition to the extent that it becomes the "only game in town." At the conclusion of this period, the democratic process would be better equipped to withstand ideological polarization. Ultimately, though, foundational questions over the role of Islam and Islamic law cannot be forever placed gently to the side. They will have to be addressed, and democratic outcomes will have to be respected. In conservative societies—and even in less conservative ones—a prominent role for religion may be unavoidable. If there is enough of a demand for Islamization, someone will have to supply it.

To come to terms with these realities requires a leap of faith from an international community that continues to look skeptically at expressions of religion in everyday politics. In the light of the Islamic State's success as well as the Muslim Brotherhood's many failures, questions that should have been answered long ago are now being asked once again in Western capitals. Are Islamism and democracy compatible? Or even, are Islam and democracy compatible?

While any number of Islamist groups failed to meet the challenge of the Arab Spring, there is a different, deeper failure, one that is likely to plague the region for decades to come: the fundamental inability of secular state systems to accommodate Islamist participation in the democratic process. The illusion that Islamists—and even Islamism—can be eliminated through brute force is a long-standing one. It's also a fool's errand. You can try to kill an organization, but killing an idea—one deeply rooted in society—is a different matter entirely.

In the coming critical years and decades, no party, movement, or ideological current will be able to claim "victory," at least not in any definitive sense. Too much blood has been shed for that. But if the people of the Middle East are to establish—after a long period of violent struggle—a more stable and legitimate order, Islam will have to have its place. It's only really a question of what kind of "Islam," when, and at what cost.

(2)

IS ISLAM "EXCEPTIONAL"?

It may seem odd to begin exploring a modern predicament by examining a series of events that took place more than fourteen centuries ago. How much could all of that possibly matter? At Thanksgiving dinner with family and friends in 2014, I was struck by how much those events still do matter. There were eight of us, all Muslims, from assorted backgrounds and levels of religious commitment. Over generous helpings of turkey, mashed potatoes, gravy, and stuffing, we found ourselves talking about the scourge of terrorism and the responsibility of Muslims to say and do something about it. Soon enough, we were talking about Yazid, the second caliph of the Umayyad Empire, killing and beheading the Prophet Mohamed's grandson, Hussein, at the Battle of Karbala. It was like an open wound, and here we were once again, as so many had before us, trying to make sense of how and why something so unspeakable could have happened. This was the Prophet's family, his flesh and blood. And yet Hussein and all of his men were slaughtered, their bodies left to rot for forty days.

It wasn't dissimilar from the other questions we were asking ourselves that day about the rise of the Islamic State, civil wars, and the seemingly endless shedding of blood: How could Muslims do this to each other? The Battle of Karbala is only one story. We could have talked about Omar, Abu Bakr, Uthman, and Ali, the Prophet Mohamed's closest companions and the so-called righteously guided caliphs. The first caliph, Abu Bakr, died of old age, but his three successors were each assassinated by fellow Muslims. When we were growing up and going to Sunday school (yes, Muslim-Americans have Sunday school, too), Abu Bakr, Omar, and Ali didn't feel like historical figures but, rather, people who were a part of our lives, reminders of both a glorious history and the internecine killing that threatened to undo it.

The era of the righteously guided caliphs didn't last long, but it was superseded by any number of other "golden ages," which flourished for far longer. The Abbasid caliphate was one of the most successful empires the world had ever seen. From the eighth to thirteenth centuries, the empire prospered, with unprecedented advancements in science, medicine, and philosophy. Students from Europe flocked to Muslim universities, hoping to study with the world's greatest doctors, thinkers, and theologians. Muslims today, particularly in the Arab world, enter into tortured debates over what went wrong, with this history as subtext.

The dismal state of the Middle East is all the more difficult to accept knowing that, for much of the past fourteen centuries, there was a great deal to be proud of. This dissonance is unsettling. Perceptions of decline were often overlaid with a kind of theological determinism. Was the decline some sort of divine retribution? After centuries of dominance, the various Islamic empires were gradually eclipsed by a rising Europe.

Then came the trauma of colonialism, when much of the Muslim world fell under direct, and often brutal, European control. Hard-won independence offered a gleam of hope, but the promise of secular nationalism ultimately disappointed, with young nations descending into dictatorship. Perhaps God had forsaken the Muslims, punishing them for straying from the straight path. After all, God had promised glad tidings for those who followed his commands, and he had, seemingly, delivered for centuries. The most devout—the Prophet, his companions, and their earliest followers—had enjoyed unimaginable success, conquering the entirety of North Africa, then spreading out through Spain and into France within a hundred years of the Prophet's passing. This *must* have been evidence of their righteousness. That, though, could only mean that the territorial contraction of once great empires must have been evidence of sin and decadence.

The Ottoman Empire, hoping to stave off decline in the nineteenth century, launched a series of internal reforms, known as the *tanzimat*. Though this wasn't their intent, the *tanzimat* hastened what Wael Hallaq calls the "evisceration" of the sharia.[1] In an attempt to codify and control what had been an organic and constantly evolving body of law, the state was strengthened and centralized, its authoritarian tendencies exacerbated, and the clerics weakened. Secularists, meanwhile, believed that the Islamic state couldn't be reformed and that holding on to religious foundations would only stand in the way of progress. If embracing secular nationalism had led to Europe's ascendance, they argued, then why shouldn't it do the same for the Middle East? Among elites, assorted secular ideologies—Marxism, socialism, fascism, and liberalism—gained currency. Islamic modernists, the precursors to modern-day Islamists, interpreted events quite differently, viewing the deteriorating state of the region as yet more evidence of God's displeasure. To regain his pleasure would require returning to the unblemished purity of Islam's founding. This notion of return, novel in the late nineteenth century, would, in mere decades, become ubiquitous to the point of cliché.

Born in 1929, the Islamist writer Muhammad Galak Kishk saw the triumph of religion nearly everywhere, even in the most unlikely of places. In 1967, Israel handily defeated the Arab nations not simply because of its military prowess, but because it had something that the Arabs didn't: the certainty and clarity of religious devotion. As Fouad Ajami writes, "In Kishk's account there is grudging admiration for the clarity with which the Israelis saw the war, for the fact that young Israeli soldiers prayed behind their rabbis at the Wailing Wall after their capture of Jerusalem."[2] Kishk's may not have been the most accurate reading of Israeli society, but it was one of the more telling.

If this clarity—this purity of vision—had been lost, then where better to regain it than at the beginning? This is what the various revivalist movements hoped to do. The Islamic modernists hoped to recapture the spirit and intent of that first generation of Muslims, while those who would come to be known as Salafis believed not just in the "spirit" but in the "letter" of the law. They wanted to imitate the particular habits of the first Muslims, whether that meant dressing like the Prophet (by cuffing their trousers at the ankle) or brushing their teeth like the Prophet (with a teeth-cleaning twig called a *miswak*). Oddly enough, for these various Islamist strains, more recent Islamic history has grown more remote. Outside Turkey, most Muslims would have trouble citing even one Ottoman-era scholar. The Abbasid caliphate is remembered fondly, but its memory doesn't necessarily inspire fighting and dying for the cause. In contrast, there is a closeness about the Prophet and his companions that belies fourteen hundred years of the passing of time. It is an odd, unusual effect—the further one goes back in history, the more intimate it feels.

• • •

MUSLIMS ARE, OF COURSE, not bound to Islam's founding moment, but neither can they fully escape it. The Prophet Mohamed was a theologian, a politician, a warrior, a preacher, and a merchant, all at once. Importantly, he was also the builder of a new state. It is difficult to know when he was acting in one role rather than the other (which has led to endless debates over whether some of the Prophet's actions in certain domains were, in fact, *prophetic*). Some religious thinkers—including Sudan's Mahmoud Mohamed Taha and, later, his student Abdullahi an-Na'im—have tried to separate these different prophetic legacies, arguing that the Quran contains two messages. The first message, based on the verses revealed while the Prophet was establishing a new political community in Medina, includes particulars of Islamic law that may have been appropriate for seventh-century Arabia but are not applicable outside that context. The second message of Islam, found in the so-called Meccan verses, encompasses the eternal principles of Islam, which are meant to be updated according to the demands of time and place.[3] Taha was executed by the Jaafar al-Nimeiry regime in 1985 and his theories largely forgotten. But the basic idea of extracting general principles while emphasizing the historicity of their application has, in less explicit form, been advocated by a growing number of "progressive" Muslim scholars, many of whom live in the West.

There are reasons, though, that these theories have struggled to gain adherents in the Muslim world. First of all, they're not very easily explained to those without a background in Islamic law. For many Muslims, the point of Islam is that it is accessible and straightforward, at least in its broad outlines. The notion that the Quran contains two distinct messages is *not* straightforward and makes a "simple" religion rather complex. Why would a believing Muslim take a chance on a controversial and heterodox interpretation of scripture when he or she can fall back on a safer, mainstream approach that enjoys the backing of the vast majority of scholars?

One could go further and advocate not only for a progressive interpretation of Islamic law but also for its basic irrelevance to public life—that the separation of religion from politics forms the foundation of any pluralistic post-Enlightenment liberal society. As we will see, however, the heavy weight of Islamic history makes such a path as difficult as it is unlikely.

JUDAISM MIGHT SEEM LIKE a natural point of comparison for Islam. There is, after all, a vast corpus of *halakhic* law—the product of centuries of rabbinic interpretation. The question of how society should be governed according to God's commandments was—at least for a time—a matter of rich discussion. But a body of law or a political tradition, on its own, is rarely enough. This is a theme I will return to throughout the book: Religion, as powerful as it is, requires a conducive environment to shape political life in a significant and lasting way. And this is where Judaism parts ways with Islam. After the second Jewish temple was destroyed in 70 AD at the hands of the Romans, Jews would, for more than eighteen hundred years, find themselves living as minorities under the rule of largely Christian and Muslim powers. This meant that Jewish law could not be implemented by the state. Judaism had to make its peace, to the extent that it could, with non-Jewish rule. Delineating between the political and religious realms became necessary, sometimes even a matter of life and death. Legal thinkers had to adapt their understanding of the law accordingly. In exile, rabbinic Judaism, particularly in the Talmud and subsequent commentaries, became preoccupied with personal and communal responsibilities rather than political rule.

As the great political theorist Michael Walzer explains, "since writers in the [Jewish] diaspora could not recapitulate the experience represented in that text [the Hebrew Bible], they were forced into a radical reinterpretation or, better, a series of reinterpretations, of its meaning."[4] Rabbis increasingly distinguished between civil and economic matters, on the one hand, and nonnegotiable religious principles, on the other. As the editors of the seminal four-volume work *The Jewish Political Tradition* note: "We may read this as a more or less straightforward distinction between secular and religious regulation."[5]

With the founding of the state of Israel, Jewish law and its relationship to the state became relevant once again. By this time, however, what Israel's first prime minister, David Ben-Gurion, called the "ingathering of the exiles" meant that many of the Jewish state's earliest citizens were just as much a product of European conceptions of religion and state as they were their own (whatever that now meant, almost two millennia later).[6] The new state, being democratic, was a reflection of the preferences of its citizens, and these had now been indelibly marked by secularism. Religion would play an important role in public life, just as it did in the United States, but few questioned the basic, and mostly secular, foundations of the Israeli state. On this there was a wide-ranging consensus, even if it has eroded somewhat with time. Meanwhile, Ultra Orthodox movements, as illiberal as they may be, have little interest in re-creating or returning to an invented past. They seek to guard, rather than dismantle, the long, rich tradition of rabbinic Judaism, a tradition that had, for nearly two thousand years, little to say about law and governance. As the Brookings Institution's Natan Sachs, a leading expert on Israeli politics, puts it, "While there are extremists, there aren't truly 'fundamentalist' Jews in the literal sense. I don't know even know what that would look like."[7]

Judaism and Islam's approach to governance is a fascinating and important topic that deserves greater attention from researchers. For our purposes, however, Christianity provides a more fruitful point of comparison, since it is the only other monotheistic faith that has aspired to the same level of univer-

sality as Islam, seeking to expand its domain among nonbe-
lievers and enjoying centuries of sovereignty to experiment with
matters of religion and state. Across a wide stretch of territory,
Christianity was dominant, infusing itself in every facet of
public life and politics. Yet, after considerable resistance, it
eventually succumbed to secularization. This chapter explores
why and how this secularization process came to be—and why,
for various historical, political, and theological reasons, it is
unlikely to be repeated in the Islamic context.

THE FOUNDING MOMENTS OF Islam and Christianity couldn't have
been more different. (Muslims would say that it *had* to be different—otherwise what would be the point?). Where Mohamed
was the head of a state, Jesus was a dissident against a reigning
political order, the Roman Empire. Because there was no real
prospect of governing, there is little in his message that concerns itself with governance. There was also a natural limit to
the "practicality" of Jesus's message. Jesus, for Christians, was
divine, and so emulating him in any precise way was difficult.
It was also somewhat beside the point. The spirit of the New
Testament was one, if anything, of transcending the affairs of
this world. Mohamed, on the other hand, was very much *not*
divine. While deeply loved by Muslims, there is something
prosaic—and therefore relatable—about his reign. Mohamed
would rely on advice from his companions, and he occasionally made mistakes. Instead of transcending sin through grace,
many Muslims believe that they can and should mimic the
Prophetic model in exacting, sometimes even obsessive, detail.*

---

*Jonathan Brown, a leading scholar of Islam, recounts an amusing—and telling—
anecdote from the early days of the religion: "When inhabitants of the Near East
first began encountering the Muslims coming out of Arabia, they would remark how:
'Your prophet has taught you everything, even how to shit'" (Jonathan A. C. Brown,
Misquoting Muhammad: The Challenge and Choices of Interpreting the Prophet's Legacy,
London: Oneworld, 2014, p. 19).

(No one, as far as I'm aware, talks about cuffing their trousers the way Jesus did.)

Of course, one can look back at Jesus's short life and see him as a distinctly political figure. As Reza Aslan documents in his book *Zealot: The Life and Times of Jesus of Nazareth*, Jesus very explicitly challenged the Roman establishment, preaching against both Roman officials and many of his fellow Jews, who he believed were complicit in Roman corruption. In fact, Jesus was so political, argues Aslan, that his legacy incited one of the most destabilizing revolts in the history of the Roman Empire and subsequently one of its most brutal crackdowns. Consumed by "revolutionary fervor," Jesus entered Jerusalem in his last days and cleansed the temple, which the Roman authorities treated as an act of rebellion.[8] Christianity, in this sense, offers inspiration for challenging the political and economic status quo. One example is liberation theology, which flourished throughout Latin America in the 1960s and 70s and readily tapped into this heritage. But it is a heritage that lends itself more to an oppositional posture than to any particular views about forms of government, statehood, or legal structures. It was Jesus, after all, who said, "my kingdom is not of this world" (John 18:36). As Brad Gregory, a leading historian of Christianity, notes, "In no sense did Jesus exhort his followers to seek the exercise of power— just the opposite."[9]

Given his circumstances, Jesus might not have discussed the exercise of power, but that didn't necessarily close the matter. That there is a quest for the "historical Jesus"—reflected in a voluminous academic literature—suggests a diversity and even confusion about Jesus's life and his relationship to the Roman authorities. (As Aslan notes, "there are only two hard historical facts about Jesus of Nazareth upon which we can confidently rely," that Jesus "was a Jew who led a popular Jewish movement in Palestine . . . [and] that Rome crucified him for doing so.")[10] In some ways, then, what matters more than the life of Jesus is how his successors interpreted and actualized his legacy. In the first centuries of this new Christian faith, there was a conspicuous lack of any positive vision of the state from thinkers and theologians.

There is more agreement, at least among Muslims, about Mohamed's life, in part because his companions and followers were intent on assembling a corpus of his sayings, known as *hadith*. Over time, these reports solidified into authoritative collections of "authentic" *hadith*, which in turn served to clarify and express the established practice, or *sunna*, of the Prophet, covering his words, deeds, and general conduct in every imaginable sphere of life (there are *hadiths* delineating how the Prophet ate pumpkin soup, for example).[11] This *sunna*, along with the Quran, were the two foundational sources in the formulation of Islamic law, upon which everything else was built. In understanding the development of sharia, it also helped that there was no interruption between the founding of Mohamed's state in Medina, the early caliphate of the four righteously guided companions, then the Umayyad caliphate, followed by the Abbasid caliphate. Empires and dynasties were frequently marked by sedition and infighting, but there was never *not* a caliphate (though there were often competing "caliphates").* In this respect, there is, for Sunnis at least, a continuous lineage of widely accepted and legitimate Islamic political order up until the Ottoman caliphate's abolition in 1924.

That the Christian tradition seems ambivalent about law, governance, and power is no accident. Islam and Christianity

---

*The image of Sunni political stability is all too often an idealized one. Historically, Sunni clerics emphasized respect for the ruler's prerogatives, however oppressive or unjust he might be, as long as he was Muslim. This belies a history, like all histories, which is messy and contradictory, with a long record of insurrection and legitimacy challenges. Of course, the other way of looking at it is that this is precisely why clerics erred on the side of order and stability: They had come to see too much of its opposite. For more on the question of legitimate authority, rebellion, and the caliphate in Islamic political thought, see Ovamir Anjum, *Politics, Law, and Community in Islamic Thought: The Taymiyyan Moment* (Cambridge, UK: Cambridge University Press, 2012).

are, after all, meant to do different things. Law, at least in part, is about exposing and punishing sin. Yet, when Jesus died on the cross, he, in effect, released man from the burdens of sin and, therefore, from the burdens of law. With the coming of Christ, salvation is achieved through faith in Jesus Christ rather than through observance of the law.

In the New Testament, the law (meaning Old Testament law) is often treated as something unnecessary, divisive, and heavy. In the words of Paul, it is even a "curse." Paul says in Galatians that "for all who rely on the works of the law are under a curse . . . Clearly no one who relies on the law is justified before God, because 'the righteous will live by faith.' . . . Christ redeemed us from the curse of the law by becoming a curse for us" (Gal. 3:10–11, 13). Elsewhere, the author of Ephesians writes that Christ "abolished . . . the law with its commandments and ordinances" (Eph. 2:15).

Christianity's story of salvation is one of progression, with humanity passing through different stages of spiritual development. Jewish or Mosaic law was provisional, meant for a particular place and time and for a particular chosen people, whereas Christianity was universal and everlasting. As the theologian Joshua Ralston notes, reflecting on the writing of the early Christian theologian Justin Martyr, "Christ is the new and final law, and thus the Law of Moses is abrogated. . . . Justin argues that the God of Israel had promised the Israelites a new and everlasting covenant. The Mosaic Law was never intended to be either universal or eternally binding."[12]

In short, it's not so much that Christianity has little to say about law; it's that this ambivalence, or even opposition, to law was a feature of Christian theology during its early development. In later centuries, Christianity—and particularly the Catholic Church—no doubt played a powerful role in public life, but this did not mean there was any real equivalent to Islamic law. As Ralston writes, "Simply put, there is nothing resembling a developed Christian account of public law in the New Testament."[13]

This had important implications: "Christian theology, especially in the medieval period, primarily divides ecclesial law from civil law into distinct spheres of society. Ecclesial laws govern the church and civil laws govern the public."[14]

If salvation is through Christ and Christ alone, then there is little need for the state to regulate private and public behavior beyond providing a conducive environment for individuals to cultivate virtue and become more faithful to Christ. The punishment of sins is no longer a priority, since Jesus died for them. In stark contrast, whereas theologians like Martin Luther famously fashioned a dialectic between faith and good works, these two things are inextricably tied together in Islam. Faith is often expressed through the observance of the law. The failure to follow Islamic law is a reflection of the believer's lack of faith and unwillingness to submit to God. Salvation is impossible *without* law. This has implications for the nature of the Islamic state. If following the sharia—for example, refraining from alcohol and adultery, observing the fast, and praying five times a day—is a precondition for salvation, then the state has a role in encouraging the good and forbidding evil, a role it played, to various degrees, for the entirety of the premodern period.

God's Word and God's Speech

Related to "founding moments" is the question of a text's inerrancy and infallibility. As a creedal requirement, Muslims believe that the Quran is not just divinely inspired but that it is God's actual direct and literal speech. As a foundational tenet of Islam, on which so many other tenets depend, it is difficult to overstate the centrality of divine authorship and how it affects the interpretation and practical application of Islam. Contrary to what many think, there is simply no Christian equivalent to Quranic inerrancy, even among far-right evangelicals. Throughout Christian history, no major sect or denomination has ever asserted that the Bible is God's actual speech.

The Chicago Statement on Biblical Inerrancy, published in

1978 and signed by over two hundred leading evangelical figures, clarifies what had, by then, become a contested and misunderstood word. The concept of inerrancy, in a general sense, refers to the "complete truthfulness of Scripture" and the fact that it is "free from all falsehood." It is the "infallible divine authority." This, however, does not mean that evangelicals believe that the Bible is the word of God, at least not in the literal sense of every letter and word being directly from God. As the Chicago Statement explains, the Bible is "the authoritative Word of God" but "written by men prepared and superintended by His Spirit." Elsewhere, the signatories affirm "that inspiration was the work in which God by His Spirit, through human writers, gave us His Word," and, moreover, that God "utilized the distinctive personalities and literary styles of the writers whom He had chosen."[15]

Christians also disagree about what the Bible actually is— the relative importance of various books and who exactly wrote them. The New Testament is not a single work but, rather, an anthology of various constituent books, including the Gospels and the twenty-one "epistles." Moreover, the writing and canonization of the New Testament took place over a relatively long period of time, with a commonly accepted biblical canon only emerging in the fourth century. Early Christian scholars produced critical interpretations of the scripture well before the widespread acceptance of this canon.[16]

The Quran, meanwhile, has only one "mediator"— Mohamed—and, according to Muslims, only one author—God. Muslims often criticize the Bible for being written by men, but this elides the fact that scripture is less foundational in Christianity than it is in Islam. In Christianity, the word of God became flesh in Jesus Christ, so the equivalent of the Quran in Christianity is more the person of Jesus than the texts of the New Testament. As the Catholic scholar and priest Maurice Borrmans writes, "The Word of God came into the world 'in the fullness of time' not in the form of a scripture, but in the person of Jesus Christ, the revelation of the Father and the presence of God in the world of human beings."[17] The Jesuit theologian Daniel Madigan writes, "John does not claim that his letter is the Word of life, but rather that it is about the Word of life. The Word, he tells us, is something you can see and touch and live with, not because it has been written down, but because it has become flesh."[18] If, then, the Bible seems less compelling to Muslims as revelation, that's only because God's ultimate revelation in Christianity is a man and not a book.

In short, this is a key distinction between Islam and Christianity and one that is not just a product of modern changes in taste. Throughout the history of both religions, the relationship to the text has been different in this important though often overlooked way. To put it differently, even the most liberal Muslims believe things about the Quran—direct and total divine authorship—that even the most fundamentalist Christians don't believe about the Bible.

That Muslims go well beyond Christian notions of scriptural inerrancy and believe that the Quran is God's actual speech does not necessarily mean they believe it should be taken literally. In fact, at least three of the four main Sunni schools of Islamic law are *not* literalist and emphasize authorial intent, cultural and political context, and scholarly interpretation of what is a complex and challenging revelation. The question, however, remains: Does the Muslim view of the Quran as God's speech have distinctive political implications? The notion that the actions of groups like the Muslim Brotherhood or Ennahda can be deduced by looking at seventh-century scripture seems absurd on its face, and it is. But in the modern Middle East, Quranic inerrancy matters in ways that are more basic but perhaps less obvious.

Religions and Their Resources

Of course, major religions with billions of followers across space and time cannot be reduced to any one thing. But as

Michael Cook notes, religions are neither interchangeable nor merely "putty in the hands of exegetes."[19] Every faith tradition is characterized by a diversity of ideas, methodological approaches, and theological debates. The late Harvard scholar Shahab Ahmed writes, for example, of "the capaciousness, complexity, and, often, *outright contradiction*" contained within the historical phenomenon of what we call Islam.[20] But each faith tradition is also defined by boundaries, expectations, and the accumulated "weight" of history. What religious scholars and lay believers alike have committed themselves to for centuries—in the case of Islam, since its very founding—is relevant, for the simple reason that if something has never been done before, then it is less likely that it will start being done all of a sudden, fourteen centuries later.

Another way to look at this is through the prism of "resources." After a systematic comparison of the development of Islam, Christianity, and Hinduism, Cook concludes that Islam provides richer resources for those engaged in politics. This essentially means that if a Muslim reads scripture, they will find in the Quran and the prophetic model a preponderance of commands to observe various aspects of Islamic law. If they are so inclined, they may find ways to dismiss particular rules as "inapplicable" or not meeting the conditions for implementation, but they cannot really ignore or dismiss them altogether. In the Quran, there are clear, direct textual injunctions ranging from the implementation of the *hudud* punishments to specific rules on inheritance. The verses are there, and they are God's speech, not merely inspired by him. In short, to the extent that a believer is even vaguely familiar with the Quran and *hadith*, they will, in effect, be predisposed to think about the relationship of religion to politics in a particular way. To be sure, they will also find quite a bit to support the separation between caliph and cleric, or what we might call separation of mosque and state. This, however, is quite different than the separation of religion from politics (or as Ahmed puts it, "division of labor is

not the same thing as division of product").[21] We saw earlier
how the premodern clerical class enjoyed significant autonomy
and provided a meaningful check on executive power. One
could even go further and say that, historically, the implementation of sharia law was dependent on at least some separation
of mosque and state. This, though, is unlikely to be of much
reassurance to proponents of secularization, which entails a
process through which religion becomes less, rather than more,
involved in questions of law, politics, and governance.

In Christianity's founding moment, there was Jesus's famous
"render unto Caesar what is his" (Mark 12:17), a kind of clar-
ion call for Europe's early secularists. Within Islam, those intent on finding something that offers doctrinal support for the
privatization of religion and the separation of religion from politics will struggle to find much of use. This is not to say it can't
be done—Mahmoud Mohamed Taha and Abdullahi an-Nai'm
are proof that it can—but it requires such conceptual stretch-
ing, hermeneutical acrobatics, and sheer creativity that it is
unlikely a large number of Muslims will sign on. This, I would
argue, is why they haven't.

In short, there are more resources for Muslims making
"Islamic" arguments than for those making arguments for
European-style secularism. While specific outcomes in the real
world of politics aren't fixed, the *resources* that are available
within the tradition are more or less stable, and they are fixed
in favor of one side in the ongoing debate over the role of religion in public life. It should be noted that this Islamic heritage
is available to all Muslims and not just Islamists. In other words,
Islamism doesn't necessarily require Islamists. Where "secular"
parties win in conservative countries, they tend to do so not by
aggressively affirming their secularism but by downplaying or
denying it altogether. They assert their Islamic credentials and
even—as in Indonesia and Malaysia—go out of their way to pass
and implement sharia legislation. In Egypt, the most anti-
Islamist leader in the country's history, Abdel Fattah al-Sissi,

is often portrayed as "secular," but, in reality, he openly and publicly advocates a strong role for religion in politics, going so far as to claim that the job of a president includes "presenting God [correctly]."[22] This, then, goes well beyond the question of whether Islamists or their opponents are in power. It is a more a question of how Islam—as a tradition, heritage, corpus of law, and source of inspiration—relates to politics than merely one of how Islamists relate to politics.

Is Islam the Most "Modern" Religion?

All of this might suggest Islam is a retrograde and decidedly medieval religion. Indeed, conservative Muslims and Islamists are routinely portrayed as backward fundamentalists alienated by modernity and all that comes with it. Yet Islam may very well be the *most* "modern" of the monotheistic religions and perhaps of any major religion. This presents us with a paradox: It is precisely Islam and Islamic law's modern bent that makes Islamism—so often portrayed as antimodern—all the more relevant and resonant in today's politics. Within Islam's vast legal tradition, there are a number of ideas and precedents that lend themselves to modern notions of social justice, rule of law, and democratic politics. In practice, this meant that there was no reason for Muslims to choose modernity over Islam. You could be fully Muslim, or even fully Islamist, and still be fully modern.

During the Prophet Mohamed's time, Islam brought with it a fierce egalitarianism—calling the faithful to free slaves and put away tribal allegiances—which was all the more striking considering the cultural backdrop of seventh-century Arabia. Although this would later change, the selection process for community leaders was consensus-based and nonhereditary— not quite democracy but not quite absolute monarchy either. Even on issues like women's rights, the Prophet—armed with God's speech—pushed important changes, banning the practice of female infanticide and guaranteeing women the right to own property and earn their own income. On economic issues, the practice of *zakat,* or mandated charity, redistributed income from rich to poor. In a premodern version of social security, the early caliphate's public treasury provided a stipend to elderly citizens who could no longer work. Meanwhile, the lack of a church or formal clergy allowed for direct access to God and individual agency. One could, for example, choose among different religious scholars and different legal schools of thought, or *madhabs.* Finally, as an overarching framework, the very notion of sharia—which bound ruler and ruled alike (at least in theory)—provided something resembling what we would today call "rule of law." The caliph could not claim unlimited sovereignty. That belonged to God and God alone.

All of these elements—which, again, can be traced back to Islam's founding moment and the conduct of the Prophet himself—aren't wholly removed from how people today talk about equality, egalitarianism, and democratic decision making. As Cook notes, "Where the Islamic heritage stands apart is in providing a compelling parallel to European egalitarianism. Without question this has been one of the most attractive features of this heritage under modern conditions, a source of almost lyrical inspiration to leading Islamists."[23]

While Enlightenment notions of equality, fraternity, individualism, and citizenship were no doubt attractive to many in the Middle East, including even Islamists, Muslims were never compelled to choose between their own tradition and another. Islam was flexible enough to incorporate, or even embrace, such ideas and retroactively give them an Islamic imprimatur so as to calm any fears over "authenticity." Where Islamists were at pains to justify their use of the word "democracy," they could point to a rich Islamic tradition of *shura*, or consensus. Democracy, then, could be marketed as updating or repackaging something that was already rooted in the Islamic heritage. The influential Islamist ideologue Sayyid Qutb—better known for his late-career radicalism—could write a book called *Social Justice in Islam,* essentially arguing for something resembling socialism but with a strong Islamic flavor. The same could be done for democracy ("Islamic democracy") or capitalism ("Islamic Calvinism").[24] But what about Islam and the nation-state? Could they ever truly be compatible, when the caliphate had, for centuries, implied a transnational community of believers that paid little heed to borders? Here, too, there was an answer.

A Reformation and Its Discontents

When Martin Luther nailed his ninety-five theses to the wall of a Wittenberg church, Christianity must have appeared just as politically vital as Islam seems today, infusing every aspect of public and private life across Western Europe. If we had been alive then, the same questions asked about Islam would have been asked of Christianity, about its entanglements with politics and power and whether it could ever make peace with a secular order. Christianity eventually receded from political life in ways that no one would have thought possible. In hindsight, we can say that Christianity failed in its bid to hold secularism at bay. Many, of course, would view this positively as evidence of Christianity's modern sensibilities and ability to adapt, but it still raises the question of whether such a dramatic shift was inevitable.

As political theology, Christianity could not marshal the will, the ability, or the *resources* to mount an effective challenge to secularization. In Europe, official Christianity basically conceded defeat, accepting, however grudgingly, its diminished status. There was little choice in the matter. Too many people had turned against the very idea of religion playing a central, organizing role in public life. Here, though, it is worth taking a step back. To understand how secularism triumphed in Europe— and why the same process is unlikely to take hold in the Middle East—we have to look more closely at the rise and fall of Christian politics.

As we saw earlier, Jesus had little to say about political power in this world. Christianity, unlike Islam, was a minority religion for centuries after Jesus's death. Early Christians had assumed that their savior would be returning imminently. Until then, as a matter of practical necessity, Christians could do little more than accept rule by others. Naturally, as Christians grew in number and influence, other considerations came to the fore. The Roman emperor Constantine converted to Christianity in the fourth century, which not only ended the persecution of Christians in the vast empire but also raised, for the first time, the question of what Christians could and should do with political authority.

Christians were compelled to think more seriously about the practice of politics, even if they had little to draw on from the lives of Jesus and his disciples. What resulted was a kind of improvisation that depended on local context and culture. Such efforts were complicated by the fact that Christianity was still busy establishing its foundational tenets well into the fourth century, most famously at the Council of Nicaea. The responsibilities of power were accepted not because a positive vision for what to do with it existed but because the other options were worse. Politics was embraced, with some trepidation at first. As Gregory writes, the alternative of political passivity would mean "a hydra-headed *cupiditas*"—signifying here avarice and prideful power—receiving "unrestrained sanction by default."[25] The ambivalence would persist. In the words of the historian Peter Brown, "power was redeemed."[26] But the word "redeem" here suggests that the pursuit of power was not necessarily a natural, welcome enterprise for the Christ-loving believer. As Saint Augustine wrote in his masterwork *City of God*, the city of man and the city of God, though they inevitably overlapped, were separate, and they were sometimes even portrayed as walled cities in opposition. The gap could not be erased, and, more important, it wasn't meant to be erased.[27] These influential strains of Christian theology—emphasizing dualism and even "separation"—could lead to passivity where the temporal world, with its mundane politics, was accepted as the fallen realm of sin. As one leading scholar of Protestantism, John Witte, Jr., writes, "This apostolic ideal of separationism found its strongest and most enduring institutional form in monasticism, which produced a vast archipelago of communities of spiritual brothers and sisters, each walled off from the world around them."[28] This early ambivalence over temporal rule was less surprising than it otherwise might have been. After all, "render unto Caesar what is his and to God what is God's" suggests separation between realms of activity but doesn't specify what is God's and what is Caesar's.

With the Papal Revolution, beginning in the eleventh century, the church's influence and political reach grew considerably under the "two swords" doctrine, where temporal and spiritual authority, however distinct, would be wielded in tandem in the service of Christendom and Christianity. With more land, riches, and political privilege, there were, inevitably, more abuses. With the church becoming ever more pervasive in the everyday lives of believers, those abuses became increasingly difficult to ignore. One notable example was the practice of clerical concubinage, which "was so widespread in parts of Germany and Switzerland that bishops profited from the practice by selling pardons of the offense."[29]

The church, powerful as ever, may not have provided an easy target for the disenchanted, but it provided a clear one. To the extent that Christians were angry, their anger could be directed at the one, dominant church. Well before the Reformation, the Spiritual Franciscans faced persecution for deeming the pope "the antichrist," a prelude to the intense passions aroused by the Reformation and then, predictably, the Counter-Reformation. The church provided a rallying point for all those who had lost faith in its authority, but a problem soon became apparent. If the church and all of its elaborate pomp and power had obscured Jesus's truth, then it made sense to go back to the word of God. The question that the Dutch humanist Erasmus faced was one that Luther and a long line of reformers would have to contend with. As Diarmaid MacCulloch writes in his seminal history of Christianity, "Did the Bible contain all sacred truth? Or was there a tradition which the Church guarded, independent of it?"[30]

The Bible, by itself, could only go so far. As we saw earlier, the New Testament—and Jesus—had relatively little to say about governance. The tension between the two kingdoms, that of God and that of man, was left unresolved. Not only that, the question of authorship and transmission of scripture was far from clear-cut. The Bible, then, was not necessarily strong enough to provide the sole foundation for a new Christianity, as reformers like Luther initially hoped it would. In *The Unintended Reformation*, Brad Gregory offers a fascinating, revisionist account of the resulting fallout, and how it paved the way for Europe's secularization. "Against the intentions of its protagonists," he writes, "the Reformation ended more than a thousand years of Christianity as a framework for shared intellectual life in the Latin West."[31]

The Reformation—so often associated with the liberal sensibilities that would later define Europe—was neither peaceful nor liberal. It was an intensely violent process and unleashed a wave of unabashed puritanism. It brought about what Witte calls "the rapid deconstruction of law, politics and society."[32] The fact that there were Lutherans and Calvinists—but also Anglicans, Anabaptists, Mennonites, and so forth—suggests the scale of difficulty in fashioning coherent alternatives to Catholicism (Luther once remarked that the Protestant reformer Zwingli was more astray than even the pope, which, considering Luther's antipathy toward the church, is quite remarkable).[33] It was easy to be unified in opposition to the Catholic Church; it was much more difficult to agree on what should replace it. Protestants didn't just disagree on some things. They disagreed about *a lot* of things, including fundamental matters of doctrine:

They disagreed about the meaning and prioritization of biblical texts, and the relationship of those texts to doctrines regarding the sacraments, worship, grace, the church, and so forth. They disagreed about the broad interpretative principles that ought to guide the understanding of scripture, such as the relationship between the Old and New Testaments or the permissibility of religious practices not explicitly prohibited or enjoined in the Bible. They disagreed about the relationship among the interpolation of scripture, the exercise of reason, and God's influence in the hearts of individual Christians. And they disagreed about whether (and if so, to what extent) explicit, substantive truth claims were even *important* to being a Christian.[34]

As became apparent over time, there was simply no resolution to these differences. More and more sects and denominations appeared. The arguments persisted. Within a generation of Luther's *Ninety-Five Theses*, the Reformation had split into four principal branches, and interpretations on key theological questions would continue to proliferate.[35] Because basic doctrine had been called into doubt and undermined over centuries of intense disagreement and even war, Christianity increasingly struggled to offer a framework for understanding the natural world, law, and politics. Christianity, as a worldview, had succumbed to confusion. Reason, science, and secular approaches to knowledge came to be seen as offering more clarity and consistency on the animating questions of man's relationship to the world around him. Moreover, in order to maintain social peace, political systems needed to find a way to accommodate a seemingly irreversible doctrinal pluralism. No one group, party, or denomination in the doctrinal debate had enough people or power to realize its own particular conception of the good. It was a long, uneven process, but in the end, it wasn't that Christianity lost the battle with secularism but more that it simply couldn't win.

This didn't necessarily mean that religion was doomed to irrelevance. Although that may have increasingly been the case in Europe, religion in the United States flourished, in part because so many different—and sometimes competing—strains of Christian practice were able to coexist. In this sense, secularism and religious observance went hand in hand. As long as certain constitutional limits were respected, individuals and groups could be as fundamentalist as they wanted. They could promote their religious values through the political process, if not on the national level, then at least at the local and state levels, where abortion could be restricted and the teaching of creationism mandated. It was the state's job not to suppress religious sentiment, as in France and some other European countries, but to protect it and allow sufficient freedom for its expression.

Scholars have likened the American religious landscape to an economic marketplace, in which a wide array of mostly Protestant groups compete with each other over individual "consumers." The product is religion, and, given the nature of competition and the laws of supply and demand, groups must be willing to innovate and improve their "product." In the analogy, instead of restricting or otherwise controlling the supply of religion, the state ensures a free market. The marketplace approach is good for pluralism, because churches have incentives to cater to assorted personal religious tastes. Interestingly, the marketplace may benefit "strict" churches more than others. Strictness, writes Laurence Iannaccone, "increases commitment, raises levels of participation, and enables a group to offer more benefits to current and potential members."[36] Another way of looking at this is that, in a busy marketplace, churches have to find ways to distinguish themselves, and signaling "strictness" can do just that. In sum, if there is a demand for a niche product, then someone in the religious marketplace is likely to emerge to supply it. While this may be a boon for individual consumers—who are likely to find something that satisfies whatever religious idiosyncrasy they might have—it makes forging a shared sense of public morality more challenging.

WHILE RETURNING TO the first and ultimate source—whether the Bible or the Quran—has always provided a certain kind of fascination for the faithful, it opens a whole set of thorny questions. What about those things on which scripture is silent? Who interprets the text? What is the role of theologians, preachers, and clerics? If the answer is that each person accesses the text on his or her own, then what happens when these individuals—reading the same text—disagree with each other on the most basic of questions?

Doctrinal dilemmas, of course, didn't stop the ever-expanding list of Protestant sects and denominations from trying to establish new Christian communities and "states." They did so with the enthusiasm (and sometimes fanaticism) of the newly converted, which only sharpened the divides not just between Catholics and Protestants but also within Protestantism itself. Calvinists and other Protestant groups had relatively little use for rites and instead focused their efforts on promoting public morality and imposing social discipline.[37] Such endeavors were often dependent on the sheer force of personality of early Protestant revolutionaries like John Calvin and Oliver Cromwell, a Puritan who briefly reigned as lord protector of the Commonwealth of England from 1653 to 1658. In his seminal history of Calvinism, Philip Benedict writes that under Calvin's leadership, Geneva became "a model of the successful reformation of manners and morals."[38] Moral policing required a certain intensity, something that early reformers had in spades. For Zwingli, Christian life was akin to "a battle so sharp and full of danger that effort can nowhere be relaxed without loss."[39] Efforts to enforce moral discipline ranged from the obvious (punishing sexual deviance) to the odd (making Bibles available at pubs to encourage spiritual reflection).[40] The unacceptably large gap between professions of faith and sinful behavior was one of the persistent Protestant critiques of the Catholic clergy. Bringing outward conduct in line with inward faith was what reformers like Calvin hoped to achieve.

Meanwhile, the Catholic Church, while irrevocably shaken, retained its dominance in much of Europe. Here, too, various experiments in fusing religion and politics were embraced enthusiastically by Catholic partisans but to mixed effect. In their different ways, Catholicism and Protestantism were bound to face growing—and ultimately unresolvable—challenges in maintaining religious states, particularly with the pull of modernity growing stronger. Within the Christian tradition, there was no equivalent of Islamic law—an accumulated corpus of law concerned with governance and the regulation of social and political affairs. More broadly, as Cook writes, Christianity was characterized by the "absence of any project of state formation."[41] At some level, it is foolish to even attempt the comparison, since "law" was not, in a very basic sense, what Christianity was supposed to be about. It is little surprise, then, that Martin Luther did not view the law, as expressed in the Old Testament, in a particularly positive light. As MacCulloch notes, "The opposition of Law and Gospel, an opposition set up by God himself, remained a fundamental theme of [Luther's] theology."[42] To the extent that this tension was built into post-Reformation Christianity, there could be no resolution. Needless to say, this presented a rather fundamental obstacle when it came to religiously inspired state building. And this was why there were Lutherans, Zwinglians, and Calvinists, all named after individuals.[43] In the absence of a widely accepted legal tradition that could be called upon for setting parameters of governance, the distinctive, sometimes idiosyncratic, vision of charismatic leaders mattered all the more.

Within Catholicism, the importance—and even the very

existence—of canon law presents a similar dilemma. Canon law is essentially the system of rules and regulations for executing the church's mission. At least at first, much of it was formulated during periods when Christianity was removed from power, with little prospect of gaining it. Naturally, this body of law was primarily oriented toward running a vast, hierarchical institution. In this sense, while canon law became increasingly political and politicized, particularly after the Papal Revolution, it cannot be compared with the sharia, which is, in part, law derived directly from God's speech rather than merely inspired by him. (The large portion of Islamic law that is based on prophetic sayings is not "revealed" in the technical sense, but considering that God, in the Quran, guarantees the integrity of the prophetic model, it cannot easily be dismissed).

Without an "intrinsically Christian conception of the state," to use Cook's rendering,[44] church officials, naturally, promoted church building over state building. The church tended to advance policies that expanded its privilege and maintained its control over the religious and moral sphere. The church, then, became both the means and the end—to the dismay of those calling for reform.

There was a growing sense among reformers like Martin Luther—who started out as committed Catholics—that the church simply could not be salvaged. Later, in the post-Reformation era, the church would misplay its hand during the dawn of mass politics, further alienating Catholics. The tumult of the nineteenth century is worth considering at some length, since it underscores the doomed proposition of Catholic politics in an age of secularization. From the very beginning, the church viewed modernity and various associated ideologies with suspicion. Socialists who condemned religion as "the opiate of the masses" were demanding their rights, taking to the streets, and forming revolutionary parties. The church, on the other hand, was a status quo power that had long employed religion as a means of social control in the service of a hierarchical social order. All too often, clerics preached a kind of economic fatalism and political passivity in the face of urban alienation, mass poverty, and terrible working conditions. In Belgium, where Catholic conservatives were particularly powerful throughout the nineteenth century, the church "sternly identified itself with the oppressor."[45] "The Church's contempt for the worker," writes the eminent Belgian historian Els Witte, "was visible in the religious burial ceremony, which perpetuated social inequality in death."[46] Before the advent of civil burials (another modern phenomenon we take for granted), the church effectively controlled the most intimate moments of a person's life, those of birth and death. How to die became a key battleground between the religious and secular, stoking considerable outrage and opposition. As Witte notes, "It was the last show of contempt for any non-religious citizen when his burial in a graveyard was denied on the grounds that it would desecrate the site."[47]

Making matters worse, the fear of socialists and their ilk went hand in hand with a fear of democracy. It is difficult to imagine now, but in nineteenth-century Europe the right to vote was generally restricted to property owners (often in tandem with religious, gender, and ethnic restrictions). Electoral taxes could limit the franchise to as little as 1 percent of the population. Expanding suffrage meant that the working poor— the core constituency of socialist parties—could swing elections to the left. The masses, empowered by democratization, were something to be feared. This generally put the church and the Catholic parties it backed on the wrong side of one of the most consequential debates of the era. It was yet another losing battle that the church insisted on fighting. At their most radical, Catholic conservatives were nearly feudal in their antimodernism. The far-right Ultramontanes of Belgium, for example, agitated for a Christian state under the pope's direct control with "a medieval class structure" to boot.[48]

That the church lacked a coherent conception of law,

governance, and state building was one thing. But what doomed it was the inability to come to terms with a rapidly changing Europe, where the old foundations of social order were coming under direct assault. Here, the church's inflexibility was striking. Modernity's full and rather diverse array of political options—whether ideologies such as socialism and liberalism or political systems such as democracy—were opposed outright rather than assimilated.

MANY MUSLIM THINKERS, FROM radicals like Sayyid Qutb to reformists like Syed Attas, have written about Christianity as fundamentally dualistic, spiritual, ascetic, and otherworldly.[49] Though these writers disagreed profoundly on a whole range of issues, they shared a common interest in emphasizing Islam's uniqueness during a time of cultural encroachment and imperial domination. The assertion of Islam became a distinctly political act, and not just—or even primarily—a theological one: The Muslim world may have found itself weak and subjugated, but, at the very least, here was one thing that the colonial powers couldn't take away. Islam was *better*, truer, more vibrant, and unwavering in the face of those who sought to reduce it to a mere religion. It retained an uncompromised power and "purity" that no other major religion could claim. In this way, Christianity presented itself as an appropriate and even easy foil.

Christianity may appear decidedly "otherworldly" today, but it would be a mistake to project secularism's recent triumphs on the preceding period—running from the seventeenth to the early twentieth century—of religious violence and rather vigorous attempts to fuse religion with politics. There was a time, not too long ago, when secularists would have lost faith, resigning themselves to a world where the church appeared immovable and Christianity imbued itself, endlessly, in daily life (and death). What seemed impossible then came to pass more quickly than they (and for that matter, the church) could have imagined. The argument, then, isn't that Christianity, whether in its Catholic or Protestant varieties, is apolitical or uniquely "secular." Christianity *was* quite political. This posture, however, was unsustainable, for the many reasons already discussed—Jesus's "prophetic" model, the legacy of the early Christian community, the nature and role of Christian scripture, and the absence of any positive conception of divinely mandated governance.

Where a political Christianity had failed, a political—and politicized—Islam could succeed. While many Islamic intellectuals looked at Christianity with skepticism, or worse, many—and sometimes they were the same people—also drew inspiration from its Protestant variants, arguing that Islam had inspired the Reformation. Martin Luther was portrayed as a sort of "latter-day Muslim," someone who had washed away Catholicism's sins and decadence and restored the power and purity of original scripture.[50] The preeminent Islamic modernist of his time, Mohamed Abduh, saw his own project of reform as continuing in that spirit. Jamal al-Din al-Afghani, often mentioned in the same breath as Abduh, argued that Europe had progressed "from barbarism to civilization" because of "the religious movement raised and spread by Luther."[51] Not surprisingly, then, while Luther might have been a latter-day Muslim, Afghani fashioned himself a modern-day Luther.

In the light of recent years and decades—with the Middle East an apparently unceasing source of religious conflict and fanaticism—it is easy to overlook what came before. In the late nineteenth and early twentieth centuries, the region underwent a wide-ranging and often fascinating process of reform and modernization. To the extent that the Middle East today seems hopelessly violent, it is a product of, rather than a precursor to, modernization. As we will see, this process was for both better and worse, but in ways that may not seem obvious at first. It also offers a useful reminder to be careful what you wish for. Reform doesn't necessarily lead to reformation. Good things don't necessarily go together.

(3)

ISLAM'S REFORMATION

The church came to accept democracy and, to an extent, liberalism, but these were concessions from a position of weakness rather than strength. The various strains of Catholic conservatism were ill suited for a rapidly changing Europe, where ideas like egalitarianism, mass politics, and universal suffrage were becoming ubiquitous. Meanwhile, Protestantism claimed to depend on a sole scripture (*sola scriptura*), which was ultimately unable to provide a workable foundation for a distinctly Christian conception of law and governance.

Within Islam, the idea of a return to scripture—which had inspired Luther centuries before—was more practicable. The Quran, in a way that the Bible never was and never could be, was unimpeachable in the eyes of believing Muslims. The fundamentals, then, were stronger, and where the fundamentals were stronger, "fundamentalism" had more of a fighting chance.

But fundamentalism, or what would later become known as Islamic revivalism or Islamism, had another unlikely advantage:

Islam, oddly enough, happened to be the most flexible and modern of the Abrahamic religions. Not only that, Islamic law, or sharia, proved more "secular" than Christian conceptions of law and politics. This is a critical point of departure, since it is the sharia's very secularity that makes it more relevant and resonant in today's politics. How, though, could this be? This unlikely reality can help us solve the puzzle of Islam's continued relevance in a secular age.

It is not so much that premodern Islamic law was a bad fit for modernity; it is rather that, almost by definition, any premodern legal system—being based on an entirely different set of assumptions—was bound to be inappropriate and irrelevant to modern realities and expectations. In short, Islam had to change, and the story of how it came to change and, importantly, why it was *able* to change is the subject of this chapter. As we will see, where official Christianity came into conflict with mass politics, pluralism, and democracy—a conflict it ultimately lost—Islam was able to accommodate and even incorporate these supposedly Western secular ideas, recasting them as authentic and "Islamic."

TO GRASP THE IMPORT of the debate that would soon rage—over the problem of modernity and what to do about it—we first need to understand the massive geopolitical shift that took place in the eighteenth and nineteenth centuries. The Ottoman caliphate, deemed the "sick man of Europe," was entering a slow but unmistakable decline. The territories that were ostensibly part of the empire were coming under the effective control of colonial powers, which brought with them new notions of European nationalism. Russian and Austrian campaigns gradually eroded Ottoman territory in the predominantly Christian areas of the empire. Bosnia and Herzegovina—where neither European policies nor Ottoman reforms were able to quell restive Christian and Muslim populations—saw uprisings in the late nineteenth century and soon fell out of Ottoman control.[1] Meanwhile, colonialist encroachments on Muslim territories continued with French attempts to seize control of Egypt and the Levant.

These setbacks prompted the *tanzimat* reforms in the nineteenth century, the empire's final, desperate attempt at modernizing the caliphate's ailing structures. The *tanzimat* were the Ottoman response to the nationalist ideologies that were gaining momentum in imperial territories. The reforms sought to offer a more inclusive Ottoman "nationality" that would counter the appeal of new national identities, say in Lebanon or Egypt, by easing discriminatory policies toward religious and ethnic minorities. The *tanzimat* ushered in wide-ranging changes in the Ottoman military, political, and economic bureaucracy, but it was too little, too late.

The religious innovations of the Islamic modernists would have been impossible to understand outside this particular political context. Theirs was a modern response to modern problems. When they looked around themselves at the turn of the century, religious thinkers like Jamal al-Din al-Afghani and Mohamed Abduh saw the success of the colonial project on the one hand and the many, varied Muslim failures on the other. Profoundly troubled, they asked—and then tried to answer—the question of what could be done. If Muslims were now weak, how could they once again become strong, just as they had been in centuries prior?

For centuries, Muslim thinkers had looked down on Christian Europe, taking refuge in the uninterrupted success and dominance of Islamic empires. This posture of knowing superiority became untenable as Europe closed the gap, soon enough eclipsing the Muslim world altogether. Certainty was replaced by insecurity and resentment. Simon Wood remarks that the writings of the influential modernist Rashid Rida reflect "an overwhelming awareness of Muslim weakness relative to non-Muslim strength. The calm confidence of classical Islam is lacking."[2] Rida, the prolific editor of the influential journal *al-Manar*, was born in Ottoman Syria in 1865. It is interesting to note these Levantine origins, since, in the various accounts of his life, Rida seems almost rootless. He traveled throughout the Muslim world with apparent ease. That he wasn't Egyptian mattered little in what would become his adopted home. The nation-state was slowly asserting its dominance, but Rida was among the last of a generation that could be—and not just aspire to be—pan-Arab and pan-Islamic.

Rida migrated to Cairo in 1897 to study under the Egyptian jurist and al-Azhar scholar Mohamed Abduh.[3] Rida and *al-Manar* served as the intellectual bridge between Afghani and Abduh's Islamic modernism and later movements like the Muslim Brotherhood. The Egypt to which Rida migrated, despite nominally remaining part of the Ottoman realm, had by 1882 succumbed to the effective control of the British Empire. In the 1880s, Rida's mentor and teacher Abduh, along with Afghani, founded a society with a strong anti-British bent, called al-Urwa al-Wuthqa, or the Indissoluble Bond. The name they chose was no accident.

Europeans were able to subjugate Muslims because Muslims were weak, and Muslims were weak because they had abandoned the true, original Islam. It was this conclusion that reflected the essential premise behind all revivalist movements, from the modernist to the most literalist. Naturally, the next question was why, exactly, had Muslims strayed from the straight path?

The tragedy of Muslim paralysis in the face of an overwhelming cultural and political assault wasn't just a problem for Islamists, but for so-called secularists as well. Secularists, though, had a different interpretation of the Muslim world's fall from grace. Their solution was not only to appropriate the scientific and technological progress of Europe, its work ethic, or the trappings of parliamentary politics but also to go further and embrace elements of European culture, including at least some separation of religion from politics. Religion, in their view, could no longer remain at the center of public life. These being conservative societies, secularists rarely called for a wholesale separation, but they hoped to shift their societies toward less, rather than more, religious politics.

As this chapter will show, the claim that Muslims rejected modernity fundamentally misinterprets this critical phase in the Middle East's evolution. If anything, nearly everyone across the ideological spectrum was grappling with modernity and all that it entailed. Some, to be sure, didn't like what they saw, but they were irrevocably changed by it nonetheless. Meanwhile, those "traditionalists" who still held to premodern approaches to law were overtaken by events, either unable or unwilling to mount their own challenge. Many if not most traditionalists, including large segments of the clerical class, were co-opted by the state, accepting their fate—and reduced influence—with little resistance.

One Man's Reformer Is Another Man's Fundamentalist

The Islamic modernists were the original Salafis—a group usually today associated with ultraconservative literalism, theocratic rule, and religious violence. But for these first "Salafis," the basic thrust was quite different. First, they hoped to return to the unadulterated Islam of *al-Salaf al-Salih*, or the early, righteous generations of Muslims who were closest, in both time and proximity, to the Prophet Mohamed. This, though, did not necessarily suggest an obsession with the past. After all, as Jonathan Brown notes, the Islamic modernists believed that "Islam had always been modern . . . and it had to be returned to its proper form."[4] For them, the purity and purification of Islam meant moving away from bland imitation and literalism, not toward it. As the memory of the Prophet faded, Islam became ossified, buried under layers after layer of highly technical

Quranic and legal commentaries. Scholars wrote commentaries about other commentaries. This was the work of self-indulgent elites who had lost sight of the essence of religion and what it could offer to the hearts—and minds—of men. Something had gone wrong "in between," and only by reconnecting to the Quran as the source could the spirit of Islam be revived. For someone like Rashid Rida, the abandonment of the Quran was an "ugly abandonment."[5]

The modernists looked at the passivity of the traditional religious establishment with dismay and even disgust. It wasn't that the clerics had rejected modernity as much as it was that they were simply indifferent to it, and in some ways indifference deserved less respect. They had little to say about a world that was changing so rapidly around them. Stuck in their books and their circular legal commentaries, the clerics could not muster anything resembling a coherent response to the twin challenges of colonialism and secularism. The implications of their weakness were far-reaching. The traditionalists, with old, outmoded modes of thinking, had left Islam—and Muslims—vulnerable to external conquest.

Losing territory was one thing but losing faith quite another. Rida and his contemporaries were alarmed by the influx of Christian missionaries. They feared that ordinary Muslims—many of whom held to superficial and superstitious understandings of Islam—would fall under the sway of arguments about the contradictions of the Quran or the inferiority of Islamic civilization. As they saw it, the loss of territory, threat of secularism, and assaults on Islam were inextricably linked, all part of a larger colonial enterprise.

In the writings of the Islamic modernists, there was a simple, repeated refrain, one that would color nearly every Islamist movement to the present day. Muslims were most successful in the temporal world—in their conquest of territory, in their knowledge of the sciences, and in their technological prowess—when they were close to Islam. The more they moved away from religion, the more they suffered in this world, just as they would in the next. As Rida wrote in his refutation of the missionaries: "Indeed, [the Muslim] community was at its high point of civilization and science when holding most strongly to its religion, whereas it became distanced from the religion as it distanced itself from science."[6]

The modernists hoped to arm Muslims with the tools to resist missionary arguments. The solution wasn't literalism—far from it—but rather an effort to affirm, as they saw it, the inherent rationalism of Islam. In this respect, Rida's refutations are perhaps most illustrative. For Rida, Islam is the "religion of reason" and "the ally of the sciences." Islam is "nearer to mankind's innate disposition and intelligence."[7] He advises his readers, "You may come to know your religion's truths through logical proof and evidence." The Quran, meanwhile, "furnishes evidences and rational proofs through which it demands certainty in faith from people of reason."[8] If it seems as if Rida had something to prove, it is because he did.

Christianity, in contrast, was portrayed as otherworldly, irrational—a religion of magical thinking. "[The word 'reason'] is not mentioned in the bible," Rida writes, his disdain palpable, as it so often is in the apologetics of Muslim writers at the dawn of the twentieth century.[9] For similar reasons, Rida and other modernists looked at the more "mystical" of the Sufi orders with skepticism and even scorn. The practice of Sufism had been a venerable tradition, and one that was indelibly linked to the development of Islam over a millennium. As Albert Hourani notes, "Throughout the eighteenth and nineteenth centuries . . . the most influential currents of thought and action still flowed within the channels of the Sufi orders."[10] This made Rida's attacks on various aspects of Sufi practice all the more striking. The Sufi emphasis on the inner, the unseen, and the nonpolitical was seen as contrary to the modernists' insistent, self-conscious rationalism. It was an early sign of what would prove to be one of the most defining shifts within Islam: the at first slow and then rapid decline of Sufism.

Interestingly, Rida uses the incidence of miracles, or the lack thereof, to underscore Islam's rational bent. In his book *The Muhammadan Revelation*, Rida opines at length about Mohamed's prophethood, which had little need for miracles. Although Mohamed was associated with some supernatural acts, he "certainly never ordered that these be mentioned to people." "The reason for this," Rida argues, is that by the seventh century "humanity had entered that stage of maturity and independence in which men's minds are not given to submitting to the incredible or unnatural. To expect this would be to hamper their intellectual progress."[11] It seems odd to hold seventh-century Arabia as a font of intellectualism or a place inhospitable to a belief in miracles. But Rida was a product of a very different age; he was trying to make Islam appear as modern as possible, at a time when it was being attacked for being the opposite.

This obsession with demonstrating Islam's rationality and, by extension, its superiority helps explain the modernists' anti-clerical bent. The curriculum at al-Azhar—the Sunni world's premier institution of Islamic learning—had fallen behind the times. The clerics of al-Azhar contented themselves with teaching an avowedly premodern curriculum. Rida castigated them for failing to teach secular subjects, particularly the social and biological sciences.[12] They had "rendered the religion tradition-bound."[13] And so Islam had to be freed from tradition and reaffirmed with evidence and reason. Only then could Islam be made safe for modernity and modernity safe for Islam. This led to some controversial arguments. For example, according to Rida, if divine revelation appears to be in conflict with "clear-cut" rational evidence, then the latter takes precedence and the revealed text would have to, in effect, be interpreted allegorically rather than literally.[14] Elsewhere, Rida reinterpreted military jihad, or "struggle," as primarily defensive in nature, analogous in many ways to just war theory.[15] Again, the implications were clear. Just as missionaries argued that Islam was irrational and full of contradiction, Western scholars had long argued that Islam was a warlike religion, inherently predisposed to violence. Rida, through unorthodox methodological and hermeneutical techniques, hoped to cast Islam in a different light. It was neither brutal nor bellicose.

Of course, Islamic modernism had its limits, and the modernists weren't quite liberals, nor did they want to become liberals. Islamic law still provided the foundation for social and political life, but it had to be reinterpreted in the context of new norms of nationhood, democracy, and human rights. Their vision of Islam and Islamic law still fell well short of Western liberal norms, at least as Western liberals would understand them. This makes it challenging to take stock of the modernist legacy more than a century later. As the legal scholar Mohammad Fadel notes, "Modernist Islamic political thought takes the appearance of a thoroughly secular movement from the perspective of other Islamic traditions of political thought, but viewed from the perspective of humanistic political philosophy, it takes the appearance of a thoroughly religious movement."[16] In other words, it really depends on how you look at it.

KHAYR AL-DIN AL-TUNISI, the chief minister of Ottoman-ruled Tunisia in the 1870s, proposed *shura*, an Islamic concept meaning "consultation," as a solution to autocracy, which he viewed as the primary sickness of the Muslim world.[17] Every other Islamic reformer during this period—and up to the present day—has held *shura* as either the analogue or equivalent of Western-style democracy. This served the objectives of the reformers quite well. They could embrace what were effectively Western ideas and norms without compromising their traditions and heritage. After all, if *shura*, at its core, was about deliberation, discussion, and consent, then it wasn't too different from democracy and could easily be used to justify democratic practices.

Most modernists saw creeping autocracy as one of the great ills of their time. As the traditional clerical class was either swept away into irrelevance or co-opted by powerful regimes, it could no longer play its historic role of checking executive authority. In this sense, the weakening of the clerics had already happened, and unlike in Europe, it was not necessarily in the service of pluralism or democracy. As Noah Feldman argues, it was the self-regulating clerical class that, as keepers of the sharia, ensured the ruler was constrained by something greater than himself.[18] But if the clerics could no longer check executive power, it was time to adopt a different approach, and, here, the modernists hoped that the "people," through elected parliaments, could serve a similar function. Consultative mechanisms and institutions, even if they weren't quite democratic in the full sense of the word, would balance the burgeoning power of the executive.

This is where Islam and Islamic law's aforementioned flexibility came in handy. Islam, at least as the modernists saw it, could appropriate anything from the West as long as it was good while discarding the cultural excesses that prioritized the individual over the community. This made enough intuitive sense: If the Quran was a book for all times, then its laws and principles should be appropriate for the modern era just as they were appropriate for seventh-century Arabia. If God in his wisdom had revealed Islam as a complete and comprehensive religion, that could only mean that the text and the tradition had an inherent power to renew themselves, even if it meant going where Islam hadn't quite gone before. And this is where they went.

The state is at the center of our story, and here too the modernists were willing to come to terms with new realities. Premodern Islamic law, by definition, was incompatible with the modern nation-state. There had to be a way to square the circle, even if that meant going well beyond what textual literalists were comfortable with. It's worth remembering that until 1924, the idea that there should be a caliphate—even if its authority and reach had been significantly weakened—was relatively uncontroversial. More than that, there was an "overwhelming" scholarly consensus that establishing and maintaining the caliphate was obligatory for Muslims.[19] Al-Azhar's Council of Senior Scholars went so far as to expel one of their own, Ali Abdul Raziq, for writing a book, published in 1925, deeming the caliphate unnecessary. Yet while Islamic union was and would remain an ideal, the modernists spoke in terms that were readily intelligible to nationalists. They recognized and acknowledged state power but hoped it could be harnessed for religious ends.

Like any movement, the Islamic modernists, while maintaining the core ideas of Afghani and Abduh, would evolve and become something other than what they were. Modernist thought was an attempt to reconcile the irreconcilable, so a certain tension wasn't merely inevitable; it was inherent to the very enterprise. Abduh's students, of which there were many, would come to differ on what to prioritize: Islamic identity and authenticity, on the one hand, or what Albert Hourani calls the "irreversible movement of modern civilization," on the other.[20] Some such as Qasim Amin, who wrote passionately about the emancipation of women, gravitated toward secular and liberal ideas. Others, however, provided the link between Abduh's ideas and what would come to be called "Islamism." The nature of this evolution is a controversial one, and that controversy can be captured in the changing views of Rashid Rida.

Rashid Rida was either a reformer or a fundamentalist—or both—depending on whom you asked. As discussed, Rida very much saw himself as a rationalist and was adamant about demonstrating Islam's alignment with science, technology, and civilizational progress. But in his later years, largely for political rather than religious reasons, he became fascinated by a new experiment in statehood in what would become Saudi Arabia. In the 1920s, Abdelaziz Ibn Saud united large swathes of the

Arabian Peninsula with the help of a religious militia inspired by Wahhabism, a particularly harsh, puritanical strain of Islam.

Rida, who was in some ways more conservative than his mentor and friend Mohamed Abduh, had a major influence on Hassan al-Banna, the next major personality in the modernist lineage. Just as Rida was, or became, more conservative than his teachers, Banna was more conservative than Rida. And this is where our story of modernists and modernism leads to the Middle East's present predicament. In 1928, Banna founded the Muslim Brotherhood, the largest and most influential of the world's Islamist movements. More than eighty years later, the Brotherhood remains controversial—perhaps more controversial than ever.

The Muslim Brotherhood's Message

Understanding who came before—and what they hoped to accomplish—is crucial to understanding the basic thrust of the Muslim Brotherhood's sociopolitical project and, by extension, the ideas that continue to animate mainstream Islamist movements across the Muslim world to this day.

The irony is that modernity and Islamism were, and are, inseparable. In fact, it's nearly impossible to imagine one without the other. The very idea of Islamism—that Islam and Islamic law should play a central role in political life—would have been met with confused looks and blank stares at any point before the nineteenth century. But with the advent of the modernists, Islam, for really the first time, became a distinct political project. It never had to become one before because Islam's role in public life was inescapable—it imbued nearly everything—and, more important, unquestioned. It went without saying, so it wasn't said.

Islamism only made sense in opposition to something else—and that something else was secularism. Islam was no longer just a way of being. It was no longer the natural order of things, and so it had to be reaffirmed and reasserted. In the process,

Islam became a political theology of authenticity and resistance in the face of an intertwining and overwhelming brew of secularism, colonization, and authoritarianism. This, then, is a story of how religions become religious ideologies. Islamism was inherently oppositional and unless it had something to oppose, would there really be a need for it? For now, though, the need was clear enough.

Rida's simple formula—that the fortunes of Muslims rise and fall with their commitment to Islam—was updated and extended in the Brotherhood's even simpler slogan "Islam is the solution." Again, it was logical and intuitive: If losing Islam was the problem, then finding it again would undo the damage, returning Muslims to a position of strength and self-confidence.

During his lifetime, Rida's (potentially) populist message remained confined to a relatively small number of people. Abduh and Rida were intellectuals who mostly addressed themselves to other intellectuals and elites. They were focused on reforming institutions and elite discourse. Hassan al-Banna, a schoolteacher, was interested in reform on a wider scale.[21] Translating what was previously a vague idea into a program of action was his most important and lasting legacy. Far from an Egypt-centric movement, the Brotherhood's message spread throughout the Muslim world, with affiliates, descendants, and offshoots soon emerging in dozens of countries. Today, there are Libyan, Syrian, Jordanian, and Yemeni Brotherhood branches, to name only a few, each attempting to adapt Banna's core ideas and principles to their own local contexts.

Although his collected writings, including his "epistles," are still pored over by Brotherhood members, Banna had little interest in developing a reputation as an author or scholar. One of his tracts—titled "Are We Practical People?"—was emblematic of his hands-on approach. As Khalil al-Anani notes, "Banna held that it would be significantly difficult to revive the Islamic identity without engaging the whole populace in a debate over such an important issue."[22] In Banna's early years, he traveled across the country, visiting coffeehouses and talking to ordinary Egyptians about Islam and what Islam could do for them. Banna recounts in his memoirs:

> I selected three main coffeehouses which were always overcrowded with people. I made a program to deliver two sermons in every coffeehouse every week. And I delivered my sermons in these coffeehouses regularly. My way of preaching proved to be a matter of astonishment for the people in the beginning. But soon they got used to it and took great interest.[23]

The Brotherhood was to be a mass movement. Anyone, regardless of class, social background, or occupation, could join the movement, as long as they believed in the organization's ideals and were willing to adhere to strict standards of moral conduct.

In a mass movement like the Brotherhood's—which could claim as many as half a million members by the 1940s—what was the role for the individual? The Brotherhood stood apart with a deceptively simple yet intricate model of social change. It began with each and every Egyptian, who was called on to reform the mind and the heart and return to Islam, embracing it as a comprehensive way of life. The reformed Muslim man would raise a good Muslim family. Enough Muslim families, in turn, would give rise to an Islamic society. If society was sufficiently Islamic, then it was only natural that the government would become Islamic as well (assuming there was some level of popular representation).

The Brotherhood needed numbers before anything else, so recruitment was a high priority. Each member was expected to introduce the organization to friends and family and to recruit supporters for specific initiatives. The Brotherhood's tiered membership structure, something like the Boy Scouts on steroids, is one of the organization's most innovative elements.

For the truly committed, it could take as long as eight years to become a fully fledged member and reach the level of an "active" brother. But not everyone needed to become a full brother, and not everyone would want to. The membership structure reduced barriers of entry while allowing for different levels of individual commitment and interest. But for an organization whose bedrock was supposedly individuals, the Brotherhood—a massive, plodding, inflexible body—would take on a life of its own. The organization—or *tanzim*, as it is known in Arabic—became not just a means but also an end unto itself, a problem that would persist throughout the Brotherhood's checkered history of success and disappointment.

From its founding, the Brotherhood was meant to be a big-tent organization that could be everything to everyone (of course, as long as you believed in the basic premise of political Islam). In his epistles, Banna writes of the inevitability of disagreements on "minor" matters. Even the Prophet's companions had such disagreements, after all, but this didn't keep them from their mission. A far cry from Abduh and Rida before him, Banna's epistles are fairly straightforward and self-consciously so. "I decided to write as I speak," Banna explains, "and to discuss my topic . . . without any false pretense or complexity. I simply wish people to understand me as I am, allowing my message to reach their minds devoid of any fancy ornament and decoration."[24]

The basic thrust of the message was simple enough. Banna looked around and saw passivity and fatalism. This infuriated him. Muslims had fallen. Muslims were weak, divided, bickering, and in the thrall of foreign ideologies. Banna wrote of his fellow Muslims, "[T]heir faith is anaesthetized, lying dormant within their souls, one to which they do not wish to submit and act accordingly. Whereas it is a burning, blazing, intense faith fully awakened in the souls of the Muslim Brotherhood."[25]

How "Modern" Is Islamism?

Centuries ago, Islam and the sharia were the natural order of things. And by sharia here, I don't just mean "law" or specific rules and punishments. Sharia was a moral as well as a legal system, a social order, and a source of legitimacy.[26] In its everyday import, it was pedestrian and prosaic, and it must have seemed to ordinary Muslims that it had always been and always would be. If you appeared in court over a business dispute, the judge, or *qadi*, was religiously trained. He would rule in the context of sharia. The sharia was a dynamic, living thing, which didn't necessarily offer easy answers, and in interpreting it, the *qadi* enjoyed considerable leeway. Still, there was no doubt that he—and it would be a he—was working within a particular moral, legal, and religious framework. In this sense, the sharia, as commonplace and mundane as it was, reflected something deeper. The scholar of Islamic law Wael Hallaq, for example, refers to an "overarching moral apparatus" and a "hegemonic moral system."[27] Hallaq and other chroniclers of medieval Islam—and no doubt many Muslims—have a tendency to idealize the sharia for what it claimed to be rather than what it actually was. But they are right to point to a kind of enveloping power that has so far been lacking since its demise.

During the ebbs and flows of the historic caliphate, no alternative source of legitimacy was devised or even considered. Of course, within this Islamic framework, there were competing philosophical approaches to Islam, different legal schools, warring leaders, and would-be revolutionaries. There were ongoing, and occasionally violent, debates and disagreements over the relationship between the caliph—the locus of executive authority—and the clerics, who, as we have seen, enjoyed considerable independence and autonomy.

Because the law was everywhere, it, in a sense, didn't need to assert itself or to intrude into the private lives of believers. A society imbued with Islamic law and tradition was *not* synonymous with intolerance and harsh restrictions. For example, the drinking of wine may have been forbidden, but many still consumed it during various periods in Islamic history.[28] Great poets valorized it and royal courts flowed with it. Even as he upheld the prohibition on alcohol for the Muslim masses, as great an Islamic thinker as Ibn Sina (Avicenna) was known to enjoy wine, and without shame.[29] Such behavior, as surprising as it might seem today, was not a threat to the overarching moral culture and legal structure.* An Islam that was already dominant had less need to dominate. It also *couldn't* dominate, because the premodern state, unlike modern states, was simply incapable of monitoring the minutiae of everyday life.

In the premodern era, an "ordinary" Muslim could be more (or less) observant and leave it at that. Hassan al-Banna was essentially saying that this would no longer do. With the advent of modernity, secularism, and tyranny, Islam was no longer the natural order of things. Because it was taken away, it would have to be regained. Because it was weak, it would have to be strengthened. It was doubted, so it would have to be affirmed. This was an Islam that was self-conscious, and this is what made it different from what had come before. This was a distinctly *modern* Islam. And it would come to be known as Islamism. But this is the irony of it all: In order to retrieve something that was lost—this supposedly pure, original Islam—it would become transformed into something new and unprecedented.

In his epistles, Banna isn't talking about a religion in the

---

*The distinction between private and public domains is worth mentioning in this context. As Rudi Matthee writes: "Because public deviance affects fellow believers and ultimately undermines Islam itself as a communal faith, Islam requires its followers to comply with the rules of the public sphere as well as to be vigilant in their maintenance. . . . The existence of a private sphere of sorts . . . has always made life livable in Muslim societies, allowing people to behave as they wished while maintaining the pretense that society continued to pursue the idea" (Rudi Matthee, *The Pursuit of Pleasure: Drugs and Stimulants in Iranian History, 1500–1900*, Princeton University Press, 2005, p. 296).

sense it's understood in the West, but about a *program* to be applied and implemented. A new phrase, *al-mashrou al-islami*, or the "Islamic project," entered the Islamist lexicon. It was a clinical way of looking at God and spirituality, that something as inevitably complex and varied as Islam could be a "solution" for the mundane problems of everyday life.

It was little surprise, then, that Banna's message resonated with Egypt's professional classes. Engineers, doctors, and lawyers would be the leaders of this new movement, with the rank and file drawn from the middle and lower-middle classes (rather than Egypt's most destitute). The organization's can-do attitude was appealing to upwardly mobile Egyptians, particularly those who had just moved to cities like Cairo and Alexandria and had no preexisting social or professional networks.

As massive as the organization would become, it remained, in another sense, local and personalized. As long as the movement operated in different fields and served different purposes, there would be a long list of reasons to join. Some joined it for the simple reason that being part of the Brotherhood provided moral purpose and guidance. This, in turn, would help them "get into heaven." For others, it was the sense of belonging and, well, brotherhood. For the charity-minded, there was the Brotherhood's social work—providing health care, youth activities, educational and "self-help" courses, and even assistance finding jobs. Still others were interested in the group's explicitly political work, whether it was street protest, parliamentary advocacy, running for office, or (in the 1940s) sending volunteers to fight against an incipient Israeli state. But, more likely, it was a combination of all of these elements, with some being more important than others, depending on each member's inclinations.

Being so many different things to so many people—with hundreds of thousands of members from wide-ranging backgrounds—presented its own set of problems. In the long run, the Brotherhood, and its members, wanted an "Islamic state." But no one knew what exactly that state looked like. And how could they? To the extent that "Islamism" was something new, their conception of the Islamic state would be new as well. How would it be organized and how would it execute its policies? How would it come into being?

When it came to the form and content of their preferred end state, Brotherhood leaders had an interest in remaining vague. Hovering within generality and abstraction is the task of any big-tent movement. Getting into too much detail would inevitably provoke disagreement among the group's varied membership. It was better for the Islamic state to remain an inspiration and an aspiration, but not too much more. Armed with the haze of nostalgia, members could project their hopes and dreams on the blank canvas of a state that would likely never come into being in their (or their children's) lifetimes.

It also helped that the Brotherhood's leaders were gradualists par excellence. They were playing the long game. (I was always struck by how, even in their darkest moments, they would maintain an unwavering—and, as far as I could tell, sincere—belief in their eventual victory.) They believed that history—and God—moved with them, and so it was never a question of whether but when they would prevail. This is a theme that repeats itself. Just two months before the Arab uprisings began, Egypt was experiencing what, at the time, seemed like an especially hopeless period. I was in Egypt for those November elections—arguably the most fraudulent Egypt had ever seen. In 2005, the Brotherhood had won an unprecedented eighty-eight seats in parliament. This time around, the Mubarak regime wouldn't even allow them one seat. But they accepted their fate in stride. I spoke to Hamdi Hassan, head of the Brotherhood's parliamentary bloc, at his campaign office in Alexandria. "In the lifespan of mankind," he told me, "eighty years isn't long; it's like eight seconds."[30]

Little did the Brotherhood know that just months later, Mubarak, in power for more than thirty years, would fall after just eighteen days of mass protests. And even then, at the height of euphoria, it would have been absurd to suggest that the

Muslim Brotherhood's Mohamed Morsi, a man relatively few Egyptians had heard of, would become president the following year. The arc of history moved in unpredictable ways, yet it seemed to bend toward the Brotherhood. Or at least that's how they wanted to see it.

AS DARK AS THEIR history may have been, there were few moments darker than August 14, 2013. The Egyptian military—the bedrock of the state since modern Egypt's founding—staged a coup against President Morsi on July 3. Just a year after their crowning achievement, it was yet another striking reversal of fortune for the Brotherhood. Knowing that the army was planning to move in and dismantle their mass sit-in near Rabaa al-Adawiya mosque in Cairo, Brotherhood members wrote their wills and prepared their families for what was to come. But in Rabaa, there was, oddly enough, a sense of relief and calm. They believed they were right.

When the blow came, it came as a shock. They knew it would be bad, but this—over eight hundred killed in mere hours—was worse than anyone had expected. Human Rights Watch called it the worst mass killing in modern Egyptian history.[31] After the massacre, it was only natural to ask why. For the faithful, believing that God created man and simply left him to his own devices—even if that led to terrible evil—wasn't really an option. There had to be some meaning, however hidden. This is the province of "theodicy," which seeks to explain why God permits evil in the world. Far from just an esoteric exercise, the problem of theodicy impacts very real questions of how religious movements, Islamist or otherwise, interpret evil and, perhaps more important, how they respond to it.

The post–Arab Spring era has featured quite a lot of "evil": a list of massacres too long to recount, bloody civil wars (including more than 400,000 killed in Syria), the Islamic State's apparent pleasure in savagery, the resurgence of a brutal authoritarianism, and so on. The brutality is often shocking, but brutality, even on such a scale, is not new. What is perhaps more troubling is how the region's collapse—after a moment of euphoria and promise—undermines the liberal faith that history moves with purpose toward something better. Even the notion of evil is something we struggle to accept. As the philosopher John Gray writes, "In its official forms, secular liberalism rejects the idea of evil. Many liberals would like to see the idea of evil replaced by a discourse of harm: we should talk instead about how people do damage to each other and themselves."[32] It becomes more challenging, however, to see evil as something exceptional and contrary to history's arc when it is always around you.

To the extent that evil exists and is making a comeback of sorts, how do the people of the Middle East process it? What, if anything, is God trying to tell the faithful? In this sense, the problem of theodicy has assumed a renewed urgency. There is little to suggest that violence, and the dehumanization that leads to it, will diminish anytime soon in the Middle East. How Muslims answer the question of theodicy, then, has considerable practical import. It's not a topic that comes up naturally, in part because it can arouse some very personal and trying questions about one's faith in God. But it is often lingering somewhere there in the background.

One Muslim Brotherhood activist—who had quite literally prepared for death in Rabaa—was able to leave Egypt shortly after the massacre. A year and a half later, when I met him over Indian food at a London mainstay for Islamist exiles (the restaurant, for one, didn't serve alcohol), he recalled a debate he had had with some friends. Was this a test—the righteous, after all, have always had their faith tested—or was it a punishment for having strayed from God's path? He wasn't sure. I could tell that he was torn. But he floated the idea that, perhaps, the Muslim Brotherhood had been tempted by power, that they had diverted too much of their attention to politics and lost sight of their original, animating mission—to be among the people spreading

God's word. He wondered whether the purported rise in atheism in Egypt was a sign that something had gone very wrong.

But, in reality, a lot had gone wrong well before the coup in
Egypt. Let us to return for a moment to Rida's words. He had
said that the Muslim world was "at its high point . . . when
holding most strongly to its religion."[33] But weren't Egyptians, and Arabs more generally, doing just that, holding more
strongly to their religion? The Brotherhood and other Islamist
movements had made substantial inroads in society. Secular
nationalism and socialism had been discredited while Islam
and Islamism filled the vacuum. Starting in the early 1970s,
more and more women began donning the head scarf. Men
grew their beards. Universities became hotbeds of Islamist protest, challenging—and soon replacing—a long-dominant left.
The Brotherhood, whose organizational structures were wiped
out by Gamal Abdel Nasser in the 1950s and '60s, was granted
another lease on life when President Anwar el-Sadat released
its leaders from prison. But it went well beyond the Brotherhood, which was more a reflection than the cause of Egypt's
religious revival. Buoyed by these changes—and with hundreds
of thousands of Egyptians returning from work in the Gulf
both wealthier and more conservative—the Brotherhood grew
more assertive and influential, further driving a bottom-up Islamization of society, which spread across social class, geogra-
phy, and economic background. There was little doubt: More
and more Egyptians, even those who disliked the Brotherhood,
were heeding at least part of the Brotherhood's call.

After all the suffering and sacrifice, this was a great, unlikely
victory. But it laid bare the challenge—some would say impos-
sibility—of translating "Islam is the solution" from rhetoric into
practice. If Islam was the solution and if it began, before anything else, with the individual, the family, and the community,
then how come the growing piety of Arabs wasn't translating
into more tangible improvements in living standards, scientific
advancement, or regional unity?

This is where the slow, plodding gradualism—and the long time horizon—of groups like the Brotherhood come into play. If eighty years were like eight seconds, as Hamdi Hassan had said to me, then it would be too soon to judge the Brotherhood's success. The long game was built into the Brotherhood's message as well as its organizational structure, and its members knew from the moment they joined that patience would be the most prized of virtues. Banna had warned his followers that this would be a "long, enduring, and continuous struggle," and it was a struggle consisting of different stages, some more explicit than others.[34]

The Long Game

The "politics of stages," or *siyasit al-marahil*, is one of the Brotherhood's more controversial ideas and one that can be interpreted in a number of different ways depending on whom you ask. For an organization as ambitious as the Brotherhood, gradualism almost went without saying. Some of the early extremist groups that went their own way in the 1970s hoped to surgically seize the state apparatus through armed insurrection or military coup. The Brotherhood was interested in something quite different: the reform of society. There was no obvious shortcut, since the state couldn't simply force people to become more religious. Instead, the groundwork had to be laid, and that could only happen when enough Egyptians experienced a change of heart. If the masses were ready and willing to embrace the Brotherhood's message, then—and only then—could there be a serious discussion of the next step: a change in government or even regime.

At the Brotherhood's fifth annual conference in 1939, Banna urged caution:

> If anyone of you wishes to pick a fruit before it is ripe and to pick a flower before it blossoms, I shall never agree with them. . . . If, however, you exercise

patience and wait for the seed to germinate, the plant
to grow, the fruit to ripen and then the most suitable
time for the plucking of the fruit, then your recom-
pense shall remain safe with Allah.[35]

This is what happens when absolute religious ideals—and
hopes far out into the future—run up against the realities of
everyday, mundane politics. Something at one stage might not
be appropriate for another. Why contest the majority of parliamentary seats when parliaments are weak and subservient and
when doing so only serves to provoke the regime anyway? Why
go into any great detail about what an Islamic government
might look like when there is no real prospect of governing?
Why talk about changing the international system and promoting Islamic unity, or even use the word "caliphate," when
the international system won't allow it?

Until you were ready, the temptations of power were to
be resisted. While Banna railed against British colonialism, he
worked, at least initially, to build a working relationship with
the British-backed monarchy, and particularly Ali Mahir Pasha,
the royal councilor, who developed a reputation as the Brotherhood's patron in the king's court. The Brotherhood was willing
to strike controversial deals with the authorities, so long as it
allowed them greater organizational freedom and furthered
their objectives. In 1952, the Brotherhood provided crucial lo-
gistical support to the Free Officers on the day of the military
coup that made Egypt into a republic. The leader of the Free
Officers was none other than Nasser. Later, the Brotherhood
put its support behind Nasser's Revolutionary Command Council when it was most vulnerable, during a brief but critical phase
in 1954, when the forces supporting a return to parliamentary
life appeared to have the upper hand.[36] Nasser's consolidation
of power, at the expense of the political parties, parliament,
and other vestiges of the ancien regime, was the prelude to his
brutal dismantling of the Muslim Brotherhood.

The Brotherhood's history, then, is a history of questionable alliances and fairweather friends, of playing the long game well but playing it almost too well. Although it is not widely known, Nasser himself was briefly a Muslim Brotherhood member, having joined the Brotherhood's "secret apparatus" as a young officer in the 1940s. Khaled Mohieddin, a friend and associate of Nasser's in the Free Officers, recounts the moment of initiation in his autobiography:

> We were taken into a totally darkened room where we heard a voice and, placing our hand on the Quran and a gun and repeating after the voice, we took an oath of obedience and total allegiance for better or worse, to the Grand Master [Hassan al-Banna], swearing by the Book of God and the sunna of the Prophet.[37]

President Sadat—who would turn against the Brotherhood in the late 1970s—also had a complex relationship with the movement as a young man. In 1940, on the night of the Prophet Mohamed's birthday, Banna first met the young Sadat, who thereafter served as the primary liaison between the Brotherhood and the Free Officers. Sadat recounts the sense of mystery that enveloped Banna. Sadat left the meeting overwhelmed, his admiration for Banna "unbounded."[38] The man was "like a saint," Sadat recalled. "It seemed strange to me but here was a theologian with a sense of reality, a man of religion who recognized the facts."[39] The two men—Banna was thirty-four and Sadat only twenty-two—met regularly for two years and developed a close friendship.

Success and failure were thus inextricably intertwined for the Muslim Brotherhood. What then does it mean to claim victory, when the movement's greatest victories were followed by its worst disappointments? Other Islamist movements have struggled with many of the same questions. Here, the ghosts of Algeria loom large. In the landmark elections of 1991, Algeria's main Islamist party, the Islamic Salvation Front (FIS), stood on the brink of a historic victory, winning 47.5 percent of the vote and 188 of 231 seats in the first round. However, there were mounting fears that the military was preparing to move against them. In the tense days that followed, FIS leader Abdelkader Hachani addressed a crowd of supporters. "Victory is more dangerous than defeat," he told them.[40] But it was too late. The military made its move, aborted the elections, and plunged the country into a bloody civil war.

This decades-long experience of repression has tended to make mainstream Islamists even more cautious and circumspect than they would have otherwise been. As Islamists rose to newfound prominence and influence in the 1990s and 2000s, the world—including the West—began to pay closer attention. Regional and international powers were skeptical of Islamists in the best of times; they could be outright hostile in the worst. Being more explicit about their intentions and going into detail about what "Islamization" might entail could prove dangerous for Islamists. And what was the point of getting ahead of themselves and alienating potential allies, including liberals and secularists at home, when they would gain little in return?

It was a delicate balancing act: the need to say different things to different audiences at different times. The gap between what Islamists believed and what they could realistically do seemed to grow larger and more pronounced the closer they approached the halls of power. For any ideological movement, the tensions between untethered objectives—what you would want in an ideal world if you had unlimited resources and few domestic constraints—and political reality is a disorienting one. It is even more so for Islamists, since they have to contend with an unusually inhospitable environment. Islamists obviously take scripture seriously, and that scripture includes rules and regulations. Some of these rules—particularly the *hudud* criminal punishments—are controversial in a way that they never would have been in the premodern period. But even more "realistic" proposals, such as restricting alcohol consumption, segregating the sexes in public schools, or Islamizing educational curricula, are bound to attract unwanted controversy. In countries that receive little Western attention, such as Indonesia and Malaysia, Islamists and secularists alike can experiment with sharia ordinances at the local level.

The Middle East, however, is different (and, in any case, Middle Eastern states tend to be centralized and top-heavy, so sharia by way of under-the-radar local councils isn't much of an option). Threatened with repression and fearful of provoking Western opprobrium, there were simply some things Islamists could not say. As we will see in the following chapters, this would reach tragicomic levels, as in Turkey, where the then mayor of Istanbul—and future president—Recep Tayyip Erdogan was imprisoned for reciting an overtly Islamic poem. In effect, Islamists in Turkey had to cease being Islamists. This suppression of self proved both unhealthy and unsustainable. In Tunisia, the Islamists of Ennahda adopted a similar approach, downplaying their Islamism and making a mad dash for the center.

The unique situation Islamists find themselves in leads to confounding debates: What do they *really* believe? Does it even matter what they believe in their hearts? This presents a problem for Islamists if and when they try to moderate their rhetoric and adopt "liberal" positions. Their opponents look at these changes and wonder if they're merely tactical, a product of domestic and international constraints. Among secular elites, attitudes toward Islamists tend to be "inelastic," meaning that what Islamists do—or don't do—has little effect on how their opponents view them. Islamist moderation can even have the opposite effect of what is intended, exacerbating instead of lessening distrust. This is a particular problem in Tunisia, where Ennahda's sanitized visage—including tailored suits and skinny black ties at the party headquarters—and always on-point messaging seem almost too good to be true. To a skeptical eye, it might appear insincere and perhaps even evidence of bad faith.

With the very foundations of the state in question, there is little incentive to believe the best of your political adversaries.

Although perhaps frustrating for outside observers and political opponents, the politics of stages serves a purpose for Islamist organizations, helping maintain internal morale and cohesion. As Khalil al-Anani notes, stages give the Brotherhood leadership "room for maneuver and manipulation as the temporal link between the stages is blurred."[41] In addition, they encourage patience, since the latter stages may never be reached in a member's lifetime. At the same time, they provide the illusion of progress and offer something to aspire to and hope for, always near but just out of reach. And when that isn't enough, there's the promise of glad tidings in the afterlife. That, after all, is the only guarantee. As Banna writes, "One carries out a duty firstly for the sake of doing so, then secondly for a reward in the hereafter, and thirdly for personal advantage. If he works in this way and performs his duty, he will thenceforth win Allah's approval."[42] There is also the famous saying of the Prophet Mohamed: "Actions are judged by their intentions." In other words, the faithful aren't responsible for outcomes that are well beyond their control. The best they can do is prepare and work to the best of their ability. The rest is in God's hands. If Muslims don't experience his reward in this life, then no matter: They will experience it in the next.

There is always an out, particularly if you have faith. Failure is in the eye of the beholder. After the 2013 coup, the Brotherhood experienced an unprecedented crackdown. The movement was discredited by its own failures in government. The top tiers of the Brotherhood were either thrown in jail or forced to flee, starting new lives in other countries, all the while wondering if they'd ever be able to set foot in Egypt again. Yet I was always amazed by the ability of many in the Brotherhood to cast a debacle of historic proportions in a more positive light. One London-based activist pointed to the unexpected death in January 2015 of the eighty-one-year-old Brotherhood leader

Gomaa Amin. He died in exile. When Amin was wasting away in Nasser's dungeons as a young man, he never would have dreamed that, after three or four cycles of repression, there would be a Brotherhood president in his lifetime, but there had been. For the Brotherhood activist, Amin's story meant one thing: This was not the end. It was just another stage. Just as there would be other cycles of repression, there would be other political openings.

The Illusion of Unity

One of the great ironies is that a movement that saw itself as a unifying force in a time of division became one of the most divisive movements of the modern era. Banna wrote that the competing ideologies of the twentieth century—liberalism, nationalism, communism, fascism—had "arisen like a stormy sea, dividing men's hearts and throwing their minds into confusion."[43] The basic premise of Islamism was that Islam was the natural, authentic setting for all believing Muslims. In Rashid Rida's words, it was "the religion of innate disposition."[44] In that sense, Islamism wasn't meant to be an ideology among others; it was meant to *resolve* the problem of ideology. But while a return to the spirit of the first Muslims was possible, a return to a time before ideology was not. Islam, in the premodern period, was a source of unity. No one, then, questioned the organizing premise that Islam and the sharia were the order of things. But that will never be the case again: The modern era—and the introduction of what were originally Western ideologies—has irrevocably changed the region, as well as the religion itself.

As scholars of political culture are quick to note, culture is not something that changes quickly. Culture is made up of the symbols, norms, and values that resonate with ordinary citizens. These are the things that are deeply embedded, drawing on the accumulated weight of history. Depending on your perspective, this can be good or bad. The Brazilian sociologist turned president Fernando Cardoso spoke of the "dead weight of the past,"[45] a weight that would have to be lifted, likely under duress. For others, the past is something to be embraced. Either way, everything that comes before has an effect on what comes after—what political scientists call "path dependence." In other words, once a particular path is chosen—and the longer one walks on it—the more difficult it is to go back to the original fork and start over.

It doesn't happen often, but this cultural inertia can be broken by external or internal shocks to the political system. When nations or even empires become stagnant, there is the possibility of revolution from within. But, failing that, the most that can be hoped for—or feared—is that foreigners will provoke or force fundamental changes through military attack or invasion. Crises can be imposed on countries that want nothing of the sort. One such moment was September 11, 2001, when a horrifying attack executed by a few men ended up changing the course of American history.

External shocks helped bring about the transformation, and ultimately the demise, of the Ottoman caliphate. The most basic assumptions of religion and state—the order of things as they had been for the better part of fourteen centuries—were dismantled with the advent of modernity. What transpired were decades of sustained cultural and political assault, including, in some instances, the brutal colonial occupation of Muslim lands. If this couldn't break the religious and political status quo of the Middle East, then nothing would.

To say, though, that these changes were simply a matter of foreign intervention would be a mistake. The confrontation between East and West entailed considerable violence, of course, but it also brought a more intense exchange of ideas. It was no accident that the works of the great Islamic modernists were influenced by their time spent traveling and studying in Europe. As we saw earlier, the new ideas being introduced into the region—ideas of democracy, popular sovereignty, universal rights, and women's empowerment—were genuinely attractive (within limits), even to the most pious. Not only that, the colonized made good use of these "Western" ideas, turning them against their European occupiers in wars of national liberation. Many of these insurgent groups, particularly in countries like Algeria, were deeply influenced by Marxist and nationalist intellectuals and philosophers. They weren't fighting to restore the old caliphate but for their own independent nations. It wouldn't have made much sense to fight for something that had ceased to exist and that the Turks themselves had agreed to abolish.

It is difficult to overstate how radical these changes were. The rerendering of the region was experienced as a series of shocks—invasions, revolutions, anticolonial struggles, military coups, and world wars—touching the lives, to one degree or another, of every Arab and Muslim. For the first time, there were real intellectual and philosophical alternatives to the old legal, moral, and social order, a far cry from when the sharia stood uncontested. The decline of Islamic empires and the rise of Europe forced the people of the Middle East to ask themselves difficult questions they hadn't previously thought to ask. For the first time, there were alternative notions of political community that were just as compelling, if not more so, to a growing number of Muslims. Once ideas of democracy, nationalism, and the nation-state were introduced, the effects couldn't be undone. Muslims now lived in an increasingly interconnected world, where they were bombarded with new images and ideologies. For non-Muslim minorities, the idea of "citizenship" in a secular state held the promise of full equality. They could never truly be members of the worldwide Muslim community, or *umma*, but they could be part of a new Arabist project. Across the Arab world, the British and French introduced constitutions, parties, and parliaments (although they rarely allowed these institutions to challenge their rule). For those who preferred more militant approaches, there was the rise of nationalist and even fascist parties, which were experiencing unprecedented success in Europe between the world wars. There was no choice but to engage with these new "Western" ideas, even if to ultimately reject them.

Islamists, for their part, were not among those who counseled simpleminded rejection. They recognized that certain concepts developed in and by the West could be worth embracing. For example, as Banna writes:

> Nobody can ignore the freedom [the democratic system] has secured for peoples and nations alike, and the justice it has introduced to the human mind in allowing it to think freely, and to the human being as a whole in allowing him the freedom to fulfill himself; and, apparently, giving power to the people. Indeed, international relations after the First World War came as a proof of the legitimacy of these ideas and most of the world turned towards them wholeheartedly.[46]

Of course there was a "but," as there almost always was when saying something nice about the West. Banna, for example, railed against the "unlimited freedom" that undermined the family structure, but he was clearly willing to acknowledge that aspects of democracy reflected human progress and could be used to build on and advance his own mission. There was a conscious attempt to incorporate these new ideas into an Islamic framework or, put differently, to Islamize them as if they were intrinsic and inevitable elements of the Islamic tradition.

This was yet another sign that political Islam, for all of its seemingly reactionary tendencies, bought into that most modern of assumptions: that history moved with purpose and that progress was inescapable. The Ottoman-era caliphate, then, was a relic of the past. It had failed to evolve with the times, and so it was little surprise that the Ottoman Empire found itself unable to compete with Europe's success and soon crumbled from within. The new ideology that Banna was offering was meant to be an improvement on what came before, building toward a new Islamic synthesis.

But there would be others—liberals, socialists, secularists, and nationalists—who, for various reasons, did not feel a need to base their political identity on Islam. This didn't mean they were impious—some of them, in fact, were quite devout. Islamism was a step beyond merely being an observant Muslim, and it required a conscious commitment. If you wished to join the Brotherhood, it meant pledging loyalty, or *baya'a*, to the general guide. But the more important point here is that in this new era, there were alternatives to the *umma*. Socialists and liberals alike believed that membership in a political community should be based on secular grounds. Islam could still play a role, but it needn't be the defining consideration.

Any ideology was bound to be divisive, no matter what the original intentions. Ideologies are purposeful constructions. They can only be recognizable as ideologies insofar as they oppose other ideologies. If there were something called "Islamists," then there would always be those who weren't and were called something else. To the extent that Islamism was synonymous with the Brotherhood's version of it, even those who might have been sympathetic to its basic premise might find themselves in the opposing camp for more mundane political reasons. They may have been uncomfortable with the Brotherhood's insular nature, its requirement to pledge loyalty to the leader, or its neoliberal economic orientation. This might have weakened, perhaps fatally, the unifying potential of Islamist parties, but it was a boon in other ways. Islamists drew strength and support from their underdog status. Hoping to unseat the elite, they were the counterelite. They seemed most at peace when their backs were to the wall. The struggle for survival became its own kind of victory. In short, Islamism was *supposed* to be different. It needed Gamal Abdel Nasser just as much as it needed Hassan al-Banna. For Islamists, religion had to be politicized, but doing so came at a price.

4

THE MUSLIM BROTHERHOOD

FROM REFORM TO REVOLUTION

The Muslim Brotherhood eschewed revolution. They were the ultimate gradualists. But the Arab Spring would show, yet again, that however careful and cautious they were, a fundamental divide remained. That gap—over the role of religion and the nature of the state—was deepened with the Brotherhood's unlikely rise to power in 2012, when Mohamed Morsi became Egypt's first democratically elected president. For the first time, the prospect of prolonged Islamist rule became more than just a theoretical consideration, provoking considerable fear among Egypt's economic and political elites. And so they took action and worked with the military to unseat the Brotherhood—this time, they hoped, once and for all.

The weeks and months leading to Morsi's demise will forever be remembered in a haze. This is the haze of nostalgia, tragedy, hatred, and, of course, hindsight. This makes it all the more important to try to remember things as they really were. And that is where we can begin our story of the Brotherhood's unlikely transformation from plodding gradualists into budding, if not entirely convincing, revolutionaries. Mohamed Morsi was many things—incompetent, polarizing, and profoundly uncharismatic—but a radical wasn't one of them. There was little doubt that the Brotherhood had veered to the right during its brief time in power. Yet the real debate in the organization, at least after the fact, was whether it had veered far enough. Where those outside the Islamist fold argued that Morsi had overreached, Muslim Brotherhood supporters often made the opposite argument—that the president was too deferential to the state and that he should have used his powers more, not less, aggressively.

From the day Mubarak fell, whenever the Brotherhood had a choice between reform or revolution, they chose the former. They wagered that it was better to avoid direct confrontation with the military, long considered the guardian of the Egyptian state. This meant sometimes turning a blind eye to the army's disastrous management of the transition period. Even when the military and judicial establishment threatened hard-won gains—such as with the dissolution of the democratically elected parliament—the Brotherhood may have talked tough but it ultimately abided by the decision. It would push, but only up to a point.

Once he assumed the presidency, Morsi—described by those close to him as "doing things by the book"—opted to work within the state apparatus rather than fight it, at least at first.[1] Even his most dramatic move a month into his tenure—forcing the retirement of military chiefs Hussein Tantawi and Sami al-Annan—was relatively restrained. At the height of his powers and popularity, there was no real purging or restructuring of the army. Tantawi's replacement was none other than Abdel Fattah al-Sissi, another creature of Egypt's bloated military— and its spymaster to boot.

Morsi's goal was to slowly solidify power and gradually wrest control from Egypt's labyrinthine bureaucracy. The longer

Morsi stayed in power, the thinking went, the more state institutions would come to accept him. The thinking was wrong. Brotherhood leaders allowed their earnestness and naïveté to color some of their most consequential decisions. To be sure, they could play hard-nosed Chicago-style politics with the best of them, but they were also products of a religious movement whose basic premise was that change began at the individual level. The founder of the Muslim Brotherhood, Hassan al-Banna, believed that even skeptics could be won over to the cause if Brotherhood members held themselves up as models of moral and ethical conduct. When Brothers tell the stories of why they joined, there's usually that one person with exceptional charisma and character who showered them with attention at the mosque or at school, introducing them to Banna's writings and bringing them into a circle of friendship and solidarity.

Sissi was thought to be a prime candidate for this kind of religious outreach. After all, he was devout, praying five times a day and even observing special supplementary fasts on Mondays and Thursdays. He often prayed with Morsi and other Brotherhood leaders. Intellectually, Sissi appeared to be sympathetic to aspects of Islamist thought. When Sissi attended the U.S. Army War College in Carlisle, Pennsylvania, he submitted a thesis in which he argued that the West should respect the outcomes of democratic elections in which Islamist parties come to power.[2] "The challenge that exists," he writes, "is whether the rest of the world will be able to accept a democracy in the Middle East founded on Islamic beliefs."[3]

Morsi and the Brotherhood's hope in Sissi says more perhaps about them than it does about Sissi. They believed that to truly be a good Muslim meant to be a good Islamist: If someone was devout and took the Quran seriously, they would, in due time and with the right amount of exposure to the Brotherhood's message, come to see the good in what the movement had to offer. These weren't professional politicians. Sometimes

Brotherhood leaders acted more like preachers who had the good fortune of enjoying (some) political power. When it came to their relationship with Sissi, this was a profound miscalculation.

In politics as in preaching, Morsi and the Brotherhood believed in moving slowly. They remained the calculating gradualists they had always been. Considering what they were up against—a massive, unwieldy state and an old regime establishment that had little interest in giving way—there was always the question, an almost philosophical one, of whether a slow and steady approach could ever really succeed. Take, for example, what Morsi's team had to contend with upon entering the presidential palace. According to one senior Morsi aide, the palace's wireless network was initially unsecured and could even be accessed outside palace grounds. As he recounted to me just months before the coup: "When we first got in, they gave us handwritten notes rather than proper permits [for entry]. What does that tell you?"[4]

It is a fascinating thing to speak to Brotherhood figures, particularly those who were in government during those final, fateful days of the Morsi presidency. "What happened is still like a black box to this day," one Brotherhood activist turned Morsi staffer told me more than a year and a half after the coup.[5] A senior advisor to Morsi—who continued to refer to his former boss simply as "the president"—acknowledged the confusion surrounding the Morsi-Sissi relationship. "We had strategy meetings in February, March, April [2013] in which we specifically identified Sissi as the mover behind what we called the conspiracy," he told me. "And so frankly I don't understand the discrepancy." One common interpretation, shared by this advisor, was that Morsi "had this kind of obsession that people can't handle bad news."[6] He didn't want to cause any panic, so he continued to insist until his very last moments as president that even if the others turned against him, Sissi wouldn't. We may not know—at least until, or if, he is released from prison—

just what Morsi really believed. But one thing is clear enough. Whether or not Morsi knew better is almost beside the point. Because of his aversion to conflict, his deference to the military, and his desire to work within the state apparatus, he never seriously confronted Sissi or other top military officers in those final days and weeks, despite gathering evidence that something wasn't quite right. This was the way Morsi—and the Brotherhood—did business. The spirit of revolution, or even merely a persuasive appropriation of it, was beyond them. This caution led to considerable frustration, particularly among the group's younger activists, who hadn't been chastened by long years of imprisonment and abuse.

The End of an Experiment

It may be one of the most remarkable political rants ever caught on Egyptian television. The day before the July 3, 2013 coup, opposition activist Ehab al-Khouli launched into a vociferous diatribe when asked about Morsi's final televised speech as president. "This 'former' president is addicted to his throne," he screamed, gesturing wildly. "This man is a liar and a deceiver."[7] He gasped for breath and doubled over, coughing, as the talk show host pleaded with him to calm down. But he continued—beating the table, jumping out of his chair—for nearly four minutes.

Khouli, in rather stark form, captured the anger and frustration of the millions of Egyptians who took to the streets during the June 30 protests. For many, democracy was not simply a matter of faith, or even principle, but a means to something else: a sense of dignity, the promise of economic benefit, or the freedom to dress and think as they wished. The sense that democracy had failed to bring real gains set in motion the breakdown of political order, the return of the generals, and the overthrow of Egypt's first democratically elected president.

The problem with coups is that far from resolving conflicts, they tend to exacerbate them. A coup in a country as polarized as Egypt was almost certain to lead to dueling and ultimately irreconcilable legitimacies: the legitimacy of the ballot box and the legitimacy of the street. Considering its own history of persecution, the Brotherhood was unlikely to back down in the face of the army's threats. The events of 1954 loomed large in movement lore. As Wael Haddara, a Canadian-Egyptian advisor to Morsi, explained to me,

> I think what Morsi was actually counting on isn't that Sissi was going to [stand down] out of the goodness of his heart or a set of principles or whatever. I think Morsi was counting on having conveyed to the army several times that if this happens, we're not going to back down. This isn't going to be like 1954 where people just go home.[8]

In late 1954, Nasser quickly moved against the Brotherhood, decapitating the leadership, which offered little resistance. Hundreds of thousands of members and supporters stood on alert, but they never received the call to mobilize. Plunged into disarray, the hope was that a dangerous confrontation could be avoided, a hope that appeared naive in retrospect.

This time around, the Brotherhood mobilized *before* the coup actually happened, directing supporters to gather in two key areas in Cairo. From late June until August 14, tens of thousands of Morsi supporters, including entire families, basically lived in Rabaa, the larger of the two encampments. The first time I set foot in Rabaa, just a week before the August 14 massacre, I was surprised at how self-contained everything was. You couldn't just casually stroll in. You had to *enter* it. At the makeshift entrance, about fifty feet off the street, the volunteer guards, standing next to piled-up sandbags, hurriedly checked IDs. As I walked in, people sprayed me with water. This, apparently, was their way of welcoming me. It was

August, at the peak of the humid Egyptian summer. Like many Egyptian protests, this one teetered somewhere between panic and jubilation.

More than a protest, Rabaa was an alternative city with kitchens, pharmacies, food stalls, sleeping quarters, and a "media center." That tens of thousands of people were gathered in the middle of Cairo in such outward defiance offered a constant reminder of the fact that there were now two Egypts. Rabaa, in what it claimed and what it stood for, was only the latest—and most striking—manifestation of a foundational divide that had seemingly grown larger with time. Here, in the heart of Cairo, was a ministate, where the Egyptian authorities had no jurisdiction. Something had to give.

After the massacre in which more than eight hundred were killed, a powerful mythology developed around Rabaa. Rabaa is where these young men and women came of age. Like the Prophet and his companions more than fourteen centuries ago, they were ready and willing to sacrifice for the cause, for Islam, and for God. As the standoff with the army persisted, the feeling of unity and even joy joined uneasily with fear, as the rumors of military action swirled among the protesters. This alternative universe that they had created was about to come under attack. Rabaa was where young Muslim Brothers, some of them still in college, told me of that mix of adrenaline and dread as they drafted their wills and bid their families good-bye.

With the dispersal of Rabaa, a new phase began, as Brotherhood members and leaders—at least the ones who weren't in prison—tried to make sense of an Egypt they no longer recognized. They had, of course, experienced repression before. This, though, was different. Many Egyptians supported Hosni Mubarak, but it was difficult to find anyone who was particularly passionate about him. Mubarak was the serviceable strongman—steady, solid, and devoid of charisma. As repressive as Mubarak could be, he had little interest in eradicating the Brotherhood altogether. That would have required a combination of brutality and ambition that Mubarak lacked. Sissi, however, was not lacking in such ambition. He had a messianic streak that can only be described as bizarre. In a leaked off-the-record interview, for instance, he tells his confidant Yasser Rizk that thirty-five years ago he started having dreams, like one in which he raised "a sword with 'There is no God but God' written on it in red."[9] In another, a voice comes to Sissi, saying, "We will give to you what we have given no other."[10] In still another, he is with the late Egyptian president Anwar el-Sadat. Sadat says that he knew he would one day become president. Sissi replies, "And I know that I will be president of the republic."[11] In public, Sissi presented himself as a savior who would "maximize" state power to pull the Egyptian people—"the light of his eyes"—from their sorry state. He traded his beatific, paternal tone in private. "People think I'm a soft man. Sissi is torture and suffering," he once told a journalist.[12]

Sissi was a dictator, but he was a popular one, especially in the beginning. An occasionally odd cult of personality built up around the new leader. In a colorful column, one female journalist said that if Sissi wanted her as a concubine she was more than happy to oblige.[13] A state-owned newsmagazine featured thirty smiling Sissis on its cover, all wearing different clothes—doctors, engineers, laborers—with the words "All of Egypt is Sissi" emblazoned at the top. Soon, there would be Sissi-themed pajamas for women featuring the general himself, sporting dark sunglasses.[14]

Often, Sissi was criticized for not being repressive *enough*, including in the lead-up to the Rabaa massacre. Millions of pro-coup Egyptians wondered why it was taking Sissi so long to act. When he finally did, they cheered on the dispersals and the killings, encouraged by the nonstop demonization of the Brotherhood in the state and private media. Egypt's savior had delivered. Rarely had celebrity been so inseparable from brutality.

It was frightening to watch people you knew and even loved get caught up in what can only be described as mass hysteria.

The weekend before the army moved in, I went to Egypt's north coast to visit family, hoping to escape, even if for a moment, the fear, anger, and polarization consuming Cairo. Sitting by the beach, a relative performed a morbid demonstration, pointing to the coffee table in front of him and chopping his hand down on it. The table shook. He said he wanted the severed heads of each of the Brotherhood's top leaders right there on the table, listing them each by name. I knew he was half-joking, performing a kind of theater of the absurd. However, another relative, my well-educated and sensible uncle, was deadly serious. He took to his Facebook page to publicly call for the execution of Muslim Brotherhood members *without* due process.

After the ashes settled, there was the challenge of making sense of what had happened. Again, there was no precedent in the days of Mubarak or, for that matter, Nasser. The protesters at Rabaa had seen their friends shot and killed. And yet there wasn't any mass outpouring of sympathy, at least not in public. They struggled to understand how so many of their countrymen could turn against them, including their own loved ones. This was not old-fashioned sectarianism, where different groups lived among themselves in geographic cantons, oblivious to the other's humanity. One Islamist journalist, who soon fled to Doha, recounted how her father turned against her: "My dad now calls me a terrorist—and he means it."[15] These stories have become all too common: friends, family, and neighbors turning against each other. Ominously, in a throwback to an older era, neighbors and colleagues informed on each other. The wall of fear, which had apparently crumbled during the Arab uprisings, was now being rebuilt—and the wall, if anything, was stronger. On his Facebook page, activist Abdel Rahman Zaidan recounted an experience he had on a Cairo bus. A middle-aged woman had launched into a diatribe against Sissi. A young man sitting next to her enthusiastically joined in. Suddenly, as the bus passed a church, the woman asked the bus driver to stop, stuck her head out the window, and shouted to the church guards that a "Muslim Brother terrorist" was on the bus with her. The guard immediately boarded the bus, dragged the young man off, and began beating him. As the bus drove on, its passengers "amazed," the female informer looked at her fellow passengers and said with pride as if daring them to oppose her, "Oh God, let this country be cleansed!"[16]

In another incident, journalist Sara Khorshid recounted sitting in a Cairo café, where she was casually chatting about politics with Alain Gresh, editor of the French newspaper *Le Monde diplomatique*. A fifty-something veiled woman, who was apparently eavesdropping, shouted that they were "ruining the country" and proceeded to inform the police officers outside. "The woman who informed on us looked like any average Egyptian woman—like my mother or my neighbors. . . . She sounded angry and sincere," writes Khorshid. "I've seen many like her in the past months, even in my own circle—ordinary people who really believe they are serving their country by doubting the loyalty of fellow citizens."[17]

Reform or Revolution?

After a failed stint in government, a coup, and a massacre, it was time to take stock. It was clear that the Brotherhood would change in important ways, not necessarily because it wanted to but because it had to. What, though, would that change look like? Crises, especially unexpected ones, force a process of political learning. But just because lessons are learned doesn't mean they're the right ones. As we saw earlier, the Brotherhood did, in fact, learn something from the trials of 1954: When threatened with eradication, don't stand down. Applied to the events of 2013, however, this approach only served to compound a growing list of errors.

In the early months after the July 3 coup, the Brotherhood's leaders seemed to be in a daze, repeating empty statements about impending victory. It was just a matter of months, maybe a year at most, before the coup would "break." With so many killed, many more in prison or in hiding, and others organizing weekly, even daily, protests, it wasn't the right time to offer apologies or ideological revisions. It was a time to resist.

The vast majority of the Brotherhood's first, second, and third-tier figures were arrested. By late 2014, there wasn't a single senior leader inside Egypt who was still free. The leadership in exile, based in London, Doha, and Istanbul, stubbornly insisted on the language of politics, even after politics had ended. The president, the constitution, and the parliament needed to be reinstated, they said. "Legitimacy," meaning here electoral legitimacy, was the watchword. There was little in the way of new, creative ideas. A series of strategy sessions, bringing together Islamists from various countries, was held in Istanbul in the fall of 2013. As one London-based Islamist figure recalled, "We sat with [Brotherhood secretary-general] Mahmoud Hussein for three days. They were still in a state of a shock a year into the coup. It's fine to be in a daze for a month or two, but . . ."[18]

One of the more interesting ideas which emerged from the discussions was that in exchange for a return to democracy, the Brotherhood would withdraw from direct political participation for a set period of time. But such a radical proposal could not gain the support of the Brotherhood's conservative old guard. The more forward-leaning members of the Brotherhood-led National Alliance for the Support of Legitimacy—which included the centrist Islamists of the Wasat Party, the reformed Salafis of the Watan Party, and the ex-jihadists of Gama'a Islamiya—grew increasingly frustrated, leading to the alliance's effective collapse by the end of 2014.

Throughout its long, varied history, the Brotherhood remained a top-heavy, hierarchical organization. While there was significant decentralization and internal democracy on the local and regional levels, when it came to overall political strategy, the Brotherhood's executive body, the Guidance Council, dominated. It made sense, then, to follow the public state-ments and initiatives coming out of Istanbul and Doha, look-ing for subtle shifts in direction or signs of dissent within the Brotherhood-led alliance. But the coup had punctured the old way of doing things. The real change was happening elsewhere.

THE SEEMING STASIS of the leadership in exile belied an increas-ingly fluid and volatile situation in the one place that mattered most. Inside Egypt, younger activists and university students were leading anticoup protests and demonstrations. They had to. There was no one else. Older Brotherhood leaders, after all, were imprisoned or in hiding. These realities created a new and fascinating dynamic—a dynamic that wasn't directed or even really intended.

Brotherhood and other Islamist youth were acting first and thinking later. On the tactical level, this meant considerable improvisation. The more they were able to evade the security forces, the more their confidence grew. During a short-lived Arab Spring, the entire organizational infrastructure of the Brotherhood had become consumed by electoral politics, as hundreds of thousands of members entered into a phase of near-constant mobilization, working to get out the vote in five major elections (two referenda, parliamentary elections for the lower and upper house, as well as presidential polls). This led one prominent Egyptian liberal, who ran on the Brotherhood's parliamentary list, to offer a backhanded compliment. "If you give the Brotherhood a piece of shit," he told me, "they'll ask: where is the electoral angle of the piece of shit."[19] Soon, he, like so many others, concluded he could no longer stay in Egypt, taking up self-imposed exile in the United States.

In the postcoup era, politics, in the normal sense of the word, lost its relevance. Few in the Brotherhood thought seriously of trying to contest elections under military rule. They had put their lives on the line and watched their friends die. After all

of that, what would be the point of fighting for a few parliamentary seats in elections that would be anything but free and
fair? "Politics" had become a battle of wills, waged on Egyptian
streets and in Egyptian homes. In late 2013 and 2014, the repression intensified, as tens of thousands were arrested and
hundreds of Islamist businesses and social-service organizations
were shut down. After the Muslim Brotherhood was declared a
terrorist organization in September 2013, the Cairo Court for
Urgent Matters leaked a list of 1,142 social-service organizations
and entities linked to the Muslim Brotherhood either directly or
indirectly, as Steven Brooke details.[20] The state immediately froze
the assets of those organizations, as well as those of eighty-seven
Brotherhood-affiliated schools. Prominent Muslim Brotherhood–
affiliated organizations like the Islamic Medical Association,
which had operated twenty-two hospitals and seven specialized-
care centers across Egypt, gradually came under state control
by 2015.[21]

For young Brothers who had come of age during the Mubarak
era, the scale of repression was unprecedented. Yet, even as the
regime moved to eradicate it, the Brotherhood's new generation
of de facto leaders—the ones actually organizing the marches
and sit-ins—were able to sustain small but significant protests
across the country. Contrary to claims that the Brotherhood organization had been decimated, the Brotherhood was able to
maintain, at least initially, much of its traditional activities. In
many parts of the country, Brotherhood "cells," or *usras*, continued to meet; financial stipends were distributed to relatives of
the imprisoned; and, in January 2015, internal elections were
held. And at the forefront was a new generation of Islamist youth.

The shift from slow, gradual reform to confrontation, "revolution," and even occasional violence wasn't something they intel-
lectualized until well after the fact. In those first months after
the coup, whenever a Brotherhood figure would even so much as
hint at offering concessions or entering into dialogue with proregime figures, the backlash was immediate and overwhelming. If,

for example, the reinstatement of Morsi wasn't explicitly mentioned in a public statement, activists would take to social media to attack leaders for betraying the revolution. As one senior Brotherhood official who sometimes found himself at the receiving end complained to me, "We have to be able to make concessions, but there's always the concern that our base won't be supportive."[22]

When critics insisted that the Brotherhood learn from its mistakes and "evolve," one doubts that becoming *less* gradualist is quite what they had in mind. In this new Egypt, compromise with the regime was tantamount to dishonoring the dead. There would be no pact with the military and other state institutions as there was after Mubarak fell on February 11, 2011. That day, the throngs of protesters gathered in Tahrir Square went home, thinking that victory was theirs after just eighteen days. The military assumed responsibility for the transition, a role that the Brotherhood readily accepted. For many in the movement's younger ranks, this, at least in hindsight, was the original sin. Knowing what they knew now, it wouldn't be enough to go back to July 2, 2013, the day before the military coup. They had to go all the way back to February 11, 2011, and embrace revolution in the fullest, total sense, before the Egyptian state co-opted it. They shouldn't have gone home that night.

SISSI'S BRAND OF REPRESSION was the most dangerous kind—it was populist *and* popular. But, more than that, his campaign against the Brotherhood reflected the unity of the Egyptian state. In the first year after the coup, at least 2,500 civilians were killed and 17,000 wounded.[23] By March 2015, security forces had arrested more than 40,000 people, the majority of them on grounds of suspected support for the Muslim Brotherhood, although leftist activists, journalists, and university students were also detained.[24]

One might have expected such high levels of repression—

surpassing the darkest days of the Nasser era—to sow doubts within the regime and among allies and supporters. But when the military led, the rest of the Egyptian state followed, sometimes with over-the-top aplomb. There was the April 2014 sentencing to death of 529 Brotherhood members, one of the largest-ever mass death sentences anywhere in the world. The court seemed to make no pretense of transparency or fairness in the case: The attorneys of the accused were denied access to the "evidence," and those who protested were threatened. The verdict was handed down after only two court sessions, each lasting less than an hour.[25] In May 2015, the same court sentenced Mohamed Morsi for his alleged role in (his own) prison break during the 2011 uprising. The former president faced execution. More than a hundred others were sentenced alongside him. Morsi's co-conspirators included a Palestinian man "who has been in an Israeli jail since 1996" and two Palestinians who had reportedly already died, writes Emad Shahin, a leading Egyptian political scientist who himself was handed a death sentence in absentia.[26]

Morsi's death sentence came a year after Egypt's courts had broken their own record, sentencing 683 people to death on April 28, 2014. The judiciary was a full and willing partner in the war against the Muslim Brotherhood. The courts were instrumental in first banning the Brotherhood and then declaring it a terrorist organization, seizing its financial assets and closing down hundreds of Islamist civil-society organizations. In shuttering hospitals, clinics, and charitable organizations affiliated with the Brotherhood, the government effectively cut off thousands of needy Egyptians.[27] The crackdown extended to mosques: The Ministry of Endowments boycotted preachers not licensed through al-Azhar and instituted a license-renewal requirement to ensure that all preachers were vetted by the state.[28] Some institutions, such as privately owned schools, were harder to bring to heel than others. But the regime used all the weapons in its arsenal. In January 2015, the

Ministry of Education appointed new directors for every school owned by a Muslim Brotherhood–affiliated individual.[29]

As Nathan Brown and Michele Dunne write, "Under Nasser as well as Sadat and Mubarak . . . the judiciary sometimes acted as a brake on the government's most authoritarian impulses. Now, all the instruments of the Egyptian state seem fully on board. Whereas Nasser had to go to the trouble of setting up kangaroo courts, today there is no need."[30] For the near entirety of the postindependence era, the army, judiciary, and religious establishment may have been politicized, but at least they offered the pretense of being above the fray, nurturing an illusion of independence and autonomy. (At its most assertive, the Egyptian judiciary became a focal point of opposition to the Mubarak regime in the mid-2000s.) That they were widely perceived as pillars of the state was due in part to Egypt's relatively well-formed sense of nationhood. The idea of the Egyptian state, with its attendant bureaucratic largesse, predated Egyptian independence.

The military, in particular, enjoyed near universal respect, becoming something close to sacred. When the army stepped in and deposed Mubarak—one of their own—in February 2011, few Egyptians objected. Defying orders from Mubarak's henchmen, the army refused to shoot into the crowds in Tahrir Square, burnishing its image of nonpartisanship. The chant that reverberated in the days leading up to Mubarak's fall—"the army and the people are one hand"—was no accident. Even if it wasn't quite true, it was the message the military brass fell back on over and over again: They represented no party or faction, they were dutiful servants of the nation, and they would guard over the interests of Egypt and Egypt alone. Even the Muslim Brotherhood, which had repeatedly fallen victim to the military's manipulations, avoided direct criticism of the army. As one Morsi administration official reflected, looking back at that critical period, "Our reformist approach led to a self-interested pact with the military."[31] To oppose the military would be tantamount to advocating revolution, and, as we have seen, Brotherhood leaders had little interest in dismantling or purging the state. If they needed to place blame, they could direct it at individuals or policies, but not at institutions. There was no need to alienate state institutions when they hoped, one day, to win them over from within the democratic process. Why defeat the state when it could more easily be co-opted?

Even with the tumult of Morsi's year in power, the military maintained the fiction of being above politics, despite mounting evidence to the contrary. As of May 2013, the army still enjoyed a 94 percent approval rating, according to a Zogby poll.[32] While there were several clashes and even massacres during its stewardship of the transitional period, the military's repression was, indeed, nonpartisan, targeting revolutionaries, soccer fans, Christians, and Islamists, and really anyone who threatened "stability."

Al-Azhar, the country's prestigious seat of Islamic learning, followed a similar path. During the democratic transition, it tried in seemingly good faith to bridge the gaps between Islamist and secular parties. At a series of meetings organized by al-Azhar's Grand Imam Ahmed al-Tayyeb, the various parties endorsed a document in June 2011 establishing a "guiding framework" for the new constitution. The memorandum stressed democratic principles and a commitment to universal rights and freedom of worship, anchoring al-Azhar's status as an influential state actor within the new Egypt.

Despite initial calls after the revolution for expanding al-Azhar's autonomy from the state,[33] since the coup it has functioned primarily as an instrument of the Sissi regime. Although uneasy with the Brotherhood's political ambitions, al-Azhar avoided clashing with Morsi during his short time in office. Ahmed al-Tayyeb reluctantly backed the overthrow of Morsi, a move that he would later describe as deciding between "two bitter choices."[34] Ali Gomaa, Egypt's grand mufti until February 2013, had less compunction, leading the rhetorical charge against the Brotherhood.[35] In several sermons and promotional videos, he offered religious justifications for killing members of the Muslim Brotherhood. "When someone tries to divide you, then kill them," he said in a video made for the military shortly after the Rabaa dispersal.[36] "Blessed are those who kill them, and those who are killed by them," added Gomaa. "We must cleanse our Egypt of this trash . . . they reek . . . God is with you, and the Prophet Mohamed is with you, and the believers are with you . . . [Oh God], may you destroy them."[37] Interestingly, Gomaa and other proregime clerics have employed the kind of *takfirist* reasoning usually associated with al-Qaeda and the Islamic State, arguing that Brotherhood members are akin to heretics and therefore their blood is licit.[38] Gomaa, Steven Brooke writes, now leads what used to be the Brotherhood's network of hospitals and clinics.[39]

This is yet another reason why the coup and the subsequent massacres (there were two others before Rabaa) would prove such a defining moment not just for Egypt but for the future trajectory of political Islam. State institutions had given up any pretense of neutrality. For the first time, the military—supported by all arms of the state, including the religious establishment—killed large numbers of Egyptian civilians from one particular political faction, in this case the Muslim Brotherhood and its allies. Once the Rabaa massacre happened, it had become, in a sense, too late. Too much blood had been spilled.

Accidental Leaders

The battle lines had been drawn more clearly than ever before. Muslim Brotherhood activists, perhaps hoping to find a silver lining in their ordeal, often cite this sense of clarity as a blessing of the coup. Gradualism doesn't lend itself to black and white and good and evil. But revolution does. They see the state, at least in its current iteration, as an enemy to be undermined. When thinking about radicalization, we tend to focus on the use of violence. But, intellectually and philosophically, attitudes toward the state and how to change it often prove more important over time. Violence is, more often than not, about means. The state is about ends.

If you were a longtime Brotherhood leader, all you likely knew was the long game, and you were probably quite good at finding creative ways to avoid confrontation. Taking the regime head-on would only imperil hard-fought gains. As we saw in the previous chapter, the Brotherhood's gradualism reflected a tacit understanding of sorts. In exchange for the Brotherhood's steering clear of regime red lines—calling for revolution, undermining state institutions, and overperforming in elections—the authorities would tolerate limited Brotherhood activity in the social and educational realms. A leader in his fifties or sixties would have spent as many as forty years of his life immersed in the organization and its ideas. Shifting into a revolutionary gear would be difficult.

The Brotherhood figures who managed to escape had little choice. They were outside the country. The best they could do was offer general directives and then let local branches inside Egypt chart their own course, based on realities that they no longer were privy to. This led to a dynamic where the leadership in exile was best positioned not to lead but to follow. Traveling to and from international capitals, their role was to reflect on and convey what has happening on the ground. If they contradicted the revolutionary spirit of their activist base, they risked irrelevance or, worse, provoking a split in the organization. Steeped in the Brotherhood and having suffered through the ups and downs of repression, leaders prioritized organizational survival above all else. And the only way to maintain organizational coherence was to give wide latitude to a new cadre of young activists. A strategy oriented around continuous and confrontational protests may have been "revolutionary," but, more important, it was good for morale. It gave Brotherhood members something to do and something to fight for.

The alternative was going home, lying low, and waiting, which ran the risk of plunging the Brotherhood into irrelevance. As Steven Brooke writes, referring to this period of mobilization: "By demonstrating the organization's strength, the Brotherhood is likely striving to convince the regime that they must be taken seriously, as an equal to be negotiated with rather than a minority to be exterminated."[40]

For a new generation of activists in their twenties and thirties, protests were their training ground. Forced to improvise, evade detection, and outsmart the police, they developed new methods and, in the process, got a crash course in how to be leaders. If they needed to quickly change locations for a protest, they would use fireworks to simulate gunfire to frighten the police and then scurry away. If they wanted to post pictures of a human chain on social media or needed a record of the inevitable police brutality, select Brotherhood members would loiter on the margins and pretend they were *against* the Brotherhood, shouting insults at the protesters, all the while taping as much as they could.

Even in the best of circumstances, taking part in a Brotherhood-affiliated protest came with the risk of significant jail time. But many figured that if their names weren't already on some police dossier, they'd be soon enough. They had less to lose. As difficult as this period was, it served as a political coming of age. These activists came to believe that the future of the movement depended on them, in part because it did. If they were detained, then at least they knew their families (and legal expenses) would be looked after by the Brotherhood—one of the many "perks" of membership.

These accidental leaders had adopted revolution as their call. Not surprisingly, they now looked back at the Morsi era through the distorting prism of revolutionary purity, judging the Brotherhood's actions against that lofty standard. The thirty-five-year-old journalist Asmaa Shokr, a local Brotherhood official and media spokesperson in the posh Cairo suburb of

Mohandiseen, was one such activist. When I sat down with her in Istanbul in February 2015, she was getting used to her new life, settling into a routine of dropping her kids off at school, talking strategy with fellow exiles, and meeting with reporters and researchers like me.

Exile is an odd thing. Many Brotherhood leaders left for Doha in the summer and fall of 2013, often fleeing Egypt through excruciating treks to the Sudanese border. The easier journeys involved "thousands of dollars in bribes to airport security officials."[41] It was early then, when they still held to the belief that Sissi's days were numbered. Sitting in a Doha hotel lobby, I remember asking the Brotherhood's Hamza Zawba, "So you're in exile now?" He laughed, and then said, "Let's see if we can find another word for it!"[42] But the second wave of political refugees like Asmaa Shokr had both the benefit and the burden of knowing they wouldn't be returning anytime soon.

Unlike her more prominent counterparts in Istanbul, Asmaa had struggled for nearly a year in Egypt, organizing weekly protests, before managing to flee the country ("No one knew I was leaving, even my family," she recalled). She had suffered more than any of them. "Do you know how many funerals we've attended?" she asked me.[43] She had witnessed two massacres. Asmaa took it one day at a time, worrying about what might happen to her children if she was imprisoned. Having been on the front lines, she had earned the right to speak—and to criticize. Hers was a revolutionary legitimacy that no one could take away.

She loved the Brotherhood. "I grew up with the Brotherhood. It's like you feel like you're part of this big family," Asmaa told me. But looking back at the Brotherhood's rise and fall, she felt more anger than regret. The incompetence of the Morsi government baffled her. It was obvious, for instance, that the military was preparing to stage a coup. Why, then, did Morsi hold on to the hope that Sissi would protect him? "They kept telling us not to worry, that everything was just dandy," she recalled.

A year and a half after the coup, it was time for an accounting. "These are the people who brought us to this disaster," Asmaa said. "Any leader who held a position of responsibility—I can't have confidence in him. With respect, it's time for you to leave, if you were an official, if you were a minister under Morsi, whatever. They're not going to change. That's the way they think." Their crime, as Asma saw it, was naïveté coupled with a lack of revolutionary fervor:

> We should have purified state institutions. Let's put to the side for a moment the decision to run for the presidency. You have the presidency; you control both the executive and legislative branches. So what do you do? You purify the state television channels. When a channel spreads a rumor about the Brotherhood, investigate it, and if it turns out to be fabricated, close the channel down.

She wasn't about to be fooled again. Asmaa was now calling for revolutionary courts, trials for military leaders—including, of course, Sissi—and overhauling the state. On how to actually get there, Asmaa was lacking in details. Sure, it didn't sound practical, but, as she understood it, revolution wasn't necessarily something you planned; it was something that *happened*, when the time was right and any number of factors came together in a perfect storm of action and purpose.

Asmaa and others like her were critical of nearly every Brotherhood leader, but they reserved much of their scorn for a shadowy figure named Mahmoud Hussein, the Brotherhood's secretary general and one of the only members of the organization's Guidance Council who wasn't in prison or on the run. Hussein shied away from the limelight and avoided reporters, yet, based first in Doha and then Istanbul, he was the Brotherhood's strongman, wielding considerable power. Stubborn and immovable, Hussein was notorious for a seeming inability to admit fault. Meanwhile, his tendency to operate in the shadows clashed with the unabashed, transparent anger of the rank and file. Mahmoud Hussein's allies in the anticoup National Alliance for Supporting Legitimacy would complain that they never quite knew what Hussein was thinking and whether he was up to something behind their backs.

Hussein's influence was likely overstated, but, as an embodiment of all that had gone wrong, his specter served a purpose, offering a focal point for the burgeoning anger of the rank and file. The Brotherhood may have been hierarchical, but hierarchy was difficult when there wasn't anyone inside Egypt to oversee it. The most leaders could do was try their best to contain or channel revolutionary sentiment, which could easily become a liability if it morphed into violence.

In the 1990s and 2000s, the Brotherhood initiated a series of reforms that expanded the scope of internal democracy within the organization, particularly on the local level.[44] (Interestingly, the Brotherhood has a history of holding elections when repression is at its worst.) If and when internal elections were held in this new, postcoup era, ordinary members would have their say, and leaders on the outside would have to come to terms with those decisions. In other words, the gap between an angry, revolutionary base and a cautious leadership would have to close, one way or another. And it did in 2014, as local Brotherhood offices across Egypt began electing new leaders. With the Brotherhood's General Guide Mohamed Badie in prison, a new "secret" guide was selected. He wasn't necessarily revolutionary, but there was an expectation that he would at least respect the growing revolutionary sentiments of the membership. As Islamist activist Ammar el-Beltagy, who fled to Turkey in 2014, told me, "This is not about who the guide is. Whoever he is, he can't oppose the revolutionary wave."[45]

Neither could anyone else. Brotherhood leader Amr Darrag often found himself a convenient target because of his inability to sound anything but conciliatory and reasonable, perhaps too reasonable. He had been allowed to stay in Egypt as long as he kept a low profile, but soon enough the regime came for him, too. He managed to flee the country in a treacherous trek across the Sudanese border, ending up in Doha before moving to Istanbul. By early 2015, he had caught the revolutionary bug. It may have not been the best fit for the Purdue-educated Darrag, who had served as Morsi's minister for international cooperation and spoke confident, flawless English. In a different world, he probably would have made for a successful, even popular technocrat in a transitional government somewhere where politics was more quiet and cordial. But now he was in exile in Turkey, trying to start a new life with his family. When I saw him in February 2015, just after the Brotherhood's internal elections, he was jovial and optimistic as usual, with a hint of the sadness one sees in people who have been overtaken by events beyond their control.

"Egyptians have changed," he told me, as we sat in a café on the outskirts of Istanbul. "I'm not the same person I used to be. I'm more revolutionary. . . . If I look at the list of mistakes the Brotherhood made, this is the biggest one: trying to fix the system from inside gradually."[46] But, for Darrag, there were clear limits and, like many others in the leadership, he was worried about the growing openness to violence that he sensed among many of the Brotherhood's younger activists.

A Question of Violence

Having renounced violence in the early 1970s, the Brotherhood has been a forceful advocate of nonviolent change for decades. Yet this hasn't kept its critics from suspecting that such a shift was merely tactical and that it was only a matter of time. Jihad, after all, features prominently in Hassan al-Banna's teachings. His essay "On Jihad" is an ode to dying in the service of God and the *umma*. Even with Banna's caveat—"Allah did not ordain Jihad for the Muslims so that it may be used as a tool of oppression or tyranny or so that it may be used by some to further their personal gains"—it is not hard to see how opposition would stir to Banna's writings.[47] "The umma that knows how to die a noble and honorable death is granted an exalted life in this world and eternal felicity in the next," he writes, urging his followers to prepare themselves for martyrdom.[48]

In the 1940s, the Brotherhood established a "secret apparatus," which was implicated in various acts of violence, including the assassination of Prime Minister Mahmoud Nuqrashi Pasha in 1948. Banna, by this time, found himself unable to control the militants in his organization. He dissociated himself from Nuqrashi's murder and condemned the perpetrators, but the damage had been done. The Brotherhood also sent battalions of members to fight on the side of the Arabs in the 1948 war with Israel, but violence in the context of a war between nations was different than attacking your own government.

Many in the Brotherhood—including chief ideologue Sayyid Qutb—radicalized over the course of the 1950s and '60s, were irrevocably changed by their harrowing experiences in the dungeons of Gamal Abdel Nasser. "As the guards marched arrivals down the gloomy passageways in chains, they could hear the cries and desperate shouts of fellow Muslim Brothers," writes John Calvert, author of arguably the best English-language biography of Qutb, who was imprisoned in 1954.[49] How could fellow Egyptians—fellow Muslims—be capable of such brutality toward their brothers in Islam, Qutb and his cohorts wondered. Soon enough, they managed to find a way to make sense of their ordeal, in an intellectual shift that would reverberate for decades to come: Perhaps those guards—and rulers like Nasser—weren't *true* Muslims. The 1957 prison massacre of twenty-one Brotherhood members was a defining moment. Qutb, writes Calvert, "was in the infirmary when the guards brought in the injured. The floor would have been covered with his comrades' blood. The massacre elicited terrible emotions in Qutb."[50] Again, we find ourselves face-to-face with the problem of theodicy, and how trying to make sense of evil can pave the way for yet more evil. Qutb's successors took his arguments several steps further with their condemnation of most Muslims as "disbelievers," thereby making their blood licit. The Brotherhood, though, was moving in a different direction by the late 1960s, and the group's general guide at the time, Hassan al-Hudaybi, issued a disavowal of Qutb's most controversial ideas in the book *Preachers, Not Judges*.[51]

As the question of violence dogged the Brotherhood, it went out of its way to highlight its gradualist, nonviolent approach to political change. In the 1990s, extremist groups waged a low-level insurgency against the Egyptian regime. The Brotherhood came under growing pressure to distinguish itself from the perpetrators of the increasingly brutal attacks, including the killing of foreign tourists. With the world paying greater attention, the Brotherhood's leaders made the case to domestic and international audiences that they were a different breed of Islamist that pursued nonviolence, spoke the language of human rights and democracy, and sought gradual rather than revolutionary change.

To be a Brotherhood member meant to be immersed in an ethic of nonviolence, which went hand in hand with the organization's insistence on gradualism, the long game of politics, and the centrality of electoral competition. This ethic was on display in Rabaa. Facing a likely massacre, one might have expected protesters to smuggle arms and return fire when the military moved in and launched its attack. But, with only a handful of exceptions, this did not happen. At the end of the day, security forces had confiscated fifteen guns from the sit-in, hardly a match for twelve hours of the military's indiscriminate gunfire, teargas, and bulldozers.[52] Eyewitnesses reported isolated gunfire on the part of protesters; those who responded to the attacks threw rocks or Molotov cocktails, while a few car-ried sticks or clubs.[53] Looking back at those early months after the coup, what's remarkable isn't how many Brotherhood sup-porters turned to violence, but how few.

After the coup, in a speech that became a rallying cry, the Brotherhood's general guide, Mohamed Badie, who was pre-sumed until that point to be under arrest, emerged to tell fol-lowers gathered in Rabaa that "our peacefulness is stronger than their bullets." He promised to resist nonviolently until Morsi's reinstatement. The struggle "is peaceful, and will remain peace-ful," Badie said.[54]

In practice, however, peacefulness didn't seem to be work-ing particularly well. The presumption—naive in retrospect but sensible at the time—was that the military wouldn't be able to sustain high levels of violence and brutality. Unlike, say, Syria or Iraq, the army didn't represent a particular sect or ethnic-ity. The army was made up of Egyptians from every family (young men with at least one other male sibling are required to serve). Would conscripts really be willing to turn their fire on fellow Egyptians, and for how long? Egypt didn't have a his-tory of this kind of internecine conflict. There was also the role of the international community to factor in. Would Egypt's patrons, including the United States, be willing to turn a blind eye to wanton abuses, with the whole world watching?

Outside contexts of civil war, nonviolent resistance is gener-ally considered to be more effective than violent alternatives, precisely because of the role of international actors.[55] As Maria Stephan and Erica Chenoweth note in an important 2008 study, "Externally, the international community is more likely to de-nounce and sanction states for repressing nonviolent campaigns than it is violent campaigns."[56] The regime's use of excessive force against nonviolent groups can be critical to the latter's suc-cess, resulting in "sympathy and a possible increase in legitimacy" as well as political and financial support from the international community.[57] Yet what might apply in normal circumstances was unlikely to apply in Egypt. When Islamists are the ones being repressed, the calculus changes considerably. Over the past twenty-five years, there have not been any instances of anti-Islamist repression in the Arab world that have elicited significant international outrage.[58]

As Brotherhood leaders saw it, though, while peaceful protests may not have quite brought down the regime, any turn to violence was almost certain to fail. Asmaa Shokr recalled one telling example of the leadership's fear of starting down the path of violence, even as a reaction to overwhelming regime violence. "On the day of the Rabaa dispersal," she told me, "someone tried to torch a car, and a Brotherhood leader was close by and told him to stop. I was shocked that day. Your children are dying in front of you and you care about a car?"[59] There was a bitterness, and that bitterness would only grow.

Portrait of a Young Man in Prison

What does it look like to come of age in the Brotherhood, to find yourself skipping classes and revolting against the state? In an organization that prioritized the principle of "listening and obeying," how did Brotherhood youth decide enough was enough and start questioning not just the decisions of their leaders, but some of Brotherhood's most basic assumptions about violence and political change? The story of one of these activists—I'll call him Karim—reflects a journey that has become all the more common. These are young men and women who grew up in the Brotherhood's embrace, dedicating their lives to the movement. But a series of unlikely events—the revolution, Morsi's rise to the presidency, then a coup, followed by a massacre—led them, however slowly, from certainty to doubt. Their commitment to the Brotherhood is so deep—the Brotherhood after all is not so much an organization as a way of life—that they would never think seriously of leaving. But they questioned nearly everything else: tactics, strategy, and even what it meant to believe in and fight for an Islamic state.

For the twenty-three-year-old Karim, a dentistry student, the shock started the day of the coup. "It was June twenty-eighth," he recalled. "I was in Rabaa, and a Brotherhood official was talking to us, telling us not to worry, that 'the army is in our pocket.' Great. I believed them because I didn't have the information to come up with a different opinion. That's why when the coup happened, it was such a big shock."[60]

Karim generally agreed with the Rabaa sit-in, but the surrounding circumstances worried him. "I started to have questions," he recalled. "Okay, what if they came in and hit us? Then we'll defend ourselves, but we don't have anything to defend ourselves with. If so, then we're just offering ourselves for death." Despite his doubts, there wasn't a protest he would miss in those few first months after Rabaa. But what he described as the Brotherhood leadership's "radical peacefulness" continued to grate on him. "Your job is to get killed and that's it," he told me. "I don't want violence, but at the same time I don't want that kind of peacefulness. So if we let them kill us and we lose two hundred thousand people, okay, and then what? He has no compunction to kill. Nothing will stop him, except if the people he's killing can resist."

In early 2014, he was arrested. It was an ordinary day (to the extent that life on the run can be ordinary). Karim joined a protest, as he always did after the weekly Friday prayer. He was, by now, fairly skilled at this sort of thing, having attended protests at least weekly, sometimes daily, though his enthusiasm was starting to wane. This time, when the police came, his friends were able to get away, but he found himself surrounded on both sides by officers. He laughed and then told me, "I was the only one who got arrested!"

Even in the best of times, Egyptian prisons are notorious for their subhuman conditions. These were not the best of times.

There were thirty people in a small cell, probably not much larger than four by six meters. The prisoners couldn't sleep on their backs, only on their side. "You can't even spread your legs out or else you'll end up hitting someone," Karim recalled, his voice steady and reflective, as if remembering a field trip gone awry. There were ten Muslim Brotherhood members. The rest were also political prisoners of various sorts, most of whom had been rounded up at street protests. The Brotherhood assumed leadership of the cell, offering religious classes to the other prisoners on the Quran and the life of the Prophet Mohamed. It was ideal for recruitment. You had thirty people in close quarters, together twenty-four hours a day. There was nothing to do but talk to everyone else about everything—religion, politics, tactics, and strategy.

Three months and three weeks into his four-month prison stint, he was moved to another prison unit. This is where Karim's evolution would continue, his doubts heavier than before. In a neighboring cell, there was a charismatic Salafi preacher named Ahmed Ashoush. After returning from the anti-Soviet jihad in Afghanistan, Sheikh Ashoush spent nineteen years in prison, from 1992 until the start of the Arab Spring. He was an unrepentant Salafi jihadi. Before the coup, Ashoush had gained modest recognition in the Egyptian press as a "controversial" and open critic of Morsi and the Brotherhood. In a 2012 talk show appearance, he described Morsi as an "illegitimate" president. Morsi, he added, was no different from the other Egyptian presidents that came before him— even if he happened to be a more observant Muslim. Ashoush instead called for a true Muslim ruler to run a true Islamic state.[61]

The prison guards would open the cells for about ten minutes, and Karim would sneak off to Ashoush's cell and stay there the rest of the day. He only had four days with the sheikh, but he made the most of it, spending every waking hour with him. Before his arrest, Ashoush had memorized dozens of books. He spent much of his nineteen years in prison going over the details in his head, making sure he didn't forget a thing. This was also how he stayed sane. "[Ashoush] was just so knowledgeable that he was able to influence me to an extraordinary degree," Karim told me. Ashoush challenged him on the ideological origins of the Brotherhood, linking Banna to Jamal al-Din al-Afghani and Mohamed Abduh. He viewed the two leading Islamic modernists as dangerous innovators who had fallen under the allure and influence of Western colonialism. Not only that, they were *murtadeen*, or apostates. Ashoush challenged his eager student on the Muslim Brotherhood's 2012 constitution. "Morsi's constitution is far from the ideas of establishing sharia and Islam," Karim recalled the sheikh saying. "I wasn't able to say much in response because he was telling me things I didn't know in the first place."

In just a few days with Sheikh Ashoush, the doubts began to gather. One of Karim's friends, who joined our conversation at the coffee shop, jumped in. "With Brotherhood youth," he said, "there is a deficit of religious education. We weren't raised well intellectually. So when we sit with people like Sheikh Ashoush and hear big talk, about this book and that book, naturally we're overwhelmed." Contrary to popular perception, Salafis are at least in some ways more theologically sophisticated than their counterparts in the Brotherhood. For reasons inherent to their particular brand of Islamism, theology isn't as important for Brotherhood-inspired groups. This is why Salafis like Ashoush tend to look at the Brotherhood with suspicion: Because of their modernist pedigree, they're too flexible, too pragmatic, and too willing to use sweeping *maslaha* (public interest) arguments to justify or rationalize what are ultimately political imperatives.

Karim had also been wondering whether the Brotherhood's long-standing methods could be effective against a regime that was oblivious to the moral and human costs of violence. Arab prisons—and the fact that Egyptian authorities were quickly building new ones to meet demand—embodied the failure of politics and the triumph of force. For would-be prisoners, it didn't matter whether they were peaceful or violent; they'd be arrested all the same, and the peaceful ones would often find themselves slapped with longer sentences.

Prisons were ideal incubators for radicalism, providing a space for hardened Salafis to preach the gospel of purity and jihad. The bitterness that builds during a long prison term isn't something that goes away easily. Karim was lucky that his sentence was short. After his release, he continued to grapple with the questions that had been nagging him. He decided to stay in the Brotherhood but promised himself he would learn as much as he could about the group's history and keep an open mind about ideas coming from outside the movement. To the extent that he could, he—along with thousands of young activists who shared at least some of his doubts—would try to change the organization from within.

Like many of his comrades, Karim had given considerable thought to the question of violence. Nearly nine months after his release from prison, he still believed that taking up arms would be a mistake. He instead proposed a path somewhere in between armed insurrection and the "radical peacefulness" he had so derided. First, as he saw it, defending yourself against the violence of others was a moral and legal right. This was "defensive" violence—to be distinguished from "intentional" or "offensive" violence. But morality aside, violence had to serve a purpose. Karim realized that violent acts, embraced only out of necessity and even then reluctantly, weren't going to bring down the regime. Rather, the objective was to establish "red lines" and to "reach" members of the regime who were oblivious to the consequences of their actions. The example raised by Karim, echoed by many others I spoke to, was perhaps the most obvious one, as it captured the indignity, outrage, and horror of Brotherhood members: that of a police officer who raped a sister ("sister" here being either literal or figurative or both). "If there's a person known to take girls and sexually assault them, find out where he lives and then torch his car," Karim told me. "Leave a message not to do it ever again; otherwise, the punishments will be more serious."

Beyond the burning of police cars and the targeting of security personnel, Brotherhood youth were asking themselves what next. Beyond supposedly serving as deterrents against future police brutality, what was this sort of low-level, anarchic violence meant to accomplish? To answer such a question, more systematic thinking was required, and so Karim walked me through his thought process. "What are the elements that strengthen or weaken the coup?" he asked me rhetorically. "That's what we have to think about." "The violence I support," he went on, "is the violence which targets the coup's sources of strength without spilling the blood of innocents. I don't want anyone to die. So, for example, we can target companies with close ties to the regime and military as well as multinationals. These are the ones who can force Sissi to change his policies. If their economic interests are threatened, they may be willing to pressure Sissi to rethink his approach."

An Unlikely Ideologue

It was no accident that Karim's ideas sounded similar to some of the missives of an unlikely, eccentric ideologue named Shahid King Bolsen, who had become semipopular in revolutionary Islamist circles around the same time. The story of Bolsen, a forty-three-year-old convert to Islam and native of Boulder, Colorado, sounds like something out of a film noir. He was convicted of murder in the United Arab Emirates in a bizarre incident where he posed as a woman and lured a German man to his apartment ostensibly to help him see the error of his ways. What actually happened isn't entirely clear. "We fought," says Bolsen, "and I unfortunately caused his death."[62] After a lengthy appeals process, his conviction was reduced to manslaughter. Bolsen was released from prison—where he had spent seven years—after paying blood money to the victim's family. He soon moved to Istanbul, where he began attracting a cult following for his unusual mix of Islamism and leftist rants against neoliberalism. Since adolescence, Bolsen had been moved by economic and social injustice—he had even adopted "King" as his middle name after Martin Luther King, Jr. His financial difficulties—he struggled to find work after an Internet café venture in Dubai failed—and an idiosyncratic reading of anticapitalism add to the evident bitterness in his writings. "The pyramid economy has become an obelisk, in which a tiny number of billionaires own approximately twice the total value of currency in circulation on the Earth," he wrote on his blog in late 2014.[63]

Bolsen, a college dropout, had no religious training and spoke little Arabic. He had no real media platform, at least not until his supporters began distributing his translated writings through various Islamist networks. Mostly, he shared his thoughts on the evils of the neoliberal world order on his Facebook page, which slowly accrued more followers. His message was simple enough, that Egypt's revolutionaries "can prove that collaboration with the coup is bad for business."[64] Addressing the revolutionaries, he tells them to "inflict loss, decrease profit, increase expense, lower investor confidence, deflate share values."[65] In another post, he explains the logic as follows:

> When you strike KFC, or any of their companies, your message goes directly to the top of the pyramid. If the investors who work through Vanguard alone are convinced that the Coup cannot secure their capital, they easily have the power to demote Sissi from the presidency of Egypt, to washing dishes at KFC.[66]

Bolsen also offers detailed instructions, for example suggesting the use of homemade caltrops to disrupt transportation and close down roads. Bomb scares are another do-it-yourself method. "Hundreds of work hours, profit loss, disrupted operations, and increased expense . . . because of a phone call," he writes.[67] Bolsen hailed the early closure of the telecommunications company Etisalat in early 2015—caused by threats on the company, most likely a bomb scare—as an ideal act of civil disobedience: "There was no bloodshed, and no arrests, but the actions sent a wave through the entire system of corporate control. . . . May Allah bless those responsible, they have not only struck a blow against the stability of the Coup, but also against the corporate imperial system itself."[68] Inside Egypt, activists associated with an obscure group called the Popular Resistance Movement apparently took Bolsen seriously enough, staging an attack on a KFC in the town of Quesna and using slogans he first popularized.[69] While there is no evidence—contrary to regime claims—of Brotherhood involvement, plenty of the group's members either sympathize with or, like Karim, support such acts.

It all sounded incredibly naive to me, so I pushed back. Karim acknowledged that the "targeted" violence of the kind he was describing might provoke a very different response than the one intended. Targeting multinationals, of course, might only harden the business community's position, pushing them even closer to the Sissi regime. Moreover, the military would use such attacks as a pretext to move even more aggressively against the Brotherhood and its interests, provoking a terrifying wave of violence and counterviolence. What if that happens? I asked him. He hoped that it wouldn't. But if it did, at least it would clarify matters—"if the military becomes a combatant against the Egyptian people in such a blatant way," Karim told me, "then we will turn it into Syria." He knew this would be a disaster, but he sounded resigned. "If only ten thousand have died, then that's nothing in the context of a revolution."

The very fact that young Brotherhood activists might take someone like Bolsen seriously was itself a sign of the changing times. Even if Brotherhood leaders were learning to speak the language of revolution, they were still temperamentally cautious, preferring slow deliberation over sudden political shifts. But if Bolsen was anything, he was reckless. Speaking for no one but himself and ultimately unaccountable for the consequences of his ideas, Bolsen frequently contradicted some of the more fundamental elements of the Brotherhood's political strategy. For example, in one January 2014 Facebook post, he argues that "it is a mistake in Egypt to focus on changing the government, and trying to return Morsi to power." He goes on: "The form and features of the government do not actually matter that much, and that's not what the problem is in Egypt. It is only a distraction to become obsessed with 'restoring democracy' and so on."[70] This is a rather obvious criticism of the Brotherhood's priorities. But, more than that, Bolsen's exclusive focus on neoliberal economic policies over political institutions goes against the entire premise of the group's approach to politics. (While more than comfortable with the rhetoric of social justice and equality, the Brotherhood tends to avoid more sweeping critiques of neoliberal economic structures.)

Fundamentally, Bolsen had little interest in the Egyptian state as such and was more likely to see the Sissi regime as the inevitable by-product of economic imperialism. The Brotherhood, meanwhile, had come to see the modern nation-state—and the economic order that went along with it—as constants or, in the words of legal scholar Wael Hallaq, "timeless."[71] The state was indispensible because it was the state, through parliaments and presidencies, that could redirect and re-render society through the modification and changing of laws. As Shahab Ahmed writes, this was not an Islamist problem as much as it was a modern problem. The centralization and codification of law—and the control and monopolization of power and territory that comes along with it—has been essential to the process of state building. Why, Ahmed asks, should modern Muslims assume "the constitutive centrality of law to the constitution of Islam" and not focus just as much, if not more so, on rethinking "theology, philosophy, ethics, poetics, and Sufism"?[72]

Losing Faith

The openness to ideas that violated the Brotherhood's basic understanding of political change reflected a deeper shift in the world of political Islam. Everywhere, and not just in Egypt, Islamists and the so-called "Islamic project" were evolving. Islamism has never existed in a vacuum; it draws on the peculiarities of time and place. The Arab Spring and its quick demise forced Brotherhood-inspired organizations to rethink their basic assumptions. For decades, they had streamlined their focus considerably, settling into a comfortable though inconclusive routine of contesting flawed elections, pushing autocratic regimes for greater freedoms, and hoping that when a political opening finally came, they'd be there to reap the rewards.

A succession of events called into question any "elections-first" approach to politics, particularly in states that now lacked not just elections but also functioning governments. Meanwhile, Egyptian and Tunisian Islamists' brief experiences in government showed that, far from a blessing, the promise of power could prove a burden and even a curse. The rise of Islamists provoked an especially hostile response from regional power brokers like Saudi Arabia and the United Arab Emirates, which saw the Brotherhood as an existential threat and a challenge to its own religious and political legitimacy. With Turkey and Qatar as the two leading supporters of Islamists across the region, an Arab cold war emerged, with each bloc wading into an ever-multiplying number of proxy battles.

The collapse of central governments, as in Yemen, Syria, and Libya, and their ceaseless politicization elsewhere, as in Egypt, challenged the basic building block of modern politics: the nation-state. If the nation-state was no longer a given, then neither was mainstream Islamism's slow-moving, gradualist approach to politics.

As if that weren't enough, the rise of the Islamic State—portraying itself as the standard bearer of not just Islamism but Islam—presented yet another challenge to the Brotherhood's state-centric approach. It was little accident that just a month after Egypt's coup, the Islamic State singled out the Brotherhood in an official statement, calling it a "bankrupt" model.[73] The ballot box and the purple-stained finger were appropriate symbols for the first phase of the Arab Spring, capturing the euphoria of those who thought they finally had reason to hope. In its second phase, it might as well have been the black banners of the Islamic State, embodying the dark turn in the region's fortunes. Across the region, Arabs were losing faith in politics. By "politics" here I mean something quite basic—the belief in the possibility that divides over what we hold most dear can be resolved through peaceful competition. The coup in Egypt was a gift to the Islamic State and its extremist ilk, further fueling an already potent message that fundamental change could only come through bullets and brute force.

In such an environment—with coups, extremists, cold wars, and proxy battles—it was little surprise that the likes of Shahid Bolsen would get a hearing from angry young activists looking for something, anything, to believe in. Much of Bolsen's message may have sounded nonsensical, but it wasn't necessarily any more unrealistic than believing in the return of democratic politics, winning a presidential election, and actually being allowed to govern.

A State Beyond the State

One of the main themes of this book is that the divides at the heart of the Arab state are difficult—perhaps uniquely difficult—to resolve. Mainstream Islamism has offered a particular response to the problem of the state, hoping to fuse Islamic law with modern state structures, but at the price of emphasizing the prerogatives of the state over the integrity of the law. Some would say it is a contradiction without a resolution. Islamic law wasn't designed for the modern state. Over the centuries, the sharia developed into something organic and autonomous, a self-regulating and constantly evolving body of laws, norms, and traditions. In its considerable diversity, range, and scope, an anything but monolithic sharia wasn't an intuitive fit for a powerful, all-encompassing state that sought to control and codify.*

The state as a fact of life couldn't really be undone, at least not entirely. Even where states had failed, as in Iraq and Syria, the Islamic State found itself mimicking the nation-state despite its protestations to the contrary. It called itself *the* Islamic State, itself a rather audacious choice for a name. It had a flag and it collected taxes with a statelike bureaucracy. It sought to fulfill the basic social and economic functions of the modern state while rejecting the classic compromises of statecraft and international relations. Perhaps most important, it hoped to control the lives of its subjects in ways the premodern caliphate never could.

Some of it was awfully mundane, suggesting a kind of normalcy in the midst of a raging civil war. Here was the group's would-be state fixing potholes, maintaining electric lines, opening food kitchens, and leading vaccination campaigns.[74] In doing these things, the Islamic State sought to instill a sense of belonging and loyalty—a kind of nationalism—in its subjects. This "belonging," however, was to be manufactured, constrained, and controlled. To the extent that there was something called "society" in the Islamic State's version of the Islamic state, there

---

*As Knut Vikør notes, "We see in the Islamic case that the law is drawn away from the state, personified by the sultan, and so presents in many ways an anomaly compared to the theoretical model of state power as the embodiment of state law," *Between God and the Sultan: A History of Islamic Law* (Oxford: Oxford University Press, 2005), p. 185.

was nothing particularly organic and autonomous about it. Society was meant to serve the state, something that premodern scholars would have found unfathomable. When the clerics of the Islamic State's vaunted sharia courts—which were supposedly independent—produced problematic rulings, they were promptly dismissed. When an Islamic State cleric in the Syrian town of al-Bab ruled that the group's February 2015 immolation of a Jordanian fighter pilot was un-Islamic, he was put on trial.[75]

As confrontational as they might be, Muslim Brotherhood youth express little sympathy for the Islamic State's "model." Instead, there is unanimous condemnation. They will often point out (correctly) that the Islamic State considers them, by virtue of being Brotherhood members, to be apostates. "Every time I look at ISIS, I wonder if Sissi is the least of our worries," the London-based Brotherhood activist Abdullah El-Haddad told me. "Imagine ISIS coming to power in Egypt. What would they do to us?"[76]

More and more Brotherhood youth are expressing interest in a sort of Islamist third way, between the election-focused state centrism of the old Brotherhood and the self-conscious maximalism of ascendant extremists. They don't quite know what it looks like—it's never been done before—but they know what it doesn't look like. At its most basic level, the vision that people like Karim and Asmaa Shokr have in mind is "revolutionary" and somewhat anarchic, accepting temporary destabilization and perhaps even bloodshed as the necessary price for long-term political change. What they share with a leadership whose stomach for confrontation has its limits is a new take on existing state structures. Amr Darrag, the former Morsi minister, sees this as one of the unintended benefits of an otherwise tragic turn of events. "It took a revolution and a coup to fix things in an organization that otherwise would have never changed," he says.[77]

That the coup was a blessing is something that Brotherhood

figures have said since the day it happened. Perhaps some of it was about trying to answer the question of why God permits evil. There had to be something behind the madness, the killing. Could it really be that more than eight hundred innocents not only died but died in vain? What may have initially sounded like wishful thinking and after-the-fact rationalization now had an air of plausibility. The coup and its tragic aftermath *were* forcing the Brotherhood to change. For the believer, accidents of history are never just that. And so it must have seemed like a greater plan was set in motion. Perhaps God was sending a message that the old ways of doing business had failed and that the Brotherhood's assumptions needed to be reassessed, not necessarily because they were wrong then, but because they were wrong now.

AMR DARRAG WAS a moderate's moderate, at least by Brotherhood standards. In an organization suffering from a dearth of intellectual and strategic thinking, Darrag at least had a good grasp of the political. In the weeks leading up to the Rabaa dispersal, he was the Brotherhood's main interlocutor with the international community, meeting with senators, ambassadors, and diplomats as they scurried—and almost succeeded—in brokering a deal between the Brotherhood and the military that was based on a series of confidence-building measures.[78] But that was all in the past, as Darrag settled into his new life as a political exile and the director of a new Istanbul-based think tank focused on Egyptian and regional affairs.

While studying at Purdue, Darrag must have gotten used to the snow in Lafayette, Indiana, but it had been a while. When I saw him in Turkey, it was an unusually cold winter. It had been snowing heavily, making my trek to the outskirts of Istanbul all the more challenging. This was, indeed, a different world, even as Darrag tried to make it his new home. He had lived every day since July 3, 2013, either fearing arrest or living in exile, which had given him considerable time—alone and away from Cairo's stifling embrace—to ponder what came next.

He took it for granted that there would be a political opening, even if he didn't quite know when. On this, he was correct. No autocracy lasts forever, and postcoup regimes in polarized societies tend to be fragile. It was a question, then, of what to do when the opening came. As Darrag saw it, any "elections-first" strategy would need to be scrapped entirely. New Brotherhood forays into electoral politics would polarize the country just as they had before. If they limited their ambitions and contested only a partial slate—say 25 percent of parliament seats—then that wasn't exactly a great solution either, since a mix of old regime elements, Salafis, and a few corrupt liberals would likely win the rest. His model instead was what he called "partnership without elections," where the focus would be on laying the foundations of a new Egyptian state. Elections would have to be postponed for a few years. The appropriate focus wasn't who was in charge but what they would be in charge of.

"The overall structure of the state has to be rebuilt," Darrag told me. The point of departure was Egypt's sadly repeating history of political manipulation by and for the state. The centralization of power may have been an essential element of modern state building, but it was also a recipe for repression. The balance of power could be shifted away from the state by granting expanded authority to local governance structures. In effect, this would also reduce ideological polarization. On the local level, issues around the role of religion and the "foundations" of the state could be put to the side. Instead, the focus would be on the more immediate needs of communities, including improved social services, transportation, healthcare, and education. As Darrag saw it, this was a way of building trust between Islamists and non-Islamists by essentially agreeing not to fight over ideology, at least until greater trust and confidence could be built between the two sides. Instead of concerning itself with running for president and taking power, the Brotherhood would serve as the "guarantor" and guardian of the revolution. For the duration of the transition period, the Brotherhood would make decisions based on whether those decisions served one and one goal only: overhauling and even "purifying" the state. Of course, it was one thing to advocate such ideas while in the opposition; it was quite another to live up to them when tempted by power. And there would never be any way to know for sure until you had the choice.

Darrag's ideas may have sounded original—and they were certainly more "revolutionary" than the Brotherhood's precoup politics—but there remained the question of the ultimate purposes of the state, however decentralized and localized it was. Matters of religion could be postponed, but they couldn't be postponed forever. Politics is also about what happens *after* you get what you want, whenever that might be.

I COULDN'T EXPECT BROTHERHOOD leaders to do what they hadn't properly done for decades: outline a clear, coherent end state. They couldn't be expected to offer a detailed framework for the establishment of a mythical Islamic state that might never come to be. This was not the time for treatises on Islamic political theory. The overriding concern was to ensure the organization's survival and relevance at a time when it was threatened with extinction. Moreover, as we saw in the previous chapter, the Brotherhood benefitted from "constructive ambiguity" over the exact nature of its mission; it was a big-tent movement that couldn't afford to alienate a large swath of its own supporters, especially when they were the ones keeping the organization alive.

But if young activists were willing to question the Brotherhood's long-standing obsession with the state and if they were willing to question the very nature of political change, then perhaps they'd be willing to push the boundaries on what an

Islamic state might look like, whether it was ten, twenty, or a hundred years into the future.

Here, too, I return to my conversation with Karim, who took the critique of the state several steps further. In so doing, he put into words what many Brotherhood youth hint at and gesture toward: a more avowedly and unapologetically "Islamic" end state. Of course, this isn't particularly surprising—Islamists are Islamists for a reason, after all. They have a distinct ideological project that involves at least some "Islamization" of society. This Islamization, however, has been purposely downplayed or left vague by Islamist leaders who worry that too many details might frighten the international community and provoke a backlash among those who oppose Islamism more than they oppose autocracy.

But if their opponents, the reasoning goes, think the worst of them anyway—and have little objection to killing them in large numbers—then does it really make much of a difference if they're more explicit about their Islamism? It wasn't just that, though. If you're insisting on the need for revolution, then don't you have some responsibility to think about and explain what, exactly, the revolution is *for*? Here, Karim's statement of purpose was clear enough: "I want a revolution to change the ideology of the country." He continued, "We're not being honest in our discourse. This was the problem under Morsi. We made our message about providing 'food' and 'drink.' If Sissi were able to do an excellent job of providing food and drink, then what reason would I have to revolt? I'm revolting for a goal higher than this."

Ahmad, the friend of Karim's who had joined us, shook his head slightly. They had known each other in Egypt but had become close in Istanbul. They often disagreed in the playful way that brothers might. Two hours into our conversation, the mood had lightened as we dove into more theoretical issues, of what the Islamic state might look like and how to get there. By now, we were on our third round of sugar-doused Turkish tea. Ahmad, who had frozen his membership in the Brotherhood because of disagreements over strategy, emphasized the need to form coalitions with non-Islamists, workers, liberals, secularists, whatever. The common ground—the one thing that everyone in the opposition could agree on—was freedom. And with freedom, the Islamic state would come, but it would come organically. There was no need to get ahead of themselves. "Freedom is the first step in the long road to establishing an Islamic state," Ahmad explained. "If people are granted their political freedoms and economic freedoms, then they will inevitably choose Islam." In other words, the Egyptian people—and Muslims more generally—were naturally inclined toward Islam. This was their nature, or *fitra*, a concept with a long provenance in Islamic thought. Muslims were born pure. In their state of purity, they desired to be as close to God as possible, to submit to his will and fulfill his commandments. To the extent that Muslims deviated from this path, it was due to the corrupting influences of the temporal world, including the temptations of wealth and power.

The "freedom or Islam" debate, as they called it, was one that the two friends had been having for months. They agreed to disagree. However, when it came to the shape of the mythical Islamic state that would presumably come into being far into the future, they agreed on its basic outlines, though with the proviso that the model would require quite a lot of trial and error, since it had never really been done before.

The overarching principle was a radical shift in the relationship between society and state. "Society" would dominate, while the state—and by extension the public sector—would be weak and decentralized. Education, for example, wouldn't necessarily come from the state but would instead be community-driven. The idea was to unleash the *fitra* of each and every citizen by reducing as much as possible the distorting impact of the state on the individual. Religious scholars would be insulated from state pressures because the clerical establishment would be disassociated from executive authority. "Religion should be about religion, not the state," Ahmad said.

The state, assuming some minimal level of democracy, was inseparable from political party competition. After all, someone needed to assume power and control of the state bureaucracy. But if the state were weak, with civil society, the religious establishment, and local communities holding the balance of power, then the struggle for power would be less intense and polarizing. "In today's politics, the main goal is to be in power. The main goal of the opposition is to oppose, because they too want power," Ahmad told me. "Hopefully, in our vision, the state will be less powerful, so there will be less reason to fight over it."

At this point in the conversation, my skepticism was threatening to get the better of me. I pointed out that the Brotherhood's model was very much oriented around elections and "normal" political competition between parties. The Brotherhood likes elections "too much! That's our difference with the leadership," Ahmad responded. "We can live without elections and we did so for most of our history. Two hundred years in the history of man is nothing."

It all sounded utterly divorced from the fundamental realities of the international system. For one, the Westphalian order was one based on a rather narrow conception of the state. Even where states were weak, it was rarely, if ever, because they *wanted* to be weak. They aspired to be strong, because the logic of statehood was one of control—monopolizing territory and the use of force, to say nothing of the appropriation of economic and natural resources.

It was no surprise, then, that Karim and Ahmad weren't fans of this "secular international system," as they called it. "I want to break the international order," Karim insisted. "No matter how hard it is, this is the goal I want. That's what I'm living for, even if I die in the process of fighting for it." I asked him if he really wanted to be fighting such a struggle for the rest of his life: He didn't want to have a family and live a calmer life, taking a step back from the disappointments of political activism? "Our understanding [of Islam] is that my whole life consists of the conflict between truth and falsehood, on the personal level between me and the devil, and between me and the attractions of the earthly life," Karim explained. "Why am I entering this conflict?" he asked me. "Not because of this life, but because of the next."

As a statement of a purpose, it was hard to argue with. As an American liberal who had no particular political cause to die for, I would always struggle to fully grasp the kind of certainty that Karim and Ahmad so clearly felt. Perhaps theirs was partly the passion of youth. Perhaps, if they were ever able to return to Egypt and if the Brotherhood became a legal party once again, they would practice normal politics within the existing international order like everyone else. Or perhaps something had really changed. Perhaps the Egyptian coup, the collapse of the regional order, and state failures from Libya to Yemen to Iraq would produce a lasting paradigm shift, one whose consequences we could only begin to imagine.

The question, ultimately, was a difficult one to answer. Could a gradualist organization—whose aversion to revolution was baked into its DNA—become something fundamentally different from what it had been for the better part of eighty years? The Brotherhood would never go as far as Karim and Ahmad might want it to go, but at least they and a new generation of Islamists could move the dial, acting as a kind of revolutionary lobby within the movement. One of the lessons of the Arab Spring was that, in times of crisis and collapse, change can happen at breakneck speed. I remember my time in Tahrir Square before Mubarak fell and asking revolutionaries if they had a plan for seeing Mubarak's ouster through. What if he refused to step down? But in a matter of days, the man who had dominated Egyptian politics for thirty years was no longer. Now, four years later, their fortunes had reversed once again, and they were in exile. "Politics is the art of the possible," I told the two young activists. Without skipping a beat, Ahmad replied, "Revolution is the art of the impossible."

5

THE TURKISH
MODEL
ISLAMISTS EMPOWERED

I walked up to the palace gates. This was Turkey's so-called Ak Saray, or White Palace. I had a meeting with Ibrahim Kalin, President Erdogan's chief advisor. The White Palace had become a headache for Erdogan and his Islamist-rooted Justice and Development Party (AKP). Built on more than two million square feet of protected forest land outside Ankara, the $600 million complex looked more like an Ottoman Versailles than the residence of a leader who came of age in Turkey's working-class heartland and who has often marketed himself as a man of the people.[1] The palace was met with outrage when it was unveiled in late 2014. Opposition parties complained that it had been built without proper court permission and shamed Erdogan's decadence in a nation that suffers from a 10 percent unemployment rate.

At the gates of the palace, I showed the guard my American passport. The guard offered a raised eyebrow and a quizzical look. "Pennsylvania?" he asked, his voice dripping with skepticism. It had never occurred to me that being born and raised in Pennsylvania would be a liability in Turkey of all places. But Turkey had changed, as Erdogan put his considerable charisma in the service of reshaping the very state that had once imprisoned him. The political environment had grown tense, and Erdogan increasingly saw his opponents not as mere adversaries but as enemies. One of those enemies was a cleric and erstwhile ally by the name of Fethullah Gulen. Gulen was living in exile in Lancaster, Pennsylvania, about an hour from my hometown of Bryn Mawr. In the progovernment press, Lancaster—better known as the home of the Amish—had become the Center of the Conspiracy.

If there was in fact a conspiracy, a palace as fortress-like as this one was only appropriate. As its name suggested, the White Palace was grand, massive, overbearing even, a monument to Recep Tayyip Erdogan's seemingly endless ambition. The question that grabbed me, and the one I hoped to answer here, was what exactly that ambition was for.

Founded in 2001, the AKP emerged from the ashes of a string of Islamist parties—the National Order (1970–71), National Salvation (1972–81), Welfare (1983–98), and Virtue (1998–2001) parties—each of which was banned and dissolved by the judiciary for "antisecular" activities. To avoid running afoul of the constitution, which enshrined secularism as one of its "irrevocable principles," the various Islamist parties downplayed their Islamism and attempted to moderate their rhetoric and policies. Such a delicate dance could sometimes prove too delicate. Their raison d'être, after all, was an embrace of Turkey's Islamic identity, but even something as mild as that could be interpreted as violating the principles of the Turkish republic.

Modern Turkey was founded by Mustafa Kemal Ataturk after the abolition of the Ottoman caliphate in 1924. Ataturk—an adopted name meaning "father of the Turks"—was the prototypical authoritarian modernizer, harnessing the power of the state to reengineer Turkish society. Others, including Tunisia's

Habib Bourguiba, tried to replicate his model, but no one managed to take it quite as far.

Ataturk saw Islamic cultural norms—and the legacy of Ottoman rule—as dangerous obstacles to his program of rapid modernization. They therefore had to be discarded. What followed was one of the most successful models of cultural and social engineering of the modern era. This included altering basic patterns of social interaction between men and women by encouraging mixed-gender interaction (Ottoman custom had put a premium on separation). Women were prohibited from wearing the face veil, while men could face jail time for wearing the traditional fez hat. Sharia courts were abolished. As part of his reforms, Ataturk ended the use of Arabic script, replacing it with the Latin alphabet, requiring a generation of Turks to learn an entirely new writing system from scratch. Arabic and Persian loan words were replaced by Turkish words. In short, Ottoman Turkish ceased to be.

Turkey's militant secularism survived Ataturk, with the military and judicial establishment settling into the role of protectors of the state, standing guard over its secular foundations. In 1960, Turkey had its first coup, and in 1997 it had its last, with two in between, in 1971 and 1980.

Not surprisingly, the Islamists, led by a German-educated engineer named Necmettin Erbakan, found themselves restricted, excluded, and limited in what they could hope to accomplish. Various center-right governments reopened mosques, legalized the Arabic call to prayer, and lifted some restrictions on religious expression, but in other ways the situation for Islamists only got worse. After the 1980 military coup, the head scarf, though it was always discouraged, was formally banned—in universities, schools, hospitals, and state institutions—for the first time. Several attempts in the 1980s to lift the head-scarf ban proved unsuccessful. In 1989 and 1991, Turkey's Higher Education Council lifted the ban, only to have their decision annulled by the Constitutional Court.[2] In the 1989 annulment, the court ruled that the wearing of the head scarf, which "lacks a modern appearance," was "increasingly becoming widespread and this is unacceptable in terms of the principles of secularism."[3] Even as the courts upheld the ban, it was inconsistently applied throughout the 1980s and early 1990s. It was only after Erbakan was ousted in the 1997 coup that the Turkish military enforced a uniform ban on head scarves in state institutions, including universities.[4]

As rural migrants flocked to the cities in the 1970s, they brought with them village customs and conservative Islamic practices. They were a natural constituency for Islamist mobilization, which started in earnest with the 1970 founding of the National Order Party. Erbakan and his cofounders reimagined Turkish history as a glorious Islamic Ottoman past that had been subverted by foreign influence. For them, the *tanzimat* reforms were the beginning of the downfall that reached a climax with Ataturk's de-Islamization of society. When National Order was banned in 1971, the National Salvation Party (NSP) was founded in its stead the following year. Alarmed by a growing leftist movement, the military demonstrated some tolerance toward Islamism, and over the next eight years, the NSP made modest gains in elections and played an increasingly influential role in parliament, until it was crushed after the 1980 coup.[5] Like its predecessor, NSP found its base among Turkey's rural and industrialized poor. NSP and its successors were informed by what Jenny White calls Erbakan's "vision of a form of modernization that was authentically Turkish and based on Muslim ethics."[6]

The Islamic revival of the 1970s and '80s heightened tensions with the secular establishment, as more women began wearing the head scarf. The economic power of Turkey's Muslim middle class—a counterelite of devout small and medium business owners—skyrocketed. But despite the party bans (or perhaps because of them), Erbakan was able to expand his base of support, increasing his share of the vote with each successive election. Erbakan nurtured the image of the outsider victimized by a state that had, for too long, neglected the silent majority of pious, traditional Turks in the Anatolian heartland. His message was clear enough: The identity and the *fitra* of the Turkish people had been denied. And Islam, both as a cultural orientation and a religious tradition, was at the center of this uniquely Turkish identity. In this reading, one could not be truly Turkish without acknowledging the debt to the Ottoman caliphate, which, as one of the world's great empires, remained a great source of pride as well as nostalgia.

The "Islamic project" in Turkey can only be understood in the context of an acute sense of loss. What it once meant to be Turkish would never be regained. Too much had happened in the interim. Turks could no longer read Arabic, the language of the Quran. Secularism, even if it was resisted and failed to take hold in rural areas, was now part of the social fabric. Norms and customs could and would evolve, as we will soon see, but a legacy of secularism was embedded, with generations having grown up with a very particular sense of what it meant to be a Turkish citizen. The visage of Ataturk was on every banknote, his statue in every city, and his portrait in every classroom. Short of a full-scale revolution, these realities could not be undone, at least not entirely.

TURKISH ISLAMISTS, LIKE THEIR counterparts in the rest of the region, were gradualists. Even in the darker days of repression, after any number of coups or party bans, revolution never figured into their discourse. While the military suspended democratic politics for periods of time, the multiparty system was never abolished altogether. And so the Islamic movement would wait, reorganize, establish a new party if the previous one had been banned, and try their hand in the next election. Before the 1983 general elections, Erbakan founded the Welfare Party, winning a mere 5 percent of the vote. After steadily increasing its vote totals in 1987 and 1991, Welfare claimed a plurality of the vote in 1996. For the first time in Turkish history, an Islamist party had won a national election. Erbakan, after thirty years of political attrition, would become Turkey's first Islamist prime minister as part of a coalition government. But what should have been a time of celebration became instead yet another instance of the secular establishment's inability to come to terms with Islamist participation. Erbakan was forced out of office in the "soft coup" of 1997, and, not too long after that, Welfare was banned. In its decision dissolving the party, Turkey's Constitutional Court cited Erbakan's own statements, including one where he said democracy was "not an end but a means."[7]

There are only so many times a party—effectively the same party—can be banned before members begin to consider other approaches. And this is where Erbakan's loyal student, Recep Tayyip Erdogan, comes into the picture. The mayor of Istanbul from 1994 to 1998, Erdogan was barred from political life for five years and spent four months in prison for reciting a religiously charged poem during a fiery speech in his wife's hometown of Siirt, a conservative, blue-collar city in southeastern Turkey.[8] The lines in question were: "The mosques are our barracks / the domes our helmets / the minarets our bayonets / and the believers our soldiers."[9] This was Erdogan at his best: rallying his base and playing the outsider. It was a brilliant move, nurturing Erdogan's sense—and that of his supporters—of victimhood. The Kemalist establishment, the so-called "deep state," had overreached, arresting a popular mayor who could now claim, with more cause than ever, that he was the underdog representing the pious masses in their struggle against an entrenched elite and a tyrannical state.

A Problem of State

A rapidly modernizing state cannot help being exclusionary. Ataturk wouldn't have been able to increase literacy from around 8 percent to 20 percent in the span of just a few years by being tolerant and pluralistic.[10] His reforms, as wide-ranging and pervasive as they were, required the centralization of power and decision making. They required a singularity of vision, and they required force. Most ordinary Turks did not share Ataturk's vision, at least not at first. To the extent that Ataturk hoped to alter the very basis of what it meant to be "Turkish," he would need to be unforgiving and relentless. In this sense, the demands of state building, which required the accumulation of authority, and the demands of democratization, which required the balancing and distribution of power, were in conflict.

A Turkish nation and a Turkish national identity did not exist under the Ottoman caliphate. Instead of the "individual" or the "citizen"—a modern invention—Ottoman subjects were governed by the rules, regulations, and norms of whatever religious group, or *millet*, they happened to be a part of. Each *millet* had its own leaders and court systems. The head of each *millet*, say, a rabbi or an Orthodox patriarch, enjoyed considerable powers, including collecting taxes, arbitrating disputes between individuals, and enforcing the community's religious laws.[11] Ottoman subjects of minority faiths were answerable not to the caliph but to their own local religious leaders who, in turn, were answerable to the caliph. The exchange was autonomy in return for loyalty.

With the decline of the Ottoman Empire, the *millet* system weakened, soon collapsing altogether. In its place, Ataturk's task was to shift the entire basis of political community. Making "Turks" out of Ottoman subjects required the pretense of homogeneity, that there were common characteristics binding all citizens, irrespective of religious or ethnic background. And so very real differences—Turkey, for example, has large Kurdish and Alevi populations—had to be papered over, ignored, or suppressed. To be a Kurd before a Turk was to challenge the entire edifice on which the new Turkey was being built. Islamism, similarly, offered an alternative conception of identity. If the state was synonymous with secularism, then Islamists were, by definition, a threat. Through their very existence, they served as a constant reminder of the gap between a resolutely secular state and a society where Islam remained a natural, organic part of everyday life. These Islamic identities, because they challenged the state, were invariably politicized by both sides of the divide, one hoping to control and suppress and the other adopting Islam as its language of opposition.

As in so many Middle Eastern countries, the "secularism" of Ataturk and other autocrats had little respect for the separation of mosque and state. If religious leaders and communities were separate and autonomous, then they would have the ability to challenge state authority. To privatize religion and diminish its relevance in public life, it would have to be made subservient to the state. Where appropriate, the state would use religion not for religion's sake but for its own. And so what followed was one of the most systematic projects of state regulation of religious practice anywhere in the Muslim world, one that would become a model for other Middle Eastern states.

Turkey's Directorate of Religious Affairs, or Diyanet, is a massive bureaucratic entity whose budget exceeds most other cabinet ministries, including both the Foreign and Interior Ministries. Diyanet staff has doubled since the AKP came to power in 2002, and its annual budget has increased fourfold.[12] The Diyanet trains imams, administers mosques and religious schools, and oversees Friday sermons. Until 2006, the Diyanet generated sermons from its headquarters in Ankara, where committees would meet monthly to determine content and draft sermons that were subsequently published on the directorate's Web site and in its monthly magazine. In June 2006, sermon production was transferred to the provincial mufti offices, over which the Diyanet maintains oversight.[13] The stated mission of the Diyanet—"to enlighten society on religion"—is inherently interventionist.[14] This is a degree of state involvement in religion that would be unthinkable to most Americans. Imagine a senior U.S. official saying it was the federal government's job to "enlighten society on religion," or try to imagine a Department of Religious Affairs approving Sunday sermons in every single licensed church in the country. This, then, is secularism not in the sense of separation of religion from politics but in the sense of affirming the supremacy of the state and ensuring that religion does not obstruct the state's prerogatives.

Learning to Love the State

Needless to say, the Turkish state's insistence on French-style secularism, or *laïcité*, rather than the neutrality of the American model of state-church relations, was a constant source of anger and alienation for Islamists. But, then again, so many things about the Turkish state—and its militantly secular bureaucratic arms—angered and alienated. The grievances accumulated, coming to a head in the 1997 coup. But instead of confronting the state head-on, Turkish Islamists opted instead for the long game, whittling away at secular dominance little by little.

Repression is often assumed to have a radicalizing effect on Islamist movements. This is in some ways intuitive—bad behavior produces more of the same. Under certain conditions, however, political exclusion can actually have a moderating effect on Islamist actors. As I have argued elsewhere, a resurgent authoritarianism in Egypt and Jordan pushed the Muslim Brotherhood to deemphasize their Islamism, moderate their rhetoric, and move to the center in a bid to stave off political isolation.[15] Strengthening alliances with non-Islamist actors offers a layer of protection against regime repression. After all, it's more difficult to repress Islamists the more diverse and expansive their support. In Turkey, a similar dynamic was at play, with each party ban forcing Islamists to regroup and rethink. With each new round of repression, the goal was simple enough: avoid getting closed down the next time around.

The 1997 removal of Erbakan was the first of the country's

coups that specifically targeted an Islamist party in power, so it's no surprise that it had a profound impact on a new generation of Islamists. The so-called "February 28 process"—named after the date of the military's intervention—went well beyond a change in government, aiming to deal a decisive blow against the broader Islamic movement in every facet of public life, particularly in the educational sphere. The military issued an eighteen-point plan that shut down religious *imam hatip* schools and extended compulsory primary education—which pushes the state's secular doctrine—from five to eight years. State institutions were purged of overtly devout officials. Thousands of Islamists faced water cannons and police batons as they protested the closure of *imam hatip* schools, which were perceived to be breeding grounds for future Islamist enemies of the secular state.[16] The extent of the assault on Islamic networks was unprecedented. They would learn their lesson. As careful as they already had been, they would need to be even *more* cautious, steering well clear of any perceived red lines, lest the regime's sword of Damocles fall once again.

After the Welfare Party's successor, the Virtue Party, was also banned, Erdogan, Abdullah Gul, and their group of upstarts parted ways with Erbakan and founded a new party that defined itself not as Islamic but as "conservative democratic." After a landslide victory in the 2002 elections, Turkey's economic transformation began in earnest. AKP leaders pledged their fealty to Ataturk's memory (which must have been difficult for them) and presented themselves as faithful proponents of the republic's secular principles. They highlighted their relative youth, juxtaposed against Erbakan's unusually long political career spanning four decades. A 2003 *New York Times Magazine* profile of Erdogan noted the AKP's younger party members referred to Erbakan's men as "the Politburo."[17] Talk of Islam was pushed to the side, but perhaps most important, AKP leaders offered a decisive break from Erbakan's anti-Western, Euroskeptic rhetoric and embraced EU membership as a core objective. Meanwhile, as much as they disliked Israel, they knew they had to accept the realities of the regional system, particularly as they worked to deepen ties with European partners.

They had an unimpeachable democratic mandate, which was renewed and broadened with successive elections. But this didn't bring the security they craved, as it might have in a normal democracy. Turkey wasn't a normal democracy. Every day, AKP officials woke up wondering if the army or the courts would move against them. To preempt such an outcome, they demonstrated an impressive singularity of vision. The Virtue Party had been banned in part because of its spirited defense of the right to wear the head scarf. For the AKP, resolving the long-standing head-scarf issue—a key demand of its conservative base—would have to wait. They were playing the long game, and, this time, they would play it to perfection. This meant keeping a razor-sharp focus on a taxing EU accession process, which required jumping over a seemingly endless number of hurdles.

Oddly enough, the EU was a godsend for a party that, in its previous incarnations, steeped itself in anti-Western posturing. The EU accession process was a classic—and particularly successful example—of "positive conditionality."[18] The prospect of joining the EU provided structured incentives for the AKP to pursue far-reaching liberal reforms, including revising the penal code, easing restrictions on freedom of expression, expanding rights for the Kurdish minority, and reining in the military. The last of these changes would prove the most important. In the name of democratization, the military would have to respect the elected civilian authorities. EU membership, then, became AKP's most important cudgel against the Kemalist "deep state."

During this period of self-restraint, the question was often posed: What did Turkey's Islamists *really* want? Were they engaging in "double discourse," hiding their intentions, and waiting for the right moment to strike? And, if so, how planned and premeditated was their strategy of defanging the military and then—and only then—refocusing on issues of identity and religion?

With the military establishment sufficiently weakened by the late 2000s and the Constitutional Court effectively neutralized by 2010, the AKP began to veer to the right on religious issues, adopting a policy of what I term "soft Islamization." When we think of Islamists and Islamization, a harsh, unforgiving picture of legislating morality usually comes to mind. At the more extreme end of things, we think about *hudud* punishments like stoning adulterers and cutting off the hands of thieves. But Islamization can be—and often is—much more subtle than that. Turkish Islamists may have been Islamists, but they were also Turks, the products of a massively successful nation-building project. And, like everyone else, they were products of a secularized society, whether or not they wished to be. Naturally, as a mass movement that prided itself on reflecting the popular will, the AKP practiced a distinctly Turkish brand of Islamism. As observant Muslims, they of course held the Prophet in the highest regard, but their golden age was to be found not in the seventh century but in the sixteenth, during the glory days of the Ottoman Empire.

IN A TURKISH CONTEXT, it wouldn't have made much sense to speak about the "implementation of sharia," which in a more conservative country like Egypt was a fairly standard and somewhat innocuous thing to say. Instead, the goal was first to "correct" the excesses of forced secularization by opening up political and economic space for religious Turks. Then, rather than imposing rules through legislative fiat, the leaders of the AKP hoped to incentivize religious behavior by, for example, increasing taxes on alcohol and providing financial stipends to young couples who married early (an effort to increase birth rates, but also presumably to discourage premarital sex). Some of it was more rhetoric than anything else, such as when Erdogan remarked that "there is no difference in killing the fetus in a mother's womb or killing a person after birth."[19] Yet, however much abortion bothered him, Erdogan didn't attempt to initiate new legislation restricting it. This was Erdogan acting in his "spiritual leader" mode, sharing his own views about the virtuous life without actually doing anything about it. As one senior AKP official put it to me, "Erdogan at times behaves like a father. Not everything that he says is a law. It is a suggestion. It is also to protect young people from bad things."[20]

While Erdogan's efforts shouldn't be overstated, the basic trajectory was clear enough. Erdogan and the AKP hoped to harness the enormous power of the Turkish state to promote a particular conception of the good. Erdogan would speak often about raising "a pious generation" of Turks.[21] The state would be the engine of change by expanding the role of religious secondary schools, Islamizing the Diyanet's preaching and outreach, and offering more elective religious courses in public schools. At the personnel level, showing outward signs of piety in the state bureaucracy was once frowned upon. The opposite was now true. As long as the AKP stayed in power, demonstrating religiosity could help with career advancement.

In one sense, using the state to establish a new "normal" was radical. It meant undoing the militant secularism that had been at the foundation of the Turkish republic since Ataturk rose to power after the First World War. But in another sense, it wasn't particularly original or creative and accepted without question some of the same problematic assumptions of Kemalism. Here, yet again, was a preoccupation with the Turkish state as the embodiment of the national will. In the early days of AKP rule, Erdogan would emphasize the need for "state neutrality toward all religions and doctrines."[22] This led Turkish Islamists to identify with American secularism as opposed to a more aggressive French-style secularism. But one objection to their otherwise preferred American "model" had to do with the role of the state. As the Turkish political scientist Ahmet Kuru notes: "The main reason [AKP parliamentarians] did not have a desire to take the American model entirely is their statist view on state-religion relations, particularly concerning the status of the [Diyanet]. These politicians have claimed that the state's coordination of religious services through the Diyanet has been necessary to maintain Islamic services efficiently and to avoid anarchy in Islamic communities."[23]

For decades, the institutions of the Turkish state tended to see Turks as children in need of a strong guiding hand. Such avid paternalism was sometimes expressed through amusing metaphors. Cevik Bir, one of the generals behind the 1997 coup, had a line he would repeat to skeptical foreign audiences: "In Turkey we have a marriage of Islam and democracy. The child of this marriage is secularism. Now, this child gets sick from time to time. The Turkish Armed Forces is the doctor which saves the child. Depending on how sick the kid is, we administer the necessary medicine to make sure the child recuperates."[24] (Notably, under Erdogan, many of the top military officers involved in prior coups were jailed, including Bir.)[25] The state was detached and inaccessible. At the same time, it was to be loved and adored. Turkish authorities promoted the idea of *devlet baba*, or "father state," which, in a simple enough phrase, captured the mix of paternalism and patriarchy at the heart of state-society relations. Until 2013, children would start their day at school with a pledge of allegiance: "I love my country more than myself. . . . I offer my existence to the Turkish nation as a gift."[26] The state, rather than religion, was something to die for, reflecting a sort of secular "martyrdom" with Turkey assuming the pose of the omniscient deity.

Every AKP leader has their own story of being excluded by their own state. When they refused to suppress who they were, there was a price to pay. For the AKP figures who were both Islamist and Kurdish, the sense of exclusion was multiplied.

One such official, Mazhar Bagli, had briefly lived in Canada as a graduate student to conduct research on multiculturalism. He clearly hadn't used his English much since then and would occasionally pause to ponder the appropriate choice of words during our interview. "There was a lot of pressure in Turkey coming from the military, on how to behave in society and within the family," he reflected. "You had to speak a certain way, behave a certain way. The main aim of the Turkish state is to design our life, at all times. The oppression was felt not only by Muslims, but by Kurds as well."[27] Bagli described being stopped by the police during his university days simply for listening to Kurdish music.

However, just because AKP leaders had been traumatized by the state didn't necessarily mean that they wanted to cut the state down to size. Without skipping a beat, Bagli would move from castigating the state to seeing state power as the solution to the problem. "Policies came from the deep state. Now the state, government, and society are hand in hand, walking in the same direction," he told me. The problem, then, wasn't state power per se but what it was used for. If it could be used for bad, it could just as easily be used for good. As long as state power was legitimated by the democratic process and was used to promote, rather than hinder, Islam, then there was little to complain about. "Before Mr. Erdogan was president, [presidents] were elected by parliament. Mr. Erdogan was elected by the people and also his power is coming from God. He is a more powerful person now," Bagli explained.

This was the only system that the leaders of the AKP really knew, and its features were drilled into them from the very beginning, in school and at the workplace. Every public building, and often every room, had a portrait or bust of Ataturk, as did many homes. The gaze of the Turkish state, embodied in his visage, was inescapable. For Erdogan, as much as he may have hated it, it was the system he had willingly joined and then embraced, first as mayor of Turkey's largest city, then as prime minister, and finally as president. Erdogan had never lived any-where but here. He spoke no other languages. He wasn't known to be much of a thinker, and, if anything, he had a mean anti-intellectual streak. This wasn't someone who was about to ques-tion the basic structures of the modern state, and why should he? He had a distinctive vision for Turkish society, one based on resuscitating Turkey's Ottoman past and returning to the Turk-ish *fitra* of Islam. Just as the Kemalist state, in its quest to reengi-neer society, had created an image of the ideal Turkish man, the state under Erdogan's leadership wished to create its own (very different) ideal of the pious Turkish citizen. What the state had built could only be unbuilt by that same state. There was simply no other way—at least not an obvious one—to do what they wanted to do. The ends dictated the means.

The state would remain in its role of guardian and protec-tor. On this, there was little doubt. Erdogan himself was quite explicit. In late 2013, controversy erupted after Erdogan said he would instruct governors to segregate mixed-gender dormi-tories. His reasoning was straightforward. "Mothers and fathers cry out, asking 'where is the state?'" he explained. "These steps are taken to tell them that the state is here."[28]

Islamism versus Authoritarianism

Some accused Turkey's Islamists of being mirror images of their secularist abusers. This was true but only up to a point. The old days of government opponents being executed, assassi-nated, or "disappeared" by the security apparatus were no more. As one Turkish journalist wryly told me, at least there were now free elections "and they don't kill people. Let's give them that." Turkey scholar Howard Eissenstat, otherwise quite critical of the AKP's post-2010 turn, warns against the easy resort to nos-talgia. "During the late 1990s," he writes, "disappearances were commonplace and police stations were the sites of grotesque torture with bastinado and electrocution, which could last for days or weeks. Romanticism about 'the good old days' when the military acted as a guiding hand behind Turkish politics is ill-placed."[29] Yardstick measures of authoritarianism corroborate Eissenstat's sentiment: Turkey dipped from a combined score of 3 in 2011's Freedom House rankings to a 3.5 in 2015, a classification of "partly free" (1 is most free; 7 is least free). But that's still a significant improvement from the mid-1990s, when Turkey scored a 5.[30]

When it came to Erdogan's authoritarian tendencies, the more interesting question was why he had them. Was Erdogan really just interested in power and simply using religion to rally his base and consolidate authority? Or was it the other way around? Determining a person's motives, of course, is a challenge. Political actors try to rationalize what they do after the fact, and they're likely to superimpose "moral" reasons for doing immoral things. One is reminded of the verse from the Book of Titus: "To the pure, all things are pure" (1:15). At first, a politician may do something cynically and even admit his cynicism (if not to others then at least to himself), but for the self-proclaimed moralist, this is unsustainable. He must come to believe that what he is doing is right.

For many analysts, the temptation is to deemphasize religion and explain the behavior of Turkish Islamists through "normal" politics: It might have had an Islamic flavor, but, underneath the surface affectations, this was authoritarianism plain and simple. Erdogan is like Chavez is like Putin. As Claire Sadar writes, "A review of the party's political legacy and current initiatives reveals a government that is more interested in expanding its power than spreading Islamist ideology."[31] Meanwhile, one of the leading scholars of modern Turkey, Jenny White, sees Erdogan as the latest in a long line of Turkish "bigmen." A bigman's position of leadership, she writes, is "acquired and augmented as he achieves status by being particularly good at provisioning and protecting his increasing numbers of followers. . . . Getting elected in Turkey involves the nationwide distribution of favors and amassing of obligations."[32] In a polarized society, being the bigman isn't necessarily conducive to promoting a pluralism of parties or ideas. It requires the steady accumulation of power and the will to subvert potential competitors.

Erdogan was, indeed, a product of a distinctively Turkish authoritarian—and statist—political culture and tradition. How could it be otherwise? Mainstream Islamists are mainstream because they don't—and can't, it seems—diverge radically from their social context. As much as they hope to change what's around them, they find themselves changed in the process. So Erdogan might be a "bigman," but that still leaves the question of why unanswered. White is closer to the mark when she notes that "Turkish society is characterized by exceptionally low levels of interpersonal trust and a pervasive, often antagonistic, 'us versus them' ethos between groups."[33] The us-versus-them dynamic, however, cannot be reduced to a war over patronage or distribution. It is also about something deeper, and therefore the battle takes on an existential edge. One would have thought that over fifty years of democratic experience would have reduced polarization and grown the political "center." Yet this hasn't happened: Foundational divides over the role of religion and the purpose of the state remain unresolved. In any country's politics, state power is a prize to be sought. But in cases like Turkey's, power is more fervently contested than it might otherwise be because more is at stake. Since the state is so powerful, it can be used to reshape the individual and reengineer society.

The Purpose of Power

To think that power is sought simply for its own sake, for megalomania or ego, oversimplifies the complex emotional tenor of modern-day Islamist politics. One way, of course, to get a better sense of why the AKP has chosen a particular course is to talk to party officials and advisors, bearing in mind that there may be an incentive to either overemphasize or deemphasize the role of religion as a motivating factor. With this in mind, let me return to where I began this chapter, at the gloriously extravagant White Palace. I was meeting with Ibrahim Kalin, chief advisor to Erdogan and sometimes described as the president's right-hand man. Kalin has been called a major player in Erdogan's "shadow" government, playing a critical role behind the scenes.[34] After defending Turkey's opposition to the Egyptian coup in a tweet, he became associated with Turkey's ongoing shift from a "zero problems with neighbors" approach to what he called a "precious loneliness"—or Turkey's choice to preserve its "meritorious position" from the poor choices of some of its troublesome Middle Eastern neighbors.[35] Kalin cut a most unlikely figure beside the brash, populist Erdogan. Previously a professor of Islamic philosophy at Georgetown University, he was bookish, soft-spoken, and self-deprecating. In our conversation that day, he seemed to be in dialogue not just with me but with himself as well, measuring his words, occasionally losing himself in thought, and expounding on the intricacies of premodern Islamic philosophy and history.

He seemed flustered by the constant criticisms, including, I suppose, from people like me. Alcohol consumption, one of the traditional Islamist-secular flashpoints, had become a kind of Rorschach test. Changing alcohol-related regulations played on the fears of secularists, who worried that seemingly minor changes—such as prohibiting late-night sales after 10 P.M. and banning sales in the vicinity of mosques or schools—symbolized a longer-term transformational project. Kalin was baffled by all the negative media attention. He said Turkey had taken an "average" and "measured" approach, combining permissive country models with more restrictive ones, like that of the United States. He went on:

> There was a very surprising reaction that this is another attempt to Islamize the country and this is

"banning alcohol" and "you are discouraging alcohol!" And I'm like, have you ever seen a government in the world that encourages people to use alcohol? Of course we encourage people not to use alcohol.

Kalin pointed to what he called a double standard: "When Britain introduces a law like that, it is considered protecting the public interest. When we introduce it, it is Islamization."[36]

This, however, is where intent may prove more important than actual policy outcomes. When Britain's Labor Party restricts the sale of alcohol, they're doing so for presumably secular reasons having to do with the public welfare. When an Islamist party does it, it's more complicated, with officials using both secular and religious justifications. And because Islamists don't necessarily see the sacred and the secular as separate categories, the two become blurred together. Erdogan went on television to defend the new regulations, saying, "I love my nation, and I want to protect them from bad habits."[37] Elsewhere, he said that "when two drunkards make a law, you respect it. But when we make a law for something that faith orders, you reject it. Why?"[38]

Clearly, Kemalists didn't have a problem with state power or paternalism as such. These, after all, were defining features of the Kemalist era. If a Kemalist prime minister had prohibited alcohol sales after 10 P.M., there would have been little outrage. It wasn't, then, the what but the why. Even if neither side was particularly original in their thinking about the state, the real dividing line was about ideas and ideology more than it was about the fact of state power, a fact on which they both readily agreed.

What worried the secular opposition most was the ambiguity around the AKP's ultimate goals. As we saw earlier, Turkish Islamists had downplayed, even conceded, their Islamism, focusing instead on expanding freedoms and moving closer to Europe. This was "post-Islamism," which became a popular term in academia, in part because of what many saw as a brave new future of Islam, secularism, and modernity merging together. But it didn't last, which left the small but influential group of Turkish liberals who initially backed the AKP "model" wondering what went wrong. One Turkish liberal who served as an advisor to AKP figures recalls the discontent of the party's conservative base in the early 2000s.[39] After a landslide victory in which the AKP won 66 percent of the seats (despite winning only 34.3 percent of the popular vote), supporters were expecting quick changes on perennial grievances such as the head-scarf ban. For those who wore the head scarf, few things were as immediate and urgent as this, affecting where you could work or study. Yet those changes were still to come. The advisor recalled an AKP leader saying in 2003 that "only after we increase the space for civilian rule can we serve the needs of the Muslim base." Politics was the art of the possible, and in 2003 many of the things the AKP hoped to do simply weren't possible.

I found this question endlessly intriguing: How conscious was the AKP's "politics of stages"? Can we really imagine party figures sitting around a table in a dark, windowless room plotting their slow but steady takeover of the state? I spoke to one of the founders of the AKP, Yasar Yakis, in the hope of finding some clarity. Yakis hadn't formally parted ways with his old colleagues, but he had grown distant from the party. "I don't recognize the ideals of the party," he told me. Yakis looked fondly upon those early days, before it all changed. Yakis was in his early sixties at the time, but it sounded a bit like college dropouts starting a tech company: "We were drafting the election manifesto and it came to the section on foreign policy and my colleagues told me they don't understand anything about foreign policy and that I can go home and write whatever I want and read it to them the day after." He smiled and I laughed. "So that's what I did. I spent hours until three thirty in the morning that night to write the section."[40] Yakis became the AKP's first foreign minister in 2002.

"We were cautious in the beginning not to threaten the judiciary, the military, and the bureaucracy," Yakis explained. "The 'tactical program' [to wait until the right moment to promote a more religious agenda] may have existed in Erdogan's mind, but not in the minds of many others." Similarly, a senior advisor to Ahmet Davutoglu brushed away the suggestion. "Even if this was the AKP's plan, it does not matter," he told me. "They needed political power first to make these changes. The AKP came out of the 1997 coup, and the party itself and the society were not ready for this kind of change in the beginning."[41] On the other hand, referring to the party's shift toward a more Islamic agenda, one AKP parliamentary candidate told me, "This was Erdogan's plan from the beginning. He just had to wait to find the right time and the right people."[42]

When we look back at recent history, it can be tempting to superimpose a certain logic and meaning to disparate events. We want to thread a narrative. At the center of the narrative is a man like Erdogan, a towering figure, whose vision—in retrospect—seems unbending and undeniable, as if it were always there. It wasn't. None of this was inevitable. Erdogan and his colleagues had no idea how successful they would be. At the time, they were driven, if anything, by fear—fear that there would be yet another coup and that their party would be dissolved once again (an outcome that was averted by only one vote in the 2008 closure case). They had to concede their Islamism, and this is what they did. The alternative was to confront the secular establishment head-on, but that had already been tried, and it had failed.

Turkish Islamists happened to live in a world where influential domestic and international actors were suspicious of and even hostile toward them. If they wanted to survive, they had to learn how to suppress at least some of what they believed in. If they crossed a red line—and it was never entirely clear where the red lines were—then that could be enough for Turkish courts to deem them a font of antisecular agitation. There will always be a gap between what people believe and what they actually do. It's become so commonplace that we barely bat an eye when politicians transparently pander to a group of voters. But it's one thing to pander in the search of votes—because ultimately those voters will hold you accountable for your performance—and another to wonder whether something you say might put you in prison or bring about the dissolution of your party.

Erdogan's shift to the right was less a premeditated plan by a brilliant, conniving politician and more a case of shifting incentives. The threat of military intervention (the stick) and the promise of EU accession (the carrot) were effectively removed. If those incentives had a moderating effect, then presumably their removal would allow the AKP to proceed along a more "natural" path. In other words, it was now possible for them to be who they were. In the words of Yasar Yakis, "as circumstances and opportunities allowed, AKP pursued its interests." When those circumstances and opportunities changed, so too did the AKP. Anyone in their position would have done the same.

Of course, this wasn't just anyone. It was Erdogan. And some individuals are better at seizing opportunities than others. Here the role of individuals becomes important and even more so when polarization is endemic. It's an interesting counterfactual: What if AKP cofounder and former president Abdullah Gul—a professor of economics with little stomach for confrontation—had become the unquestioned leader of the AKP? An aide to Gul told me that, after spending years at the man's side, he believed Gul was just as "Islamist" as Erdogan, if not more so.[43] As if talking about a dear uncle, he fondly remembered Gul's discomfort after watching a movie. "Such a passionate kiss isn't appropriate," he recalls the president saying (although I imagine it sounded less awkward in Turkish). He joked that he couldn't tell Gul about the woman he was dating, fretting over what the president would think of him. "Gul and Erdogan believe in similar things, but the difference is in how to express it," the aide told me. "Gul, for example, hates populist discourse. He's also a pragmatist. He'll look at something and say, 'There's no possibility of me doing it, so why should I take the risk?' And he wants people to be more religious, so he worries that divisive rhetoric undermines the cause." Tensions first emerged between Erdogan and Gul in 2007, after nearly a decade of partnership, when Gul ran for president after Erdogan elected not to. Eight years later, Erdogan was clearly dominant, while Gul had receded to the background.

Erdogan was many things, but a mild-mannered economics professor wasn't one of them. Even his bitter enemies describe him as one of those politicians who come around once in a lifetime. Like Ataturk, he has become, for better or worse, synonymous with modern Turkey. They speak in awe of his charisma, his way around a room, as well as his personal warmth—assuming he liked you. "If you give him fifteen minutes, he can convince anyone who's neutral to come to his side," said one such critic.[44]

As much as they matter, powerful individuals are rarely the sole or even primary cause of party transformations. They can, however, strengthen and reinforce certain trajectories. Where Gul erred on the side of caution, Erdogan was more than willing to succumb to ambition. Erdogan was fond of speaking of a society in the throes of transformation. This was the "new Turkey," as he called it, in sharp contrast to the old. Reflecting on his accomplishments in a 2015 speech, Erdogan insisted that this was just the beginning: "Change is inevitable. The building of a new Turkey is inevitable. A new constitution is inevitable. A presidential system is, God willing, inevitable."[45] Increasingly, Erdogan portrayed himself as a statesman on par with Ataturk. In March 2014, he released a video suggesting he was leading Turkey's "second war of independence," shortly after an AKP press release referred to him as the "builder of Turkey."[46]

Under Gul, the AKP would have likely drifted in the same general direction, but not to the same extent and not in the same polarizing manner. As much as Erdogan believed in a more explicitly "Islamic" agenda, he also knew that it was a good way to win votes, something that Gul would have realized as well. In democratic contexts, ideological parties often have an incentive to move to the center and reach out to the broadest cross section of the electorate. A socialist party can't rely solely on the working class because there aren't enough workers. Christian Democrats in Europe can't simply appeal to Catholic conservatives because Catholic conservatives are only a small minority, and a dwindling one at that. But this supposedly moderating effect of democracy depends on the distribution of voters. In a conservative center-right country like Turkey, the calculus shifts. The AKP's natural base of religiously inclined voters is large, so there was little to be lost and much to be gained in rallying the base. And no one did this better than Erdogan. (This strategy seemed, if only briefly, to reach its limits in the June 2015 parliamentary elections, when the AKP lost a significant share of its seats. Yet, even at its worst, the AKP still won 47 percent of the seats—about 6 percent more seats than Egypt's Muslim Brotherhood or Tunisia's Ennahda did at their best.)

During my interviews with Turkish activists and politicians, the specter of Erdogan loomed large, sometimes in amusing ways. I had met with Mazhar Bagli, the AKP official, at the party headquarters in Ankara. To get to his office, I had to pass through a wide doorway with two big blown-up pictures of Erdogan on either side. It was almost as if they wanted to make sure we never forgot: Erdogan was watching. When I met with Davutoglu's advisor, he left the television on in the background. He couldn't see it, but I could. And there was Erdogan gesturing, speaking off the cuff, giving what seemed like a fiery speech. Try as I might, I couldn't escape this towering figure of Turkish politics.

Being the populist he was, Erdogan took pride in his connection to the "people." He was just like them, growing up in a working-class family and hailing from the rougher parts of Istanbul. "Street fighter" is one of the descriptors people use, some in admiration, others in disdain. Even as the most powerful man in Turkey since Ataturk, Erdogan kept playing the role of outsider fighting a host of enemies, both real and imagined. A ruling party that sounds like an opposition party even when it's in power is an odd—and potentially dangerous—thing.

A Desire for Revenge

For many Turkish Islamists, it's personal. They were subjugated, persecuted, and made to feel like pariahs in their own country. The state told them that to be a Turk was to be something other than what they were. Finally, after waiting decades, they had an opportunity to redress the wrongs of the past. In so doing, they claimed an unprecedented mandate, having expanded their share of the vote in successive elections, reaching a peak of 49.8 percent of the popular vote in the 2011 elections. They called it "normalization"—a term suggesting that an Islamically oriented state and society was the natural state of Turkey and that the secularization that had come before was a forced aberration. This was *justice*. But what some call justice, others called revenge.

I had spent years getting to know Islamist activists and leaders in Egypt, Jordan, Tunisia, and elsewhere in the region. While the various groups differed considerably according to their local contexts, the one thing they all shared was a desire to at least *sound* conciliatory, even if they weren't particularly serious about it. They would emphasize their desire to coexist and cooperate with secularists. One can debate the sincerity of the rhetoric, but the pretense was there. What was striking about many of my conversations with AKP officials and supporters was that the pretense seemed to be lacking. Gone was the talk of compromise and national unity that had peppered

AKP statements in the early 2000s. They couldn't have been more dismissive of the secular opposition and, at times, the message was some variation of "bring it on."

Troubling as it was, there was something refreshing about their honesty. I remember when Mazhar Bagli brought out a piece of paper and scribbled a picture for me to illustrate the point. There was a small circle and a big circle. This represented the past. The small circle—the 20 percent of secularists—controlled the country at the expense of the big circle, everyone else. He then drew another pair of circles, again one big and one small, to emphasize the shift. In the new Turkey, the big circle, inside of which he wrote 80 percent, had finally gotten its due, and secularists now had to accept the reality. Not only was this "justice"—the redress of past wrongs—it was "democracy." Eighty percent may be an exaggeration, but Turkey was no doubt a nation of many observant Muslims. Sixty-seven percent of Turks claim religion is a "very important" part of their lives.[47] In a 2006 survey, nearly 45 percent of Turks considered themselves "Muslim" above other identity markers, whether nationalist or ethnic.[48] Meanwhile, in a 2012 Pew poll, only 8 percent of Turkish men say they never attend mosque, while 42 percent of all Turks say they pray several times per day, if not the full five times per day.[49]

Though Erdogan's illiberal and authoritarian tendencies have sparked significant opposition, including the 2013 Gezi Park protests, his supporters insist he is merely acting within his democratic mandate. The senior advisor to Davutoglu took it a few steps further than Bagli. "Secular idiot elites were just five percent of the population," he told me. The secular Republican People's Party (CHP)—the party of Ataturk—was a "mistake in our history." The CHP, he suggested, should change its name, since it was synonymous with blood and subjugation. "You shut down all the mosques. True? True. You burned the Quran. True? True," he said. "Everyone has a story from his ancestors" about Republican repression, and so the CHP has to "get rid of its past and say it: 'This was wrong.'" For Islamists, the greatest symbol of the trauma of secular rule was the head-scarf ban. It meant that women couldn't work in state institutions, whether as teachers, parliamentarians, diplomats, or civil servants. If you were a student, the university could compel you to take it off. Erdogan's two daughters, Sumeyye and Esra, went to school in the United States. In other words, their father was the head of government—the most powerful man in the country—yet they couldn't go to university in their own country (the ban in universities was lifted in 2010).

For the Davutoglu advisor, it was similarly personal. His wife, a doctor, couldn't work in a state hospital for seven years and was only finally able to gain employment in 2014. His bitterness was palpable. He admitted that the AKP's rhetoric was sometimes harsh and that there were excesses. "Normalization pains," as he called them, were inevitable. But I wanted to understand: What would all these growing pains amount to? What would mark the end of this process of Turkey returning to itself? "Secularists live with Ataturk's corpse," he told me, his voice rising. "If we want this normalization process to reach its maturity, we need to carry Mr. Ataturk to his grave again and close that chapter and start a new Turkey." This was a striking thing to say about the founder of modern Turkey, someone to whom successive Islamist parties had shown deference. The implications of the advisor's remark were clear enough. The struggle was ongoing, and it wouldn't end until secularists stopped believing what they believed about the meaning and purpose of the Turkish state.

THE IDEA OF "POST-ISLAMISM" was appealing because it suggested that the fault lines that threatened to tear apart Middle Eastern societies could be transcended. It was a false hope. Post-Islamism only "worked" to the extent that divides over the role of religion could be papered over and postponed. That was fine as far as it went. But it was unsustainable. When in 2010 the AKP stood victorious in its battle for civilian control of the military and secured yet another election landslide, the question of what the AKP hoped to do with its burgeoning power would reemerge.

The longer the AKP stayed in power and embraced the expansive reach of the Turkish state, the more pressure they would face from an impatient base to deliver on something as basic as a woman dressing the way that she wanted. Yet in Turkey few things were as polarizing as this, not necessarily because secularists were dead set against the head scarf itself, but more because they feared the changes were a sign of things to come.

(6)

TUNISIA

ISLAMISTS CONCEDING
THEIR ISLAMISM

Islamists' obsession with the state had blinded them in Egypt, leading them into an untenable situation. Despite protestations from its own members—as well as Brotherhood affiliates across the region—the Muslim Brotherhood decided to run a presidential candidate. In so doing, the most influential Islamist organization of the past century assumed responsibility for the management of one of the Middle East's most unwieldy states.

For a movement that sought to maintain some degree of purity, these were fateful decisions. In its original iterations, mainstream Islamism was supposed to rise above party and even state. Islamists would often say that they didn't care about power for its own sake; what mattered were the ideas that they stood for. If others could be faithful to these same ideas, then they would happily lend their support. (To this day, there is a stigma within Brotherhood movements against too readily showing your interest in power and position. Self-nomination is in bad taste. Your fellow Brothers are the ones to nominate you.)

The state, in any case, was supposed to be an organic reflection of whatever society happened to be. The state *depended* on society. Who was in power and how they wielded it was the final result in a long, gradual process of societal transformation, so, in theory, securing the presidency shouldn't have seemed so decisive and urgent. To show such desperation for power was to, in a sense, accept the inverse of the Brotherhood's original proposition that change began with the individual. It was as if the Brotherhood had lost faith in the generative possibilities of bottom-up transformation.

In Turkey, the state, as led by Erdogan and the AKP, was the focal point of an effort to raise a new Islamic generation.[1] Even the word "raise" was problematic, suggesting a state taking on a set of responsibilities normally reserved for mosque, family, and community. Tying such explicitly religious efforts to a particular partisan vehicle was a risky endeavor. If advocating a more prominent role for Islam in politics—or merely being outwardly religious—became associated with a particular party, then the party's political failures and policy missteps could reflect negatively on the piety of the pious. In Turkey, for example, 74 percent of Muslims who pray five times a day supported Erdogan in 2014, compared with 67 percent in 2010.[2] In the June 2015 elections, AKP's conservative base was large, but not large enough for a parliamentary majority, with the party experiencing a significant drop in overall support. As long as Islamist parties saw success, there was nothing to worry about. When the AKP was presiding over a doubling of GDP per capita and a near tripling of gross GDP in ten years, Turkish Islamism came to be associated with good government and improved living standards.[3] But what if it came to be associated with political divisiveness, the muzzling of journalists, and a sputtering economy?

If the AKP was the first great Islamist hope—before falling out of favor after Erdogan's authoritarian turn—then Tunisia's Islamists were the newest darlings. With the rest of the region's

descent into civil war and repression, they also had the
of being the *only* darlings. If anyone was attuned to the
of failing and falling short, it was Tunisia's main Islami:
Ennahda, or "renaissance" in Arabic.

The Great Islamist Hope

It was easy to believe in Ennahda's promise. Unlike o
lamist parties in the region, where younger members c
ously struggled to gain traction, Ennahda had nurturec
generation of leaders and activists who looked and sounc
ferent.

At just twenty-eight years old, speaking fluent Engli
French, Sayida Ounissi was one of Tunisia's youngest m
of parliament. She had grown up in exile, leaving Tun:
Paris when she was only nine. Her father, an Ennahda m
had been tortured. In early 2015, we met for the firs
over coffee at a chic bed-and-breakfast owned by a Pales1
American expatriate, who had grown up between New Yc
Beirut. Wearing a fashionable head scarf, she was proud th
nahda had "stopped" instrumentalizing religion for politic:
unlike secular parties that, despite (or perhaps becau
their secularism, were increasingly peppering speeche
statements with prophetic sayings and Quranic verses. S
the other hand, knew who and what she was. She didn
the need to overcompensate with rhetorical flourishes
for her, there was a bigger risk, and, as someone who hac
hand experience with repression, the fear that those dark
might return was always underneath the surface. "Using
gion might work in the short term, but it could just as
backfire. "If we as Ennahda keep disappointing you,
shouldn't keep you from praying," she told me. "If one da
[become unpopular] and win only ten percent of the vot
don't want mosques to be attacked, and we don't want wc
with hijab to be threatened on the streets."[4]

As with so many other Islamist parties, the long game was the only game worth playing. Ennahda's brief stint in power from December 2011 to the end of 2013, as part of a coalition with two secular parties, was a difficult and taxing experience, but it was nothing compared with their previous experiences in politics. Throughout much of the 1990s and 2000s, Ennahda had effectively ceased to exist after strongman Zine al-Abidine Ben Ali systematically dismantled the organization. Party leaders found themselves in prison or in exile, scattered mostly in England, France, and Italy. When Ben Ali fell in the first stirrings of the Arab Spring, Ennahda experienced a dizzying rise to power, claiming victory—and the prime ministership—in the country's first-ever democratic elections. Looking back, they could claim some success. They had shown that power sharing between Islamists and secularists was possible, something that couldn't be said for most of Tunisia's neighbors. Perhaps most important, a relatively liberal constitution was passed with broad consensus in January 2014.

Yet it could have easily all fallen apart, and in spring 2013, it almost did. After the assassinations of two prominent leftists, polarization reached unprecedented levels. Leftist groups such as the Popular Front held Ennahda "indirectly responsible" for the assassinations, arguing that the party had allowed extremists too much room to operate.[5] The fear of a return to repression—magnified by the military coup in Egypt—animated Tunisia's Islamists. Ennahda leaders did whatever they could to avoid any confrontation that might scuttle a hardfought democratic transition. Most of the secular opposition called for dissolving either the democratically elected constituent assembly or the democratically elected government, or both. The echoes of Egypt were hard to miss, as various opposition groups did away with subtlety. Tunisia's own Tamarrod modeled itself after Egypt's Tamarrod (Rebellion) movement, which was instrumental in toppling Morsi. Tunisia's Salvation Front, drawing inspiration from Egypt's National Salvation Front, an-

nounced a campaign to remove local and national officials appointed by Ennahda.[6]

Developments in Egypt confirmed Ennahda's worst fears, that Islamists would never be allowed to govern, no matter how many elections they won.[7] When I spoke to Ennahda cofounder and leader Rached Ghannouchi in early 2015, well after the memory of Egypt had faded, the coup loomed large in his recounting of events. As a result of Egypt, he told me, "the opposition raised its ambitions and the ceiling of its demands to bring down the system with the power of the street. . . . They even called their groups the same names as in Egypt!"[8] I would have expected Ennahda officials, speaking to a Western researcher like myself, to attribute their willingness to make unusual compromises to their being good, magnanimous democrats. But many Ennahda leaders clearly saw the downfall of their fellow Islamists in visceral, and quite personal, terms. "I was shocked by Rabaa," Meherzia Laabidi, vice president of the constituent assembly, told me, her voice rising. "They are not human beings this ISIS group, but in Egypt it was the state that did this. This cruel aspect of the Egyptian conflict—it had a big, dissuasive power in Tunisia. Nobody wants this in Tunisia. This pushed politicians to sit around the table and talk."[9] Or, as Imen Ben Mohamed, a thirty-year-old Ennahda member of parliament, explained it, "We're sorry for what happened in Egypt, but it led to a result which was in a kind of way positive for our base. They saw how the Brotherhood's insistence on unilateral acts might benefit you in the short term, but you lose in the long run. Your existence in the political scene is tied to the guarantee of democracy."[10]

With the Tunisian experiment at a standstill and threatened with collapse, Ennahda, to its credit, voluntarily stepped down from power after protracted negotiations. As positive as this was—any number of frightening scenarios were averted—this wasn't what one might expect in "normal" democratic circumstances. Ennahda had been elected in free and fair elections.

As is the practice in parliamentary democracies, the opposition could have attempted to bring down the government through a no-confidence vote. Ennahda, for its part, could have called early elections, allowing Tunisians to choose a different course if they wished. This, though, is not what happened. Sensing an opportunity, secularists weren't quite willing to let the democratic process play out on its own. Ennahda, in effect, was forced to give up power.

In this sense, Tunisia, despite all of its progress, was, and still is, very much in transition. Democratic competition hasn't been "normalized," and so a religiously oriented party like Ennahda has to play by a different set of rules. Sayida Ounissi described the Tunisian predicament as two high-speed trains—Islamists and secular hard-liners—hurtling toward each other. Someone had to choose the safer path. After stepping down from power, the compromises continued. Ennahda, the largest, best-organized party in the country, opted not to run a presidential candidate. Not only that, they didn't even endorse a candidate. Then during the 2014 parliamentary elections, there was the odd spectacle of the losing party celebrating its loss, not too dissimilar from the pre–Arab Spring phenomenon of Islamist parties "losing on purpose."[11] As one senior Ennahda figure put it, "We were relieved and relieved and relieved."[12]

It might have seemed similarly odd when Ennahda decided to join a coalition government with the secular Nidaa Tounes party in February 2015. Ounissi acknowledged that it might be difficult for Americans like me to understand. Democrats and Republicans would never want to be in the same government together, she told me. On this she was probably right, but it does raise the question of why Ennahda, once again, did something a "normal" democratic party wouldn't do. Despite coming in second place in the October 2014 elections—winning a solid 31 percent of the seats—it agreed to only one ministry (the thankless Ministry of Employment) out of a total twenty-one, as well as three junior state secretary posts. If you were going to join the government, why accept only one cabinet post? A lone minister might have seemed symbolic, but that was precisely the point: Any marginalization of Islamists would prove much more difficult with Ennahda inside rather than out.

Despite the discontent among the rank and file, Ennahda's leaders believe—almost as a matter of faith—that this is the path they must follow. One of those leaders was Said Ferjani, profiled by the late, great journalist Anthony Shadid in a 2012 *New York Times* article. In his earlier years, Ferjani was something of a radical, plotting a coup d'état against the Tunisian "founding father" Habib Bourguiba. In an unlikely twist, Ben Ali, Bourguiba's interior minister, beat Ferjani and his comrades to it, staging his own coup seventeen hours before theirs. Ferjani was later arrested, suffering unspeakable torture—including a fractured spine—at the hands of his captors.[13]

In the interviews with Shadid, Ferjani recounts his time studying with Rached Ghannouchi in the 1970s, who, he said, "was always talking about the world and politics. Why as Muslims are we backwards? What makes us backwards? Is it our destiny to be so?"[14] Ennahda's leaders hoped to answer that same question, long ago asked by the Islamic modernists, in their own particular way. Their methods, though, had evolved considerably. This was the long game par excellence. When I challenged Ferjani on Ennahda's strategy after the party's disappointing finish in the 2014 elections, he acknowledged a trade-off: "We know we're going to lose some of our popularity by being in government and accepting a cabinet post."[15] He emphasized that "this is a transition"—one that might last fifteen to twenty years—and so I would have to judge Ennahda's behavior with that in mind. He returned to this theme repeatedly. This was an exceptional period, and the goal was to solidify the transition, entrench consensual democratic norms, and guarantee basic freedoms, even if doing so meant undermining party unity or disappointing an increasingly impatient base.

. . .

DEPENDING ON HOW YOU look at it, Ennahda's approach represented either the politics of prudence or the triumph of magical thinking. Throughout the 2014 election campaign, Ennahda, unlike most other parties, played as clean as one could possibly imagine. It deemphasized its Islamism and moved to the "center," portraying itself as the party of national consensus. Ennahda's most prominent spokesmen were young, conspicuously beardless technocrats who talked endlessly about solutions to everyday economic challenges. Just from listening, there was no way of knowing that they were members of an Islamist party. One campaign organizer described the self-conscious, mannered style to me as Ennahda's "new look" and took pride in the party's conscious move away from the use of religious rhetoric.[16]

Where Ennahda downplayed its ideological distinctiveness, Nidaa Tounes played up the Islamist-secular divide with a simple, straightforward call to arms. The varied factions of Nidaa Tounes—made up of old-regime elements, leftists, and business-oriented neoliberals—couldn't agree on much, but they could agree that Islamists and Islamism were an existential threat and needed to be defeated. Anne Wolf, in one of the few studies of Tunisian secularists, wrote that the "focus on anti-Islamism is one of [Nidaa Tounes's] greatest weaknesses."[17] This may have been true in an abstract sense, but polarization, ideological sharpness, and personal attacks apparently made for good electoral politics. Nidaa Tounes, which hadn't even existed in 2011, registered a first-place finish with 37.5 percent of the vote and eighty-six seats. Meanwhile, in the presidential elections, the party's standard-bearer, the eighty-eight-year-old Beji Caid Essebsi, sailed to an easy victory. (On the other hand, as Ghannouchi became *more* conciliatory, reaching out across the aisle and portraying himself as a kind of founding father, his favorability ratings cratered.[18])

Essebsi's critics argued that his rise marked a blow to the revolution. Essebsi was an early member of Ben Ali's administration and served as minister of interior and minister of defense under Habib Bourguiba. Polling numbers indicate many secular Tunisians might not mind—a preelection Pew survey found that less observant Tunisians were more likely than religious Tunisians to support a return to authoritarianism. Fifty-two percent of those who pray five times per day said that democracy is preferable to a "leader with a strong hand," compared with 41 percent of those who report praying less frequently.[19] (In 2012, 78 percent of Tunisians said religion was "very important" in their lives, a full 63 percent of them reported praying five times per day, and 96 percent said they observe the Ramadan fast).[20]

"Our Big Trip to the Center"

As we saw with Turkey, in deeply divided societies where attitudes for and against Islamists harden, the center can't hold. It makes more sense to consolidate your base and get your supporters to turn out en masse. To say that Ennahda's electoral strategy failed, though, is to miss the point. Ennahda officials readily admit that moving to the center wasn't necessarily meant to win them the election. It was something they believed they had to do regardless of the consequences. As Ounissi told me, "We're not thinking about electoral strategy right now. It's all about Tunisia. We made a choice. If that gets us second place, then I'm fine with that." Or as Meherzia Laabidi put it, "Moving to the center has a cost, and the cost is losing part of our electorate."

Some like Noureddine Arbaoui, one of Ennahda's historic figures and chief ideologues, admitted that Ennahda's laser-like focus on policy minutiae and technocratic grandstanding was largely aspirational. "If we want to be realistic, up until now, there isn't voting for parties based on their actual programs," he told me. "There isn't one person who went to the ballot box and said this is a liberal program so I'm going to vote liberal. Our supporters voted for us because we're Ennahda. The others voted for Nidaa Tounes because they're Ennahda's opponent."[21]

For both better and worse, Ennahda had decided to carry the burden of Tunisia's democratic transition. To the extent that we can speak of a Tunisian "model," this is it: Islamists conceding their Islamism, because the alternative, which they saw all around them, was the collapse of democracy. They might have been paranoid, but they couldn't afford to take the chance, especially not with Libya, Syria, and Yemen ablaze right next door. "Yes it's true we made concessions but this wasn't a loss for us," Ghannouchi explained. "If we had held to our right to stay in government in 2013, the country would have been destroyed."[22]

This wasn't just rhetoric. "Our big trip to the center," as Ghannouchi described it to me, had significant consequences for the organization.[23] Since the start of the Arab Spring, Ennahda's leaders had veered from one crisis to another, each time persuading their base to stand down from ideological and revolutionary demands. During the constitution-drafting process, the party backed down on three controversial clauses—on sharia, gender equality, and blasphemy.[24] Ennahda's parliamentary bloc had proposed including sharia as a "source among sources" of legislation.[25] By the standards of most Arab countries, this was fairly innocuous. Islamists, by definition, believe that sharia (however one wishes to define it) has a role to play in public life, yet here was an Islamist party accepting a constitution without even a mere mention of it. This concession came despite the fact that Ennahda dominated the constituent assembly and that a more prominent role for religion was widely supported in Tunisian society. A 2014 Pew poll found that 53 percent of Tunisians believe that laws in Tunisia should "follow the values and principles of Islam," while a full

30 percent went further, saying laws should "strictly follow the teachings of the Quran."[26] Riadh Chaibi, a prominent Ennahda figure who has since left the party, recalls working to persuade conservative activists that there wasn't any particular need to include a sharia clause in the constitution: "It was challenging to convince them, and some responded with an anger, bordering on hate."[27]

The party leadership, guided by Ghannouchi's vision and charisma, stayed the course, directing considerable organizational resources to explaining why a focus on sharia would be needlessly divisive. Focused on keeping its own house in order, Ennahda paid less attention to explaining its positions to broader society, leading to confusion about Ennahda's ultimate intentions. Similar challenges presented themselves when it came to revolutionary demands. In 2013, the proposed "exclusion law"—which would have barred thousands of Tunisians, including "all members of the successive Ben Ali governments, from 1987 to 2011, as well as all senior members of the former ruling party" from holding elected office—failed to pass by only one vote.[28] To ensure the bill's defeat, Ghannouchi expended his considerable political capital to get just enough Ennahda deputies to flip their votes at the last minute. Organizations have finite resources. The fact that so much of the party's political capital was spent on resolving internal debates came at a cost.

Ennahda is an extreme example of the delicate balancing acts that Islamist movements perpetually find themselves in. These movements must demonstrate "moderation" to secular elites, international actors, and any number of other skeptics. Their conservative base, on the other hand, wants a dose of identity, ideology, and religion, and if not a dose than at least a nod to the movement's "essence." This endless balancing inevitably provokes an identity crisis. As one civil-society activist put it to me, "Ennahda aren't like the others, but they're not like themselves either."[29] In an April 2015 interview with a

French journalist, Ghannouchi himself tiptoed that tightrope. He reiterated the standard Islamist opposition to blasphemy along with traditionalist views on gender equality and inheritance but expressed surprising tolerance toward homosexuality, arguing Islam has no role "to spy on folks."[30]

How much of Ennahda's moderation was "tactical" and how much of it reflected a genuine ideological evolution? As we saw earlier, Tunisia's unique political context—the fragility of the transition and the distorting effects of repression—helps explain Ennahda's trajectory of caution and compromise. That said, the interplay between belief and action is rarely straightforward. Obviously, belief inspires action, but saying and doing something enough times can end up shaping, and changing, what you believe in, even if you don't quite realize it at first.

THE SUCCESSION OF COMPROMISES worried Sheikh Habib Ellouze, Ennahda's most prominent "hard-liner." In the 1980s, he had opposed the movement's decision to change its name from the Islamic Tendency Movement to Ennahda. More than two decades later, Ellouze—as the self-styled guardian of the party's Islamic identity—was fighting a similar battle. I met Ellouze for the first time in February 2013 on the margins of a tense parliamentary session. As one of the movement's historic figures, he had grown old (he went blind in one eye during his thirteen years of solitary confinement), but he seemed as spry as a twenty-year-old. He spoke with the confidence of someone who believed that history was on his side. He dismissed the party's move to the center as mere tactics. "There aren't any of us who do not believe in the rulings of sharia," he told me. "All of us believe in banning alcohol one day. What we disagree on is how best to present and express our Islamic ideas."[31]

When I met with him again two years later, he wasn't so sure. A lot had changed in the interim, and he seemed exhausted. He told me to meet him at the Ennahda headquarters, which took up nearly an entire block in the posh Montplaisir neighborhood. It was an odd choice of venue, I thought, considering he didn't really fit in with the party's "new look." The mostly young staff buzzed around the headquarters in a uniform of sorts: black suit, white shirt, (relatively) skinny black tie. We might as well have been at a fashion shoot—the suits seemed unusually well tailored, with the pant legs narrow and tapered. Ellouze, on the other hand, wore the traditional *jebba* along with the *chechia*, a red felt hat. We sat down off to the side of a large conference room, but a few other people were speaking loudly, oblivious to the fact that the sheikh, one of the movement's historic figures, was trying to give an interview. He asked the staff for a quiet room. After some negotiation, we moved to a tiny room on the top floor of the five-story building.

Ellouze, always loyal despite his disagreements, was, this time around, open and biting in his criticisms of the party. He had a list of grievances and detailed them one by one. First, Ennahda might as well have lost the elections on purpose, having run a vapid, uninspiring campaign replete with technocratic boilerplate. No matter how much you reach out to secularists, they'll always doubt you, he said.[32] But the disagreement over electoral tactics went deeper. He was worried about the younger party figures who grew up either in exile or outside the movement's embrace. What begins as tactics, he told me, can quickly become internalized. At some point, if you say something over and over, you start to believe in it. No one, after all, likes to think they're engaging in "double discourse" (something that Ennahda is routinely accused of by its opponents). To close the gap between what you say and do and what you believe, you may have to "shift" the latter. This, one might argue, is the essence of politics. (It can cut the other way, too, where "moderates" adopt a more conservative discourse because it's good electoral politics and, over time, start believing their own rhetoric.)

The notion of Ennahda as an "exceptional"—and exceptionally progressive—Islamist party is one that many in the leadership have embraced, and this self-perception drives them to continue along the current path, despite the discontent it has stirred among their conservative base. I heard it over and over: "We are proud." It feels good to prove the naysayers wrong, to demonstrate not just to skeptical secularists but also to the international community that "Islam and democracy can meet."

Individuals also matter. Unlike other Islamist movements, which have generally lacked major thinkers or ideologues—Egypt's Brotherhood hasn't had one for decades—Rached Ghannouchi has articulated a distinctive vision for the party. Here, the divergence with the Turkish model, often seen as a major inspiration for Ennahda, becomes clear. The two parties share similar ideological origins—a milder, more secular-friendly version of the Brotherhood "school." Erdogan, the skilled politician from the streets of Istanbul, had reembraced his religious roots, in part because it worked. Ghannouchi, the intellectual, was more interested in proving a point than in winning an election. But as the leader of the party, there were only so many elections you could lose before your followers started to wonder. As Ghannouchi's biographer Azzam Tamimi, himself a prominent Islamist associated with Hamas, told me, "Ghannouchi ended up contradicting himself at times because he needs to think as an Islamic leader, but at the same time he needs to act as a politician. It's always this tension between the two."[33]

Indeed, while Ghannouchi's vision may be distinctive in some respects, the results, when applied to everyday Tunisian politics, aren't always consistent or clear. Was Ennahda a revolutionary or a reformist party (several prominent figures have left the party because it wasn't enough of the former)? Is it government or opposition, or is it somehow both at the same time (as when it accepted a cabinet post)? Is Ennahda a movement or a party, or both (and if it is both simultaneously, is that sustainable)? And what, exactly, does it mean for a party to be a party with a religious "reference" when it insists on downplaying that religious reference?

Ennahda and the Problem of Islamist Exceptionalism

Tunisia, like Turkey, was a fascinating laboratory of what happens when decades of forced secularization come to an end. What did an Islamic revival look like in a secularized context? Ghannouchi's project, one that he had staked his legacy on, was to change Islamism and perhaps even "Islam" (assuming the two were interrelated). It was a tempting notion, this idea that ideological divides could somehow be transcended by neutralizing them. One of Islamism's greatest failures (or successes, depending on your perspective) was politicizing something—Islam—which had once, a long time ago, been a source of unity and consensus.

Ghannouchi's friend and fellow traveler Abdel Moneim Abul Futouh had left Egypt's Muslim Brotherhood in part for precisely this reason. Abul Futouh, during his insurgent campaign for president in 2012, had an interesting if counterintuitive call to arms. In an interview with a Salafi television channel, he declared: "Today, those who call themselves liberals or leftists, this is just a political name, but most of them understand and respect Islamic values. They support the sharia and are no longer against it."[34] Abul Futouh noted that all Muslims are, by definition, Salafi, in the sense that they are loyal to the *Salaf*, the earliest, most pious generations of Muslims. He seemed to be saying: We are all, in effect, Islamists, so why fight over it?

There were ample reasons to fight over it, of course. As much as Ennahda moderated, seeking the elusive center, it was still Ennahda. If Ennahda decided to throw in the towel and morph into a "liberal" party, then what would be the point? There were other liberal parties who were presumably better at being liberal than an Islamist party. Even Ghannouchi was more than willing to recognize this.[35] If Ennahda ceased to carry the mantle, then someone else would come and fill the vacuum. As long as there was popular demand for an Islamically infused politics, someone would have to supply it.

But there was another problem. Ennahda could do and say all the right things, but the doubts would linger. It wasn't something that party leaders had much control over. Secularists distrusted (or hated) Islamists not necessarily for what they did, but for who they were. Ennahda, inevitably, was going to be made up of conservative, practicing Muslims. Before and after major meetings, for instance, party leaders usually join together for prayer as a group. Islam is their starting point, even if the end point—the specific positions they advocate—may diverge considerably.

After I met with Ghannouchi, his assistant very kindly drove me to my next meeting. The assistant was a true believer, as he soon made clear. His approach to life seemed to be based on an overarching trust in the *haraka*, or movement, and the leadership of the sheikh, the honorific with which Ennahda members referred to Ghannouchi. The silence in the car was bothering me, so I tried to strike up a conversation. We soon found ourselves discussing whether someone who drank alcohol could join Ennahda. He didn't think so, and pointed out that there were conditions for becoming a member of the party. Someone had to vouch for your moral character, a process known as *tazkiya*. It was also unlikely that anyone who drank would want to become a member in the first place—unless, perhaps, they hoped that joining Ennahda would help them kick the habit and become better Muslims.

In this sense, Ennahda, despite featuring all the trappings of a modern party, wasn't quite that. It was more like a family. As the ex-Ennahda official Riadh Chaibi described it to me, "Leaving the party is almost like leaving your religion."[36] Ennahda, like most Islamist parties, is *shumuli*, roughly translated as "comprehensive" or "total." Brotherhood-inspired organizations are first and foremost movements before parties, meant to encompass every facet of life. They offer religious education and organize charity work. Perhaps most important, they provide a sense of community—of belonging and brotherhood—at a time when societies threaten to tear apart. In contexts where the state is strong and society weak, they can fill the gap. In authoritarian contexts, they offer something additional and absolutely essential—financial, legal, and moral support for the families of activists who have been unjustly imprisoned.

Academics, understandably, have tended to focus on what Islamists do. Observable behavior is, well, easier to observe. You can measure it. It's tangible. Focusing on who Islamists *are*, on the other hand, is difficult, since one can never truly know the hearts of men. That said, we can, in fact, talk in quite specific terms about what Islamist *organizations* are, rather than merely the outcomes they produce. The "encompassing" nature of Islamist parties is one of their underdiscussed yet critical distinguishing marks. Because these parties are more than just that—they are *movements*—membership takes on a weightier meaning. This is particularly the case with Brotherhood-inspired organizations, which generally have tiered membership structures. Ennahda, however, has been both a party and a movement in one, so to join the former is to be a part of the latter. Because of legal requirements governing licensed parties, this means that anyone can, in theory, become an Ennahda member. In practice, however, Ennahda, or any mass Islamist party for that matter, will stand apart for better or worse. Discussing the typical Ennahda member, Chaibi describes the dynamic: "He doesn't consider himself part of the society; he thinks he's better. This leads to love of self. He tends to think, 'We are not merely partners . . . we are the conscience of the nation.'"

Implicitly, even the most progressive Ennahda figures believed they, as individuals, were different, not so much because of what they did, but because of who they were. One particular exchange with Noureddine Erbaoui was intriguing in this respect. A close associate of Ghannouchi, he was an enthusiastic supporter of the party's "new look," downplaying the importance of religion and recasting Ennahda as the country's best technocrats. I asked him, when you talk about poverty reduction and putting people to work, why should anyone think that Ennahda would do a better job than any number of secular parties which have more economists in their ranks and more experience in government? "The program of Ennahda, the program of Nidaa Tounes, the programs of the others, they're similar," he admitted. "So, then, what makes me as a citizen vote for Ennahda? It's like what Erdogan said, 'We don't steal.'" To illustrate the point, he offered an example of why people voted for Hamas over Fatah in the 2006 Palestinian elections:

> When Hamas gets funding for job-creation programs,
> out of one hundred dinars, you know that ninety will
> go to people who deserve it. Ten dinars might get lost
> in some corruption. If you give the same hundred
> dinars to Fatah, ninety dinars will go to corruption,
> even though it's roughly the same program.[37]

I imagine that Arbaoui thought this sounded appealing to Western audiences: If people were scared of Islamists, then there was no reason to be. They were just like secularists but better, because they were less corrupt. Even if this was true, it displayed an almost endearing naïveté—that it was enough for politicians to merely be honest and come up with good economic programs. The rest would flow from that. But, at a more basic level, Arbaoui's comment, however innocuous it sounded, betrayed a belief that the religious commitments of Islamists made them not just better people but better politicians as well. It meant that Islamist parties, despite their best intentions, would never—and could never—be as "normal" as they said they wanted to be.

The tendency to stand apart isn't necessarily a major problem during periods of stifling autocracy, but it becomes an issue when Islamists assume the responsibilities of government. In established democracies, ruling parties are generally open to opportunists and influence peddlers. But if you need to be of a certain religious or moral pedigree to enter the halls of power, then this can promote the perception of exclusion. And, in Tunisia and Egypt, during Ennahda's and the Brotherhood's brief stints in power, that perception spread among the non-Islamist opposition. The charge of "Brotherhoodization" of the state became a kind of call to arms. The claims were wildly exaggerated, but they were effective all the same, drawing on latent fears that Islamist groups were insular and impenetrable, valuing organizational self-preservation over all else. In any democracy, political parties appoint party members to senior positions, but it is much less common for a closed *movement*—a movement that transcends party—to appoint other members of the movement, who are bound together by a deeper loyalty.

THIS WAS WHAT MODERNIZATION looked like, and it was a bit of a mess. The premodern ideal of Islam as a unifying force had met the modern ideal of political party competition. Political parties and the nation-state were inextricably linked. There was a state, after all, that needed governing, and it was parties that competed for the privilege. The more powerful the state was, the more contentious the struggle for power. As brittle as it may have ultimately been, the modern Arab state, with overdeveloped bureaucracies and security sectors, was "strong," dispensing patronage and providing employment to a disproportionately high number of dependent citizens.

The modern nation-state, in this sense, had no prior analogues, so there could be no prior models of reconciling Islam and the state. It was a dilemma with no obvious resolution. What was once a source of unity—an Islamic moral framework shared by all Muslims—was now the trademark of the one main "Islamic" party. That party, which came to be associated not just with Islamism but Islam, would then seek state power, further exacerbating political and ideological polarization. Ideology, party, and power were fused together in a potentially fatal embrace. Islamists themselves weren't oblivious to the dilemmas. If you asked them, they would be the first to expound at length on the empowerment of local councils and the need to distribute power away from the state. In fact, in their various political platforms and electoral programs during the 2000s, Brotherhood organizations became enamored with "decentralization."* But how did one implement an ambitious program of decentralization without first having control of a powerful, centralized state—the very state that would presumably be asked to self-limit its own jurisdiction?

A lopsided power imbalance between Islamists and secularists complicates matters further. Most Arab countries lack strong, coherent party structures, yet, during democratic openings, citizens are asked to practice politics through political parties, which are either weak or nonexistent. It can take years, if not decades, for new parties to build themselves up from scratch. Yet with "democracy"—and particularly elections—as an uncontested normative good, few democrats are willing to make the argument that elections, at least on the national level, should be shelved indefinitely. In both Egypt and Tunisia, Is-

---

*In the Egyptian Brotherhood's 2005 electoral program, the section on "financial and administrative decentralization" is among the longest and best reflects the group's apparent fixation on empowering elected local bodies to counterbalance (unelected) central authorities. Under the Brotherhood's plan, national ministries are limited to devising broad policies and strategies, while municipal governments are responsible for execution. Localities are empowered to collect taxes and fees within their own geographic jurisdiction without requiring the approval of the central government. They are also responsible for collecting *zakat* funds for poverty alleviation. If any funds remain, only then are they to be transferred to the treasury. Finally, to ensure the independence of municipal leaders, their salaries are to be paid through a private funding mechanism (*al-Barnamaj al-Intikhabi li al-Ikhwan al-Muslimin fi al-Intakhabat al-Tashri'iya* [The Electoral Program of the Muslim Brotherhood in the Legislative Elections], Cairo, November 2005).

lamists didn't have parties in the normal sense of the word. But as ideologically cohesive movements, they could easily "convert" themselves into parties, either by forming an affiliated party, as in Egypt, or by intertwining party and movement to the extent that they became indistinguishable, as in Tunisia. In their first ever free and fair parliamentary elections, Islamists (including Salafi parties) won nearly 75 percent of the seats in Egypt and 41 percent of the seats in Tunisia. The largest secular parties won only 7.6 percent and 13 percent, respectively, a massive landslide by any measure. At such an early, crucial stage, the results heightened fears that democracy would fundamentally disadvantage non-Islamists. While secular and liberal parties busied themselves playing catchup, Islamists would consolidate control over constitution, state, and parliament, making future reversals all the more difficult.

Liberals and secularists were disadvantaged in another, perhaps even more fundamental way. It wasn't clear what "liberalism" really meant in the Egyptian or Tunisian contexts beyond a generalized dislike of Islamists. It was, in any case, mostly a minority orientation, the province of well-educated urban elites. Liberals didn't have the binding organizational structures of Islamists. Or, to put it differently, liberalism wasn't—and could never be—a way of life (it was about letting individuals choose their own way of life, whatever that happened to be, free from coercion). Because liberalism couldn't offer an affirmative vision of what it meant, or why it mattered, for ordinary citizens, liberals had little choice but to fall back on virulent anti-Islamism. Where non-Islamist parties have done well in the Arab world, they have done so by building large coalitions of individuals, civil-society groups, and smaller parties, which agree on relatively little. To the extent they hold together, they do so by pointing to an enemy, whose very existence requires them to put their differences to the side, at least for the moment.

This leads to a dangerous, self-reinforcing dynamic. To justify their existence and to maintain internal cohesion in the absence of a coherent ideology, non-Islamist parties have powerful incentives to emphasize and deepen the Islamist-secular divide. In this sense, ideological and religious cleavages, once entrenched, can be very difficult to undo. In their classic 1967 study *Party Systems and Voter Alignments*, Seymour Lipset and Stein Rokkan argue that the process of state formation gives rise to differences among citizens, which provoke lasting cleavages.[38] That economic cleavages are paramount in most Western democracies is no accident, given the particular sequencing of events in the modernization process. Here, parties play an important role. If a particular cleavage gains traction, then they have greater incentive to define themselves around that cleavage, since that's how they distinguish themselves from the competition. The academic literature on political party development suggests that "parties themselves . . . are the main drivers behind party system change and stability."[39] Or, as the political scientist Nick Sitter puts it, "the parties have stolen the show."[40]

Just as secularists benefitted from the Islamist-secular divide, so too, naturally, did Islamists. As we saw in previous chapters, Islamism is a modern construct that depends on the conscious affirmation of one's Islamic identity. It would only make sense to assert your Islamic identity if it were being threatened by a competing sense of identity. If the role of Islam were neutralized—as Ghannouchi, Abul Futouh, and other "liberal" Islamists hoped it might—then Islamists would stand to lose their raison d'être. Perhaps that would be a positive outcome, but the incentives for Islamists are aligned in the opposite direction. Islam is the distinguishing mark that ensures the organizational cohesion and coherence of Islamism. From an electoral standpoint, religion is essential for rallying the base.

To hope that Islam might be neutralized was to hope that the problem—the problem at the core of the struggle for the postcaliphate order—might simply resolve itself. In any situation where ideology is a source of conflict, citizens becoming *less* ideological is certainly one solution. But is it realistic? To think that Islam can, once again, be a source of unity and consensus, as it was in the premodern period, is to succumb to utopian thinking. This is reflected, oddly enough, in the Middle East's two most successful and democratic countries, Tunisia and Turkey. The legacy of secularization, even if it has dimmed somewhat, cannot be undone entirely. In both countries, there are secular elites, significant enough in number, who disagree with Islamists not just on the role Islam should play in public life but on *whether* it should play such a role in the first place. And, as we saw earlier, when Islamic fervor, a multiplicity of political parties, and a state strong enough to be worth "capturing" are all in the mix, ideological and religious polarization isn't just likely; it is inevitable.

A prominent, even dominant, role for Islam and Islamists in the political life of the Middle East is not necessarily contrary to democracy (although it may be contrary to *liberal* democracy). Democracy, after all, is about reflecting popular sentiment in its various forms. Democracy is about letting different trends in society express their ideological preferences, regardless of whether or not we agree with them. Why should Turks, Tunisians, or Egyptians shun ideology as long as their ideological divides are real and meaningful? To paper over them or postpone their reckoning—as Ennahda has attempted—is better than the alternative, but it falls well short of a long-term resolution. If "democracy" can only succeed, or even come to be, through the marginalization of Islamists or by Islamists themselves conceding their Islamism, then this is a brittle democracy indeed.

7

ISIS

AFTER THE STATE FAILS

It was easy to get excited about Tunisia. Despite deep ideological conflict, the democratic transition survived, flawed yet intact. In the Middle East, everything is relative. Revolutionaries have the luxury—and the burden—of judging their success against some imagined standard. But the rest of us have to situate Tunisia's trajectory within a broader regional context. And with every passing day—as Iraq, Syria, Libya, and Yemen imploded—Tunisia looked all the better.

Yet in Tunisia there were darker undercurrents, if you knew where to look. We saw some of them in the previous chapter: Ideological divides hadn't yet been resolved, only postponed. But there was something else, and it confounded analysts and activists alike. As the democratic transition sputtered along, a disproportionately large number of Tunisians were looking elsewhere for hope and inspiration. More than three thousand Tunisians found that inspiration on the battlefields of Syria, forming a shockingly high percentage of an estimated twenty-two thousand foreign fighters.[1] According to the Tunisian interior ministry, as of April 2015, another 12,490 Tunisians had tried to leave to fight in Iraq, Syria, and Libya but had been blocked by the authorities.[2]

This was a different world, shrouded in silence and mystery, in the back alleys of an otherwise bustling capital city. One could spend days in Tunis and not see a single sign of it, except perhaps a fleeting mention or a muffled conversation. But if you were a young Tunisian, you almost certainly knew friends, acquaintances, and perhaps even family members who had gone to fight, or at least got stopped trying. For the average Westerner, the idea of knowing an Islamic State fighter—or knowing the brother, father, or sister of an Islamic State fighter—was the height of the exotic. For many young Tunisians, it was the new normal. It was just something that (some) people did. Friends and family of foreign fighters spoke matter-of-factly, sometimes nonchalantly, of what these young men had done. They might as well have been talking about a relative who had gone backpacking in Europe or to study in the United States. Then again, was there ever a "right" way to speak of someone you knew, and even loved, going to fight for a terrorist group?

I MET YASSINE in a quiet coffee shop in the Bardo neighborhood, near the Tunisian parliament. We found a seat tucked away in the corner. Like all coffee shops in Tunisia, the air was layered with smoke, billowing up to ceiling, creating a vaporous cloud above our heads. I have to admit that I was in somewhat new territory. I asked my friend and fixer Jihed: What was the appropriate thing to say to someone whose son had died fighting for the Islamic State in Syria? Yassine's son, a student at Manouba University, had been killed in August 2013.

"It happened all at once," Yassine recalled. The son, who I will call Hichem, began spending a lot of time at the mosque, and going to the *fajr*, or dawn, prayer. He grew a short beard and started wearing a *thawb*, the telltale dress of Salafis hoping to replicate the unadorned desert garb of seventh-century Arabia. "I told him this isn't how we Tunisians dress, and he took it off. But he got a passport without telling us. He would tell his mother everything, except this one thing. One day, it was a Sunday, he didn't come home. He called to say he was staying with a friend, although that's not something he ever did."[3]

Of course, Yassine told me, he was surprised. Clearly, their son was becoming more conservative. He was keeping to himself, spending a lot of time on the computer, but it never occurred to them that he might want to travel to Syria, first joining al-Qaeda affiliate Jabhat al-Nusra before moving on to the Islamic State.

It was this puzzle that intrigued me. How did a father, or anyone else for that matter, make sense of such a tragedy? In mourning and trying to make sense of it all, Yassine had a number of hypotheses, ranging from the lure of jihadist forums on the Internet to a Salafi preacher at the local mosque who "brainwashed" his son, inserting foreign ideas of *takfir*, or the excommunication of fellow Muslims. Any discussion of radicalizing factors lends itself to analytic confusion, particularly if you're looking for an elegant model of why people turn to political violence and terrorism. Radicalization, as it happens in real life, is inelegant. It's banal to say so, but different people radicalize in different ways. Why does one individual choose to join the Islamic State and not someone else in that same slum who experiences many of the same political and economic pressures? As terrorism scholar Jessica Stern writes, "It is difficult to make gross generalizations about what leads individuals to do what they do in any area of life; difficulty in answering this question is not unique to terrorism experts."[4] For some people, radicalization is a gradual process that takes place over many years—the product of accumulated experience. Others might be predisposed to radical politics, but it is only a catalyzing moment that pushes them not just to theorize or think about violence, but to act on it. Trying to understand why will always be something of a mystery, particularly for a grieving mother and father. This was *their* son.

In what would be a recurring theme, Yassine said that his son and other young Tunisians were initially attracted to Syria because of the unfolding humanitarian catastrophe. Watching the slaughter of their Syrian brethren at the hands of the Assad regime, they were moved to act. The groups that were most hospitable to foreign fighters tended to be the Islamist rebel factions, the most powerful of which was Jabhat al-Nusra. Far from the usual al-Qaeda franchise, Nusra, directing its fire against Assad and fighting alongside mainstream Free Syrian Army (FSA) factions, enjoyed considerable legitimacy among Islamist and non-Islamist Syrians alike. In April 2013, the leader of the Islamic State of Iraq (ISI), Abu Bakr al-Baghdadi, in an attempt to wrest control of Nusra, announced a merger between the two organizations. Nusra rejected his entreaties, leading to a split that would have dramatic implications in the world of jihad.[5] In the ensuing confusion, many Tunisian fighters, including Hichem, defected to the Islamic State after it changed its name to include "Sham," the Arabic appellation for greater Syria.

Hichem's views hardened. "In those final months, he was asking his mother to pray for him to join the ranks of the martyrs," Yassine recalls. Young fighters, with no real military experience, went to Syria not knowing what to expect. Some became disillusioned. Others, like Hichem, appear to have radicalized over the course of the fighting, particularly after joining the Islamic State. This isn't surprising. War and radicalization go hand in hand, which makes it all the more important to distinguish between the initial motivations for joining an Islamist rebel group and how those motivations and ideological commitments evolve over time. In other words, a young Tunisian might, at first, be moved to join Nusra for "secular" reasons—to fight Assad, out of a desire for revenge, because his friends joined, or because Nusra takes better care of fighters or has more advanced weapons than other rebel groups. Individuals are complex, so we should assume that their motivations are complex as well. This suggests that the decision to ally with one faction over another is based on some combination of all of the above factors. Of course, religion plays a role as well; if it didn't, we would see secular Tunisians going to fight for, say, the Free Syrian Army. Meanwhile, Salafi-oriented Tunisians are more likely to see the Assad regime as a secular, infidel regime at war with pious Sunni Muslims. They are more likely to see jihad as a religious obligation. For them, it doesn't matter that they are Tunisian and the people they're ostensibly fighting for are Syrian; they are all Muslims, bound together as members of a transnational *umma*. Religion, then, is necessary, but it is not sufficient.

In one of the earliest studies of Syrian rebel motivations, drawing on interviews with over 300 fighters in 2013–14, Vera Mironova, Loubna Mrie, and Sam Whitt found that "many reasons given by Islamists for taking up arms are not that different from FSA fighters." While 71 percent of Islamists cited the desire to build an Islamic state, only 25 percent said this was their main motivation. Interestingly, when they interviewed FSA fighters who defected to an Islamist group, "almost all mentioned reasons which were not expressly religious."[6]

However, after spending a significant period of time with a particular Islamist faction, fighters are likely to adopt and internalize more and more of the group's ideology. In other words, the "Islamism" of Islamist rebels is, to an extent, *acquired*. According to the study, 74 percent of Islamist respondents said they had become more religious since the beginning of the war. Daily immersion and indoctrination in a group's propaganda is difficult to resist, particularly when it brings with it the prospect of belonging and brotherhood. As terrorism researcher Thomas Hegghammer, curator of the Bored Jihadi Tumblr page, notes, "Look inside jihadi groups and you'll see bearded men with Kalashnikovs reciting poetry, discussing dreams, and weeping on a regular basis."[7] The natural desire to belong and be part of a cause that transcends the individual— something that grows increasingly appealing when facing death— contributes to a powerful and self-reinforcing dynamic. The most radical groups, such as the Islamic State and Jabhat al-Nusra, obviously take ideological coherence seriously. Accordingly, individual fighters, even those with reservations, have strong incentives to demonstrate ideological fervor in order to gain the favor of local and regional commanders. Fear also plays a role, particularly in the Islamic State, where openly expressing doubts about the organization can bring about an untimely death. With individual fighters demonstrating, or even overstating, their devotion to the cause, a kind of religious outbidding takes place, leading to a vicious cycle of radicalization.

While it may be more pronounced in the region, this cycle isn't necessarily unique to civil conflict in the Arab world. Moderates tend to lose out in revolutions and civil wars (or wars of any kind). The longer a society experiences chaos and disorder, the stronger radicals become. As radicals grow stronger, violence intensifies, and so on. As Samuel Huntington writes in his classic 1969 work *Political Order in Changing Societies*, "The moderates remain moderate and are swept from power. Their failure stems precisely from their inability to deal with the problem of political mobilization. On the one hand, they lack the drive and ruthlessness to stop the mobilization of new groups into politics; on the other, they lack the radicalism to lead it."[8]

Almost by definition, gradualism loses its appeal in the totalizing fog of battle. When the goal is to vanquish an opponent, or merely stay alive, everything else fades into the background. For the "moderate," the taking up of arms is done grudgingly, if at all. The radicals, however, embrace violence because they have lost faith, if they ever had it, in the possibilities of politics. Revolution is the only way, and revolution is about maximalist aims. Why, exactly, would people who are willing to kill and die for a cause care about being moderate? In their book *ISIS: Inside the Army of Terror,* journalists Michael Weiss and Hassan Hassan identify an unlikely, even odd, category of Islamic State supporter: secularists or agnostics who "express deep objections about [the group's] atrocities" but come to embrace violence as necessary.[9]

Democracy's Costs

The hope has always been that democratization and political participation would offer disaffected citizens peaceful outlets to express economic and political grievances. This notion—that the only way to effectively undermine Middle East terrorism is to promote democratic openings—was the animating premise behind the second Bush administration's Freedom Agenda in the 2000s. A growing body of evidence suggests that this is at least partly true in the long run. (Steven Brooke and I survey this literature in greater detail in an article we wrote in 2010.[10]) But Tunisia hadn't, and wouldn't, reach the long run anytime soon.

Democracy is no easy fix, and there tends to be a short-term trade-off. Democratizing countries may be more prone to instability, as the political scientists Edward Mansfield and Jack Snyder have persuasively argued in their work.[11] This is particularly the case in countries where democratic openings deepen ideological cleavages. In postrevolutionary contexts such as Tunisia's, extremist groups benefit from institutional and governance gaps. The fall of a dictator—and the euphoria of long-awaited regime change—raises expectations, yet institutions are too weak to meet rising popular demands.

In conversations with young Tunisians who have friends or relatives who went to fight in Syria, I would often point out that Tunisia, unlike its neighbors, was relatively democratic and provided channels for participation within the system. My claims were often met with skepticism and cries of "What democracy?"

When I met with the Tunisian rapper DJ Costa in a run-down district of Manouba, I suggested it was something of a paradox that Tunisia, the Arab world's democratic "model," could produce so many foreign fighters. He scoffed:

> You, because you live outside, you feel that it's a contradiction, but we know that we don't have democracy in Tunisia. It's like a man whose skin is dirty. For months he hasn't washed himself, and then, one day, he puts on nice, expensive clothes. But you know him, who he really is.[12]

DJ Costa's brother, Youssef, had gone to fight in Syria but quickly became disillusioned by growing rebel infighting. He managed to return to Tunisia but discovered that there was no place for someone like him. After constant police harassment, he went back to Syria, where he was killed by an airstrike. "Even after he died, they're still harassing our family," Costa told me.

In the city of Kairouan, a Salafi stronghold, I unexpectedly met a young Tunisian filmmaker, whose cousin was, as of writing, still in Syria fighting with the Islamic State. "I am against his decision, but I respect it," he told me, over a bottle of Tunisian beer and a seemingly unlimited supply of cigarettes.[13] I asked him if he thought that going to fight for the Islamic State was normal. It seemed to me like a big deal. "You're living in America, *habibi*, not in Tunisia," he said. "But if you lived in Tunisia and you're experiencing daily subjugation and injustice, and you have ideas, and you have principles, and you have objectives, and you have a vision for the future, and if you live in a state that doesn't embrace you, then it's the opposite. It's very normal." By the time we were winding down the conversation, he was on his fourth or fifth bottle. The seriousness of the conversation had given way to something lighter, if only because that was the easier way, maybe the only way to live with it. There were three of us at the table, and we all knew it. This was their reality, and what could they do but laugh at the absurdity? "Normal? What's normal?" he asked me playfully. "A woman walks in the street wearing a bikini. Here, it's not normal. In America, it's normal."

DEMOCRACY AS AN ABSTRACT concept was well and good, but for many Tunisians the democratic transition hadn't translated into positive changes on the ground. The economy continued to struggle, and those on the fringes—secular revolutionaries and Salafi radicals alike—felt that the political process, moving slowly because of polarization and gridlock, stifled the kind of dramatic change that was necessary.

In a 2010 article, Middle East expert Marc Lynch wrote that "when organizationally robust, the Muslim Brotherhood is well-placed to act as a barrier to incursions by al-Qaeda."[14] Here, in Tunisia, a Brotherhood-inspired organization had risen to prominence and power, yet this doesn't seem to have provided much of a bulwark against Salafi radicalization (of course, one could argue the counterfactual that if it wasn't for Ennahda, the number of foreign fighters would be even higher). For many young, disaffected Tunisians, Ennahda didn't seem to even register as a viable option. As Yassine told me, his son "wasn't interested much in politics. He didn't know the names of politicians."

Early on in Tunisia's democratic transition, Ghannouchi and other Ennahda leaders were optimistic that they could bring Salafis into the fold. Ghannouchi saw in the Salafis some of himself. "The Salafist youth reminds me of my youth," Ghannouchi said in 2012.

> This is a generation that was born with their fathers being absent and has grown up listening, like a litany, to stories of torture and suffering. The only references that unfortunately they found were religious channels from the Gulf, with a strong Salafi message.

However, I am convinced that in ten to fifteen years Tunisia will be able to welcome back the Salafis just like it did with the Islamists of my generation who have been reconciled with moderate indigenous Islam. The ability of this country to tame the toughest plants is quite incredible![15]

In retrospect, Ghannouchi's sentiments seem rather naive. The outreach to Salafis not only failed on its own terms but also heightened secular fears that Ennahda and the Salafis were ultimately two sides of the same coin. Ghannouchi hoped to keep it in the family—in one controversial video he used "we" when speaking to a group of Salafis—but this, as it turns out, was a family hopelessly divided.[16] History didn't begin in 2011. Tunisia was the only country in the Arab world that experienced both forced secularization and brutal authoritarian rule, a particularly noxious combination. Under Ben Ali, the secret police would grow suspicious if they saw a house with the lights turned on every morning. This could only mean one thing—that someone was waking up early for the *fajr* prayer, a sign of particular piety. For decades, Tunisia had little space for open and overt expressions of religion, and this, no doubt, has had a distorting effect on the social fabric in ways that are difficult to measure. If we want to understand why Tunisia has a seemingly exceptional problem with young men fighting abroad, this unusual context—which no other country in the region shares—is at least part of the story.

It was this history that made any attempt at incorporating Salafis in the social and political mainstream a particularly challenging task, although that didn't keep some from trying. In 2012, Ennahda, now a governing party for the first time in its history, pushed for the legalization of two Salafi parties, the Reform Front and Hizb ut-Tahrir. However, neither of these parties gained traction, with most Salafis opting to stay outside the democratic process. The outcome couldn't have been more different in Egypt, where various Salafi parties entered electoral politics in full force, winning a remarkable 28 percent of the vote in 2012. In a country as conservative as Egypt, Salafi ideas had acquired mainstream respectability. After Egypt's own revolution, which took place just weeks after Tunisia's, the leading Salafi groups rightly judged that by participating, they could achieve tangible gains on their core demands. Injecting religion into every public debate, they succeeded in skewing the entire Egyptian political system rightward. On the crucial question of the constitution, they served as a sort of sharia lobby, dragging the Muslim Brotherhood further to the right in a kind of "tea-party effect." Two of the most controversial clauses of the 2013 constitution (articles 4 and 219)—highlighting the role of Islamic law and empowering the religious establishment to play an advisory role on legislation—reflected the influence of the Salafi bloc.

In contrast, Salafis, given the secularized environment, weren't well established in Tunisia before the revolution, and their numbers were far fewer. The Islamists of Ennahda might have won 41 percent of the seats in the 2011 elections, but that didn't necessarily mean there would be much room for those further to their right. What could Tunisia's Salafis really hope to accomplish by joining the give-and-take of electoral politics? Despite winning by a landslide, Ennahda, because of overwhelming secular opposition, wasn't able to include a mere mention of the word "sharia" anywhere in the constitution. The kinds of things that Salafis wanted and believed in simply weren't on the table. If anything, the example of Ennahda was a cautionary tale, of how political compromises could undermine the Islamic identity of Islamists. Ennahda was technically both a political party and a religious movement, but, as a governing party, political survival became the overriding imperative—at the expense of grassroots preaching and religious education. Without established Salafi networks that could channel the outpouring of religious sentiment in a constructive direction, Tunisian Salafism increasingly adopted the language of alienation and opposition, drawing strength from the forgotten suburbs of Tunis and impoverished cities like Kairouan. It wasn't so much the government or its policies that were the problem; it was an entire structure of power that left them voiceless, in economic, political, as well as religious terms.

Like so many of its Islamist counterparts across the region, Ennahda's successes highlighted its failures. It had succeeded in being and becoming a "normal" political party. That, by itself, was a kind of victory for a movement that wanted nothing more than to be accepted as part of the fabric of political life. But, for those of a more radical bent, being and becoming normal wasn't nearly enough.

WHAT ORGANIZATIONS LIKE the Brotherhood could offer was organization, identity, and belonging. For some, accepting the Brotherhood's moral embrace meant becoming a more committed, serious Muslim, which meant not just a better life, but a better afterlife as well. This was no small thing. The all-encompassing nature of the movement, offering education, politics, and charity, supplied meaning where society had become weak and atomized in the face of an all too powerful state. In this sense, the Brotherhood, as a model, was wildly successful. But some, particularly those of a more impatient disposition, were looking for something uncompromising and dramatic. This is where the many affiliates and descendants of the Brotherhood had come up short. With the exception of Turkey, they hadn't managed to hold power for any significant period of time.

The basic project of mainstream Islamism, if it can be summed up in a sentence, was to reconcile premodern Islamic law with the modern nation-state. But in many ways—and perhaps the most important ways—the state got the better end of the deal. The very process of state building—and the state-centric international environment which facilitated that process—had an inherently secularizing effect, forcing Islamists to limit their ambitions. Working within the state meant accepting most of the basic premises of statehood, and these premises had a secularizing bias. The most obvious example was citizenship, the building block of the modern state. In the Ottoman Empire, membership in the polity was based on your religion, with Christians answering to local religious leaders and Jews to the local rabbi. After the fall of the Ottomans, to be a citizen was to become the citizen of a nation, irrespective of religion. It is difficult to overstate the implications of this shift in legal and political legitimacy. Take, for example, the issue of blasphemy. In the premodern era, blasphemy was considered an attack not just on religion but on the state as well, since the two were intertwined. Attacking the Prophet, questioning the Quran's divine authorship, or even renouncing one's Islam were treated as political rather than strictly theological acts, more or less equivalent to treason. Apostasy, in other words, was not primarily a matter of freedom of conscience or even of "religion," at least as the word is commonly understood today. Public apostasy, in particular, or calling on others to deny Islam's foundational tenets, was perceived as a threat to the basic legitimacy of the Islamic polity (yet another example of how separating between the "religious" and "secular" falls short when discussing the role of Islam and Islamic law in premodern societies).[17]

The question of citizenship wasn't necessarily insurmountable for Islamists, but it did present some problems. If all citizens were to be "equal" in the eyes of the state, then that meant Christians, like their Muslim counterparts, should enjoy the same right to lead that state. But if the goal of Islamists was an Islamic state, then could a Christian really be expected to preside over the Islamization of the state and the implementation of Islamic law? Many in Egypt's Muslim Brotherhood didn't think so, stating in their 2007 political platform that non-Muslims, as well as women, could hold any government position except for head of state. This was the traditional Islamist position, but, in an era of growing awareness on democracy, gender equality, and minority rights, it sounded decidedly antiquated. (Brotherhood leaders backtracked by suggesting that they would not pursue a legal or constitutional ban on women or Christians seeking higher office. Rather, it was simply something that they themselves would not support; others were free to do as they chose.)

Mainstream Islamists had made a decision long ago to work slowly but surely toward the vague goal of an Islamic state. Gradualism was their method. Change began with the individual. The Muslim individual, once reformed and imbued with the original Islamic spirit, would give rise to the new Muslim family, and so on, until the sentiment rose—eventually—to the top. But to get there, they would have to accommodate themselves to the realities of state power. After all, they needed authoritarian regimes to allow them just enough space to spread their message and build their organizational structures.

In the Arab world's only democracy, Tunisia, the results were mixed. Islamists survived and even prospered—but at the price of conceding their Islamism. Meanwhile, in a country like Turkey, despite the power and popularity of Erdogan and the AKP, there were clear limits to how far Islamism could go within an already secularized state and society, no matter how many elections Islamists won. The forced secularization of the past could be "corrected," but it couldn't be undone. Elsewhere, the story, at least for Islamists, was dire. Try as they might, Islamist parties found themselves excluded from politics or, worse, brutally repressed. After the Algerian military intervened against democratically elected Islamists in 1992, the debate over Islamist participation in democratic politics intensified, with little headway. The Arab Spring held out the promise that the dilemmas of Islamist participation would, finally, reach their resolution. But it wasn't to be. Secular elites and old-regime elements would do whatever they could to marginalize Islamist movements or "eradicate" them altogether. Just as important, powerful regional actors that distrusted the Muslim Brotherhood's transnational reach, such as Saudi Arabia and the United Arab Emirates, were willing to spend unprecedented sums of money—in the tens of billions of dollars—to boost anti-Islamist forces. On the international level, the United States and the European Union, even if they opposed their outright repression, weren't exactly comfortable with Islamists either.

Islamist movements, then, weren't just fighting autocratic regimes at home; the entire regional and international order seemed aligned against them, making it all the more difficult to envision not only taking power but also holding it for any significant period of time. Even if Islamists were allowed to win elections, they would still have to contend with the inevitable opprobrium from the international community or, worse, the possibility of yet another coup. For movements already predisposed to conspiratorial thinking, the events of the Arab Spring confirmed their worst fears. The fact that Islamists were "allowed" to take power in Egypt and Tunisia before the subsequent reversals only deepened the wounds, culminating in the Rabaa massacre. It was one thing to be pushed out of power; it was quite another for the world to watch quietly while a Western-funded military killed more than eight hundred Islamist protesters in broad daylight.

Everywhere, and particularly here, Islamists saw double standards. One Brotherhood activist I spoke to was incensed about the reaction to the attacks on the French satirical magazine *Charlie Hebdo* in January 2015, which took the lives of twelve staff members. "Our blood is shed day and night and no one pays any attention," she told me, her voice rising. "Our blood is licit, but theirs isn't. Our blood is cheap and theirs isn't." She disagreed with the decision of the Brotherhood's English-language Web site to condemn the Paris attacks. Like nearly all mainstream Islamists, she opposed the killings, but she wondered why Islamists needed to so publicly and loudly condemn the killings, when no one would do the same for them. "The world's balance is off," she said.[18]

The ISIS "Model"

Mainstream Islamists had quite a lot going for them. They eschewed revolution and direct confrontation with the state, which meant that joining Brotherhood-like groups was risky, but not nearly as risky as some of the other options. Perhaps more important, these movements took pride in their pragmatism (*mawdu'iyya*) and their grasp of the domestic and international realities, however unsavory. One way of understanding Islamism is as an effort to *apply* Islam. This is what makes it both important and relevant. But this also makes it vulnerable to charges of impotence. Applied Islam must be able to move beyond the wages of self-improvement and spirituality. It needs to be pragmatic and practical, which raises the question of what happens when efforts to apply Islam in the realm of law and governance fail, and fail repeatedly?

The rise of the Islamic State, then, was a new kind of threat, fundamentally different from anything that had come before. Al-Qaeda had achieved some measure of limited popularity—or at least sympathy—during the sharp uptick of anti-Americanism in the mid-2000s, but its model was never, and never could be, a real threat to the Brotherhood's method and model of political change. Al-Qaeda was proficient at staging terrorist attacks in the West and the Middle East alike, but it proved unable to carry its successes into governance. To be sure, it could point to territorial gains in the relatively lawless regions of Yemen, Iraq, and Somalia, but its flirtation with state building was just that. More important, al-Qaeda could attract support through spectacular terrorist attacks, but its governance model, to the extent it even had one, failed to wrest the attention of the world or the imaginations of tens of thousands of would-be fighters and fellow travelers.

In retrospect, this is somewhat surprising—and counterintuitive. Al-Qaeda, after all, was more attuned to the exigencies of government than the Islamic State ever was. In William

McCants's fascinating account of al-Qaeda's evolution, based on captured private correspondence, senior al-Qaeda leaders often come across as calculating politicians. One of these "politicians" was Adil al-Abab, a senior religious figure in al-Qaeda in the Arabian Peninsula (AQAP). Abab is occasionally prone to saying things like, "The largest problem that we face here is the lack of public services such as sewage and water, and we are trying to find solutions."[19] As McCants notes, one AQAP media campaign sounded like something out of a U.S. presidential primary, featuring an interviewer asking residents, "How is it working for you now?" (One man enthusiastically replies, "wonderfully!"[20]) In a 2012 letter to his counterpart in al-Qaeda in the Islamic Maghreb (AQIM), Nasir al-Wuhayshi, the head of AQAP in Yemen, counseled gradualism in implementing the *hudud* punishments. "You can't beat people for drinking alcohol when they don't even know the basics of how to pray," he wrote.[21]

This sort of talk was not something Islamic State leaders would ever countenance. Their vision for implementing Islamic law was total and unforgiving, as those under their rule would quickly learn. Yet the Islamic State, for all of its reckless abandon and apocalyptic fantasies, did what al-Qaeda could have only dreamed of. For al-Qaeda, the idea of establishing a "caliphate" was an inspiration and an aspiration. For the Islamic State, it was something that had to be done, and as soon as possible. Waiting was for the weak. There were those in the Islamic State who, in Graeme Wood's retelling, were readying for insurrection if the caliphate wasn't announced posthaste. Like many others, the preacher Musa Cerantonio, an Australian convert and Islamic State supporter, believed that the criteria for establishing a caliphate had been met well before the official announcement of June 29, 2014.[22] One of those criteria was fairly obvious: You had to capture (and hold) enough territory. After seizing Mosul in June 2014, the Islamic State controlled a swath of territory roughly the size of Hungary or the state of Indiana. The group's takeover of Iraq's second largest city led to a newfound sense of urgency for world leaders, and particularly President Obama, who had just five months before dismissed the Islamic State as a "jayvee" team.

Considering the rapidity of the Islamic State's rise, the media sensationalism was understandable and perhaps even advisable (after all, underestimating the group hadn't proved very effective). But the most interesting part of the story wasn't so much the Islamic State's studied effectiveness at capturing territory but, rather, what it did with that territory once captured.

Unlike most terrorist groups, the Islamic State had a distinctive interest in long-term governance and state building, an interest that was reflected in the group's propaganda. One 2015 study found that around 45 percent of the Islamic State's media outreach focused on building and sustaining the caliphate, with messaging on "traffic police, charity work, judicial systems, hospitals and agricultural projects." As the study concluded, "*Come to the Islamic State,* is the message. *There is fun here, and food, and services.*"[23] As Patrick Skinner of the Soufan Group commented, "They need women and children, they believe they have a state, they now need a future."[24] Of course, this is propaganda—something that we know the Islamic State is quite good at—but it does capture the group's considerable ambition and how it viewed itself in the broader sweep of history.

SINCE ITS ABOLITION in 1924, there had never been a serious, sustained attempt to reestablish the caliphate. Now, the Islamic State—and its branches in Libya, the Egyptian Sinai, and Nigeria—could claim to have been the first. Its model of governance might have been terrifying in any number of ways, but it was a distinctive model nonetheless. The Islamic State, in stark contrast to the Brotherhood and other Islamist groups, had little interest in existing state structures. These, to them, were precisely the problem. Jihadist theoretician Abu Bakr Naji's 2004 jeremiad *The Management of Savagery*—a key influence on the Islamic State and published, appropriately, on the Internet—includes a preface titled "The Order That Has Governed the World Since the Sykes-Picot Era."[25] The Islamic State, in rather ostentatious fashion, sought to subvert the First World War–era agreement between Britain and France that drew the boundaries of Iraq, Syria, Jordan, Lebanon, and Turkey following the demise of the Ottoman Empire. After taking Mosul in June 2014, the group posted images of a bulldozer quite literally erasing the border between Syria and Iraq. It went out of its way to create a new administrative province, Wilayat al-Furat, or Euphrates Province, which straddles the legal border between the two nations, encompassing the western Syrian town of Albukamal and the eastern Iraqi town of al-Qaim.[26] Underscoring its supranational ambitions, the Islamic State has administered these two towns, one Syrian and one Iraqi, as a single entity.[27]

For Islamic State supporters, the last caliphate was the Ottoman caliphate, but the last model caliphate was that of the Prophet Mohamed's righteously guided companions. However, that didn't keep the Islamic State from viewing the Ottoman Empire's portioning off into artificial states as the original sin of the modern era (when Naji refers to the "fall of the caliphate," it isn't always clear to which caliphate he's referring). To the extent that modern states depend on some secular notion of citizenship and on legislative bodies that legislate other than God's law, they are anathema to the Islamic State's Salafi-jihadi ideology. In his treatise, Naji, unsurprisingly, accuses the Brotherhood and its ilk of trying to brainwash Muslim youth into accepting their "heretical," "rotten," and "secular" plan.[28]

The Islamic State also makes repeated reference to another period oft-cited as an Islamic golden age: the reign of Harun al-Rashid (763–809 AD) during the Abbasid caliphate, centered on the glories of Baghdad and immortalized in the-not-so-pious *One Thousand and One Nights.*[29] In strictly theological terms, the Islamic State would have no doubt considered the Abbasids—who were patrons of Greek philosophy and enjoyed poetry about wine and illicit romance—to be heretics. But references to al-Rashid serve a clear tactical purpose by giving historical weight to the Islamic State's ambitions toward Shia-majority Baghdad. As McCants writes, "It is al-Rashid's power the jihadists remember, not his impieties."[30]

SALAFI-JIHADIST GROUPS SOMETIMES refer to themselves as *muwahiddun,* or monotheists. Monotheism, in the Salafi imagination, is the belief that "all of God's Attributes found in the sacred texts should be understood in a literal manner."[31] Accordingly, because God's oneness, or *tawhid*, is all-encompassing and because it serves as the foundation of the Islamic creed, his domain cannot be subdivided. Taken to the extreme, if such unity exists in the spiritual realm, then it only made sense that it should be replicated in the temporal world, including when it came to law and governance. (In other words, if a democratically elected parliament passes a law by majority vote requiring that the state cut off the hands of thieves, it would still be a violation of *tawhid* and therefore grounds for excommunication, whether or not the resulting piece of legislation was sound.)

Although the Islamic State's forerunners in al-Qaeda offered a vicious critique of the Brotherhood's accommodation of the secular state, they fell well short of constructing a coherent alternative in its place. This is where the Islamic State filled the ideological and intellectual vacuum, offering a vision for what the new Islamic caliphate could actually mean in practice. Unlike the Brotherhood, which believed in accepting the existing state and "Islamizing" it—just as they might Islamize democracy, socialism, or capitalism—the Islamic State believed in building on top of an entirely different foundation. To achieve fidelity to the text, the logic went, one had to start from scratch, since whenever Islamism and the modern state attempted to reconcile, it was always at the expense of the former. This was a new and rather distinctive take on the applied Islam of the modern-day Islamist ideologues who came to see the nation-state as the engine of Islamization.

As we saw earlier, the tensions between the mundane requirements of governance and religious absolutism make for an uncomfortable mix. One would think that such tensions are magnified tenfold when it comes to a group, like the Islamic State, with unabashedly maximalist goals. Yet in superseding the nation-state and the regional architecture, the Islamic State, which has no state patrons, also managed to supersede the endless contortions of mainstream Islamism. In other words, the totalizing nature of the Islamic State is no mistake: It's inherent to the model.

There is little to suggest that this is sustainable in the long run (although, as ever, it raises the question of how long the long run is). As McCants elegantly puts it, "The caliphate may require caution but the apocalypse requires abandon."[32] Can an individual—or, for that matter, an entire organization—be, at once, both cautious and in the throes of reckless abandon? This tension is further magnified when the Islamic State prioritizes mass-casualty operations abroad—such as the November 2015 Paris attacks—which risk provoking massive retaliatory responses that threaten its governance project. That this balancing act is ultimately unsustainable, however, does not mean that the Islamic State's model cannot inspire a small but vociferous minority throughout the Muslim world. It has and it will. More than that, even if it were destroyed tomorrow morning, the Islamic State would still stand as one of the most successful and distinctly "Islamist" state-building projects of recent decades. This is no small feat, and to the extent that one wishes to sensationalize the group, it should probably be on these comparatively mundane grounds.

Before anything else, a state—or an organization that wishes to approximate the functions of a state—must be able to provide some modicum of law and order. For ideological maximalists, this initial step is essential. Without order, there cannot be law, and the Islamic State's project, as we will see, is very much about law. The Islamic State's biggest break was the collapse of governmental structures in both Syria and Iraq in the post–Arab Spring period. With the resulting political and power vacuum, extremist groups could come in and do what discredited governments couldn't—provide Syrians and Iraqis with a degree of security, which is what they came to crave the most. A Syrian in, say, Raqqa—the Islamic State's de facto capital—might detest the group's ideology but still "support" the Islamic State because having some security, rather than none, is preferable.

Here, oddly enough, the Islamic State's absolutism served it well. Terror and state building went hand in hand. After a country collapses and descends into a state of nature with warring factions and rampant criminal activity, any group that hopes to reconstitute order must assume a monopoly over the use of force. This means roundly defeating any pretenders to the throne and, in an already brutal war zone, requires yet more brutality, something that the Islamic State displayed in spades. What makes the group appear exotic to the Western eye is its revelry in savagery. If it was interested in governing, why alienate so many constituents? There is little doubt that the leaders of the Islamic State see savagery as religiously justified and even mandated, but such savagery also serves a number of organizational interests. Instilling terror in the hearts of your opponents undermines their morale, making them more likely to stand down, flee, or surrender on the battlefield. The Islamic State has diligently built up a frightening mythology of the world's fiercest, most hardened fighters, fighters who fear nothing and welcome death. Beyond the battlefield, the ability and willingness to inflict terrible violence has a deterrent effect, raising the costs for anyone who so much as thinks of challenging the group on its own territory. In October 2014, for example, the Islamic State systematically executed more than

150 members of a single Iraqi tribe, the Albu Nimr, after conquering the village of Heet. Instead of burying or otherwise disposing of the bodies, it left their exposed bodies in a ditch—a message to any others in Iraq who might stand in their way.[33]

But there is another way to understand the brutality of the Islamic State, and it has little do with "religion" per se, something that Naji himself hinted at in his memorable line: "One who previously engaged in jihad knows that it is naught but violence, crudeness, terrorism, frightening (others), and massacring—I am talking about jihad and fighting, not about Islam and one should not confuse them."[34] Elsewhere in his treatise, Naji admits that savagery is regrettable and even tragic but that, because of the exceptional nature of modern conflict, it becomes a necessary evil. For example, he offers a justification for an act—one of the most heinous—that the Islamic State would go on to commit seven years after he himself was reportedly killed by an American drone strike in Pakistan, in 2008.[35] "Even the Friend (Abu Bakr) and Ali b. Abi Talib (may God be pleased with them) burned (people) with fire, even though it is odious, because they knew the effect of rough violence in times of need," Naji writes.[36]

As we saw earlier, the problem of theodicy involves trying to answer that most eternal—and fundamentally human—of questions: Why does God permit evil in the world? Atheists and agnostics tend to see the existence of evil, and God's seeming indifference to it, as invalidating the very notion of the divine. Islamists, and particularly those of the Salafi-jihadi strain, see the existence of evil—in the form of the oppression of Muslims, the abolition of the caliphate(s), and the brutality of war—as part of a cosmic struggle. At this basic level, they, like anyone else, are making sense, in their own twisted way, of this most fundamental of dilemmas. If there is evil, then it must be fought. To the extent that there is humiliation—and the story of the modern Muslim world is very much a story of humiliation—then there will be those who seek to address and "resolve" that humiliation through an unwavering extremism. Here it is worth quoting at some length a fascinating essay by the author Ziya Meral. He writes:

> While we were amusing ourselves with the myopic question of how religion leads to violence we have missed out on the main question: How does violence alter religion and religious believers? Exposure to violence and injustice, seeing no "why," and looking for a "how" to survive, requires theological responses in their rawest form: What is wrong with this universe? What is right?[37]

Meral considers what might motivate a religiously unlearned European jihadist. For many would-be French, British, or Belgian fighters, the first question is not necessarily one of theology. In a May 2015 audio recording, Islamic State leader Abu Bakr al-Baghdadi highlights the realities of repression and displacement when calling on Muslims to make *hijra* (migration) to the caliphate. "We call upon you," he says, "so that you leave the life of humiliation, disgrace, degradation, subordination, loss, emptiness, and poverty to a life of honor, respect, leadership, richness, and another matter that you love—victory from Allah and an imminent conquest."[38] The European jihadist's point of departure, Meral writes, is a "moral reading of the universe through personal experience, and the finding that it is corrupt, chaotic, and unfair. That is why it was only after deciding to travel to Syria did two confused British gap-year-adventure jihadists order *Qur'an for Dummies*." He concludes, "In other words, by the time theological discussion of when and how Muslims can engage in violent jihad occurs, the more important questions will have already been asked and answered. Jihad is the *last* theological question."[39]

The brutality of Salafi-jihadists, then, is in part the product of an already brutal, senseless world. Even if these would-be holy warriors don't live in failed states themselves, they see those states all around them. Because of the powerful notion of a worldwide Muslim *umma*, they come to feel that injustice as if it were their own. It is little accident, then, that Naji's exhortations of savagery came in the context of an increasingly bloody civil war in Iraq and a growing sense of subjugation among Muslims, especially Sunnis, in the Arab world.

If you come to believe that the world offers nothing but darkness, then modern notions of restraint may sound nice, but they are of little use in a state of war. More than that, they are liabilities, and dangerous ones at that. In the Islamic State statement, "The Scout Doesn't Lie to His People," the group's spokesman, Abu Mohamed al-Adnani, says, "You went out demonstrating peacefully in Iraq for one year, and we have told you then that tolerance is useless with the Rawafid [a derogatory term for Shiites], and pacifism doesn't work with them. . . . Beware [of] laying arms down, because if you lay [them] down this time you will be slaves for the Rawafid."[40]

How the Islamic State Governs

Once territory is captured, held, and consolidated, what comes next? History is replete with examples of extremist groups (and governments) that give no quarter and take apparent joy in the shedding of blood. The more challenging task is channeling and constraining the focused brutality of the battlefield into the charges of governing. In quick order, with the international community paying little attention, the Islamic State began setting up fairly intricate and well-developed institutional structures. These structures were relatively effective—in providing basic services, for example—but, more important, they reflected a frighteningly ambitious effort to rethink the nature of the state. The elaborate legal structures—oriented around interlocking sharia courts, binding fatwas, and detailed tax codes—suggested a serious effort to institutionalize and regularize the various aspects of a new rule-based order, in what Yale University's Andrew March and Mara Revkin term "scrupulous legality."[41] In an important *Foreign Affairs* article on the Islamic State's approach to law and governance, March and Revkin note that the Islamic State judiciary is divided into three different kinds of courts, including the Supreme Islamic Court and the Diwan al-Hisba, which deals with cases referred by the morality police.[42]

In Syria's Aleppo province alone, the Islamic State's religious bureaucracy was surprisingly extensive. By June 2014, the group could claim five courts; ten Diwan al-Hisba headquarters; eleven Dawa offices; ten police stations; five "Services Offices," responsible for the distribution of water, electricity, bread, and other goods; and twenty-two "Sharia Institutes"—all with carefully delineated roles to serve a population the Islamic State claimed as 1.2 million people.[43] The Diwan al-Hisba, for instance, is charged with "the promotion of virtue and the prevention of vice," which includes "drying up the sources of evil."[44] The men of the Hisba, or morality police, are responsible for patrolling to ensure that shops are closed at prayer time, preventing fraud in markets, and breaking up drug dens and other "dens of corruption."[45] The Dawa office is responsible for proselytizing, religious education, and the publication of brochures educating the population on religious affairs.[46] In one Islamic State promotional video, a smiling foreign fighter praises the efficiency of the sharia court system in Syria's northwestern Idlib province, reveling in the "speed with which cases were settled" and noting that "with Allah's help" crime rates had fallen.[47] By imposing sharia, including the *hudud* laws, the Islamic State lowered rates of blasphemy, a "phenomenon that the people of the Levant had suffered from," the video said.[48]

The Islamic State is, in many ways, the most brutal "state" in the Arab world. Its punishments are extreme and invasive, and some are nothing short of sadistic. Yet as one analysis of its public administration in the Syrian city of Manbij notes, the group's brand of brutality is relatively consistent and predictable.[49] Arab states might be less brutal—avoiding attention-grabbing punishments like stoning, beheadings, and crucifixions—but they tend to be more arbitrary in their adjudication of crimes. In a typical Arab autocracy, citizens rarely know where exactly the red lines are. The fear of not knowing is its own kind of terror. The meting out of punishments often depends on the whims of administrators and the political connections of the accused. There is little resembling the rule of law. Instead, autocrats rule *by* law, instrumentalizing the legal system for the purposes of marginalizing opponents and accumulating personal wealth. Of course, the Islamic State is not immune to such abuses, but independent accounts of Islamic State administration suggest a less arbitrary application of law. As the aforementioned article notes, punishment of crime "is consistent because Manbijis feel confident that if you just follow ISIS's rules, then you will be ok. It is effective because few crimes go unpunished (reportedly). Of course, the arbitrariness of some crimes like sorcery or cursing religion and the difficulty of knowing the real rate of crime force us to take both of these claims with a grain of salt."[50]

In their profiles of Islamic State members, Weiss and Hassan discuss the role of "pragmatists" in shoring up support for the group. One such pragmatist, a cleric by the name of Abu Jasim, seemed well aware of the Islamic State's atrocities but had little interest in discussing them. "I see them leaving people alone if nobody messes with them," he said.[51]

In a region where, for the most part, no real notion of citizenship exists, the Islamic State offered an opportunity for its partisans to play an active role—by engaging in jihad, by supporting the economy of the nascent state, or by responding to the caliph's call for more doctors and engineers. For a Salafi-jihadi who's willing to lead a dangerous and rather austere life, it is a chance to join in building a different kind of state in the heart of the Arab world. For others who might otherwise take issue with the Islamic State and what it stands for, a limited social contract is still on offer. If you're a Sunni Muslim and agree to abide by its rules, the Islamic State will offer various social services and limited legal protections. The group will prosecute thieves (brutally), ensure markets are running fairly, and provide universal education—albeit an extremely strict one.

The Islamic State is more than comfortable co-opting existing institutions in order to maintain the provision of critical services. As Mara Revkin notes, "When ISIS takes over a new area, they allow doctors and medical service providers to keep their jobs, as long as they are willing to provide healthcare to ISIS combatants."[52] The group's ultimate interest, however, is in establishing new institutions, which allows it to become more self-sufficient and to signal its commitment to long-term state building. In its de facto capital of Raqqa, for example, the Islamic State's health department opened a new medical college, issuing a call for applications to high school graduates.[53]

This isn't exactly a welfare state, but, by the dastardly standards of the region, it's more than what's on offer in parts of Iraq, Syria, Yemen, and Libya. In this respect, the ruling bargain is rather elaborate for a protostate which has only really existed since 2013. As Revkin writes, "The ISIS social contract guarantees a limited number of legally enforceable rights—for example, the right to file complaints or charges against ISIS combatants or officials—in addition to welfare services, public institutions, and police protection. In exchange for these benefits, subjects are expected to pay taxes to the state treasury (*bayt al-māl*) and comply with the many other rules of residence in the Caliphate."[54]

The Islamic State's social contract is steeped in a distinctive legal architecture. The Islamic State muftis issuing legal codes recognize, even if implicitly, that the Quran does not contain enough minutiae to govern a state. Accordingly, the Islamic State accepts and even embraces the long-standing doctrine of *siyasa shari'iya*, or discretionary law, whereby authorities are empowered to make "lawlike decisions as long as those decisions are issued solely with the welfare (maslaha) of the Muslim community in mind."[55] This requires some degree of improvisation. The Islamic State's economic policy tackles governance issues the Prophet Mohamed likely never faced. For example, how should counterfeit goods be priced? To address this, an Islamic State mufti first cites the *hadith* "whoever deceives us, is not one of us" before diving into trademark law, arguing that counterfeiting constitutes "fraud against the buyer." In Islamic State markets, therefore, shopkeepers must price counterfeit goods lower than authentic ones, and they must clearly indicate, next to the counterfeited trademark and in the same font, that the good is an imitation.[56] Seventh-century Medina was probably not dealing with an influx of fake shoes. But the Islamic State says it could have.

With this in mind, it becomes somewhat easier to understand how some people—in a region that has long lacked any real sense of law, order, good governance, or citizenship—can support, or at least remain neutral toward, Islamic State rule.[57] In Iraq, the Sunni population found itself increasingly marginalized (or worse). In Syria, civilians suffered unspeakable atrocities under a brutal dictatorship. With such a low bar, Islamic State rule could, and often did, seem like an improvement. A year into the group's rule of the city, one Mosul resident told the *Wall Street Journal*, "I have not in 30 years seen Mosul this clean, its streets and markets this orderly."[58] The problem here, however, is that judging Islamic State governance is far from straightforward. Iraqis' and Syrians' perceptions of the quality of governance depend on their baseline of comparison, and that baseline changes over time. If those like the man in Mosul initially see the Islamic State as an improvement over, say, the Shia-dominated Iraqi government, these higher expectations soon become "normalized," as Revkin notes.[59] If governance quality subsequently deteriorates—and even if it doesn't—

residents are no longer comparing their state of affairs to what it was like under the Iraqi government, but rather what it was more recently like under the Islamic State.

In addition to governing, any state must maintain some kind of posture toward the outside world, even if it is a state that no country in the world recognizes. The Islamic State has advanced a "theory" of international relations that, to the outside observer, seems mindlessly extreme. But here, too, there was a strategy at work. Historically, Islamic law made distinctions between *dar al-islam*, the abode of Islam, and *dar al-harb*, the abode of war. As the legal scholar Mohammad Fadel explains, the Islamic State drastically departs from historic Islamic jurisprudence by arguing that, with the declaration of the caliphate, the Islamic State is the only Islamic state.[60] Therefore, everyone living outside of its territory is in *dar al-harb*. This departure is unprecedented. But everything that then flows from that heterodox premise is by the book.

In the October 2014 issue of *Dabiq*, the Islamic State's glossy English-language magazine, an article titled "The Fading Grayzone" reiterates this redefinition of *dar al-islam*. "The world has split into two encampments," it reads, "one for the people of the faith, the other for the people of kufr [unbelief], in preparation for the final malhamah [epic]."[61] By defining its Muslim opponents as apostates, the Islamic State can subject them to seemingly limitless savagery. This, for example, is how the group believes it is permissible to burn a Jordanian fighter pilot alive.

The Islamic State uses the distinction between the abodes of Islam and war to aid recruitment, arguing that it is incumbent upon Muslims to migrate to Islamic State–held territory. In his May 2015 speech, Baghdadi declared: "There is no excuse for any Muslim who is capable of performing hijra to the Islamic State, or capable of carrying a weapon where he is, for Allah (the Blessed and Exalted) has commanded him with hijra and jihad, and has made fighting obligatory upon him."[62]

There are, of course, different rules and regulations for Christians living under Islamic State rule. But it is not correct to say the Islamic State simply makes them up or "uses" Islam to legitimize the naked thirst for power and dominion. As is often the case with madness, there is a method. In chapter 2, we saw how Muslims have more *resources* available to them when it comes to applying Islam to governance. Nowhere is the Islamic State's (selective) reading of these resources more evident than in its policies toward Christians, which the group has formulated by reimagining a seventh-century document that Omar, Islam's third caliph, had supposedly requested from the newly conquered Christians of greater Syria. In May 2014, the Islamic State issued a similar document laying out thirteen rules and conditions for Christians in Raqqa—but with a few revisions. In his analysis of the document, Andrew March notes that alongside "ostentatious displays of textual literalism," the group also tacks on some new demands that help it govern and keep its tight grip on the city, including demanding that Christians "report and hand over anyone conspiring against the Islamic State" and that Christians observe the same standards of "modesty in their dress" as Muslim subjects.[63]

With a reputation for unprecedented savagery, the Islamic State could roll into Raqqa and extort every Christian in the city, without reintroducing any seventh-century scripture. It doesn't. To its recruits and partisans, this is precisely the appeal.

Whether it is governing or waging war, the Islamic State is almost always self-consciously legalistic, drawing on sources and prophetic sayings from the early centuries of Islam, from later scholars like the controversial iconoclast Ibn Taymiyyah, as well as from modern scholars associated with the ultraconservative Wahhabi doctrine of Saudi Arabia. As Graeme Wood notes, "ISIS's meticulous use of language, and its almost pedantic adherence to its own interpretation of Islamic law, have made it a strange enemy, fierce and unyielding but also scholarly and predictable."[64] This is not to say that the group is

"Islamic"—whatever that might mean—but rather that it *thinks* it's Islamic and takes its own approach to scripture quite seriously.[65] Much analysis of the Islamic State's rise concentrates on its considerable income and resources: its advanced weaponry (some of it U.S.-made), its oil production,[66] and its profit from antiquities smuggling.[67] A focus on material factors and dollar figures, however, falls well short of accounting for how and why the Islamic State is both so different and so dangerous. The group is certainly a profitable enterprise. But what distinguishes the Islamic State from any other militia in Syria or Iraq is its idiosyncratic vision of law, governance, and statehood.

In one of the earliest takes on the long-term import of the the Islamic State "model," journalist Thanassis Cambanis writes that "today, there is not a single alternative vision of citizenship being offered in the region, not even a bad one. Groups like ISIS, or for that matter Hezbollah—which in all other matters is its polar opposite—thrive because they have an idea of what a citizen should do and be."[68] One might call this "bad citizenship."

To be sure, while Cambanis's basic point still applies, the appeal of the Islamic State's ruling bargain has unsurprisingly diminished over time. The group has asked more and more from its subjects in exchange for the same or less than before. International efforts to dry up Islamic State funding sources along with the costs of endless war have imposed considerable strain on the group. Like many regimes in crisis, the Islamic State has opted to raise taxes and impose heavier fines. The temptation to overcompensate for losses at home with attacks on foreign targets exacerbates tensions within a group like the Islamic State that wants to be a state but still behaves like a nonstate actor when it comes to terrorist activity abroad. As Revkin puts it: "If ISIS begins to divert substantial resources away from governance in order to finance high-profile terrorist attacks and respond to the foreign interventions that such operations will likely provoke, civilians living under ISIS rule can expect their taxes and service fees to rise even more."[69]

Eroding support for the group's governance "model," however, can only offer limited solace. Regardless of what happens to the Islamic State or its successors in the coming years (and decades), the damage cannot be undone. The Islamic State set a new standard for extremist groups, demonstrating that capturing and holding large swathes of territory is possible and that it can be achieved without the benefit of widespread popular support. This, in addition to the terror and barbarism, is what the Islamic State *means*. And what the Islamic State means is ultimately more important than what the organization is or what it does. The Islamic State succeeded in establishing a recognizably religious state—something that nearly every mainstream Islamist group before it had failed to do. Moreover, its image of a caliphate, however much it distorted the spirit and intent of Islam, aroused the imagination of a small but significant number of Muslims. Where the caliphate had for decades been a mere idea, it had now been established. If politics—even for extremists—is the art of the possible, then the caliphate, or *a* caliphate, had now, for the first time since 1924, become something beyond imagined. It was *real*. Even those who opposed it would have no choice but to contend with its legacy.

AS WE SAW IN previous chapters, the half solutions of the Muslim Brotherhood had built-in limits. The Brotherhood and its fellow travelers hoped to accommodate Islam and Islamic law within the modern nation-state, accepting many if not most of the state's basic assumptions. Their predecessors were called Islamic modernists for a reason after all. Brotherhood-inspired organizations are, with few exceptions, at pains to minimize gaps between premodern Islamic law and modern international norms. Groups like the Brotherhood in Egypt, Tunisia's Ennahda, and Morocco's Justice and Development Party have all grown comfortable using terms like "civil state," "popular sovereignty," "women's rights," and "citizenship." This doesn't mean they are liberals—there is, after all, quite a gap between believing in women's rights and gender equality—but they are keen to be recognized as legitimate and "normal" actors in the international system. Some Islamist parties, like Ennahda, are somewhat over-the-top in their presentation, deemphasizing their Islamism and adopting the language of liberalism and universal human rights in an effort to reassure skeptics at home as well as policy elites in the United States and Europe.

Since mainstream Islamists are, generally speaking, better at politics than theology, the exigencies of politics will almost always take precedence (to be justified religiously ex post facto). Being the pragmatists that they are, they believed—though that belief is now wavering—that Islamization could be achieved by working within the Westphalian order and respecting basic international red lines. (For example, as thoroughly Islamist as they are, it's very difficult to imagine the Egyptian Brotherhood executing people for apostasy even if they could vote it into law through a majority vote in parliament.)

The model of the Islamic State is to ignore, dismiss, or supersede all such considerations entirely. Not only that, the group revels in its disregard for modern norms. As Andrew March notes, "Salafi-jihadis of the ISIS stamp eagerly embrace especially those practices that can be attributed to the Prophet and the earliest Muslims that offend modern sensibilities."[70] In this sense, the Islamic State—like all Islamist groups that must pick and choose from a vast corpus of Islamic law—are cherry pickers, even when their cherry-picking aspires to some degree of internal consistency. (There are also, it turns out, a lot of cherries).

There are few things more modern than the ostentatious and

mannered antimodernism of modern-day fundamentalists. They cannot be who they are without drawing clear, unmistakable contrasts to who they aren't. If a group like the Islamic State existed in the seventh or eight centuries, many of their offensive acts—such as requiring Christians to pay a special tax—wouldn't be nearly as offensive as they are today. It is difficult to imagine a world where mass violence and the seemingly casual violation of the human rights of entire groups of people were accepted and "normal," but this is precisely the way it was for millennia. As Fadel argues:

> In enslaving non-Muslims, and executing and immolating captured Muslims and non-Muslims, the Islamic State claims to be applying the norms followed by the early Muslim community in its wars in the 7th century; but even granting that the early Muslim communities did enslave some of its captives and execute others, their practice at that time was in accord with prevailing customary standards of war that applied to both sides in any conflict, and thus are more accurately understood to be reflections of the customary law of war in the 7th century than a reflection of the permanent Islamic rules of warfare.[71]

In other words, some of what the Prophet Mohamed and his companions did fourteen centuries ago would *of course* offend modern sensibilities, because they were operating not according to modern standards but the standards of their own time and place. To expect anything else would be absurd. (A more relatable example might be the American founding fathers, who are revered by Americans even though the things they said, did, and believed more than two centuries ago—when it came to slavery and women's rights, for example—would be considered bigoted and extremist by today's standards.) To the extent that any faith tradition is universal and applicable to all times, it must evolve with a mind to the norms and customs of the particular local context at any particular time.

Such considerations are relevant to the endless, and often detached, debate about whether Islam is "violent." Mohamed was a state builder, and state building has historically been a violent process, requiring, before anything else, the capture and control of territory. Naturally, then, the Quran *had* to have verses addressing and even endorsing the use of force. How could it be otherwise? The vast majority of Islamic scholars acknowledge, however, that the verses dealing with violence and the use of force were tied to a particular set of circumstances, and it was the task of clerics to consider when war was or wasn't justified and how it should be waged. This is the jurisprudence of jihad.[72] Yet the Islamic State has little interest—with the exception of the aforementioned Ibn Taymiyyah and a handful of other clerics—in the remarkable and varied development of Islamic law that occurred over the course of the intervening 1,200 years. As Salafis, they don't consider themselves bound by centuries of classical tradition. Tradition, we should remember, is a fundamentally conservative force. Without it, almost anything is possible. Like Protestant radicals once did, the Islamic State and its ilk wish to go back to the source and to rid the source of the corruptions of "context."[73]

AT THE HEART OF debates over the future of Islamism, in general, and the future of the Islamic State, in particular, are a set of endlessly intriguing questions about what we, as human beings, really want and what we really crave. In 1940, before the severity of Adolf Hitler's crimes had become apparent, George Orwell reviewed Hitler's *Mein Kampf.* He captured what to many of us today seems unfathomable: that Hitler came to understand something deep, unsettling, and ultimately terrifying about human nature. In the parlance of Islamists, he understood a powerful element of the *fitra*—the innate character, or instinct, of men. Orwell wrote:

> [Hitler] has grasped the falsity of the hedonistic attitude to life. Nearly all western thought since the last war, certainly all "progressive" thought, has assumed tacitly that human beings desire nothing beyond ease, security, and avoidance of pain. . . . The Socialist who finds his children playing with soldiers is usually upset, but he is never able to think of a substitute for the tin soldiers; tin pacifists somehow won't do. Hitler, because in his own joyless mind he feels it with exceptional strength, knows that human beings don't only want comfort, safety, short working-hours, hygiene, birth-control and, in general, common sense; they also, at least intermittently, want struggle and self-sacrifice, not to mention drums, flag and loyalty-parades. However they may be as economic theories, Fascism and Nazism are psychologically far sounder than any hedonistic conception of life. . . . Whereas Socialism, and even capitalism in a grudging way, have said to people "I offer you a good time," Hitler has said to them "I offer you struggle, danger and death," and as a result a whole nation flings itself at his feet.[74]

I will always struggle to understand this, whatever *this* is. Although I believe in certain things, and believe in them passionately, I have never longed to join an army, militia, or rebel force. More than twenty thousand foreigners from outside Syria have flowed into the country, to fight for a cause they clearly believe in. The Islamic State revels in death. Alongside news of its imposition of sharia law and its military victories on the field, the Islamic State's public relations team publishes celebratory photos of its own soldiers: young men, bloodied, slumped over their weaponry, dead. I sincerely hope that the desire to kill, destroy, and die for something greater than ourselves dissipates. But I am well aware that, although those desires can be mitigated, constrained, and channeled more constructively, they won't—and cannot—disappear.

Mainstream Islamism will invariably be more compelling to more people than the Islamic State ever will. The Brotherhood and its many affiliates and descendants throughout the region, though they are now struggling to various degrees, are and will continue to be mass movements, with members numbering in the hundreds of thousands and supporters and sympathizers in the millions. But if the Islamic State has proved anything, it is that a relatively small number of ideologically committed individuals can have an outsized effect on the regional and international order and perhaps even the course of history. However, for groups like the Islamic State to persist and succeed, they need a conducive environment. As much, then, as religion and ideology matter—and there should be no doubt by now that the Islamic State takes its own version of Islam quite seriously— ideas, by themselves, are not enough. The Islamic State itself was perhaps inevitable, but its rise to prominence was not. It has benefitted considerably from the manifest failures of Arab governance, of an outdated regional order, and of an international community that was unwilling to act as Syria descended into savage repression and civil war. In war zones, religious absolutism offers certainty where no certainty exists. This, too, is one of the great tragedies of the Arab Spring and its bloody aftermath.

8

ISLAM, LIBERALISM, AND THE STATE

A WAY OUT?

On January 7, 2015, two masked gunmen carrying assault rifles and shouting "God is great" burst into the offices of *Charlie Hebdo*, a French satirical magazine known for its irreverent depictions of the Prophet Mohamed, and opened fire. The massacre left twelve dead, and made martyrs of cartoonists, prompting widespread calls for solidarity in the face of attacks on free speech. Two days later, the two gunmen Said and Cherif Kouachi, French Muslim brothers of Algerian descent, went down in a dramatic gunfight with police in a printing plant in an eastern suburb of Paris, where they had been holding a hostage.

The impressive and inspiring show of solidarity at France's unity march on January 11—which brought together millions of people and more than forty world leaders—was not necessarily a sign of good things to come. "We are all one" was indeed a powerful message, but what did it really mean, underneath the noble sentiment that all people are essentially good and want the same things, regardless of religion or culture? Ten months later, the Islamic State carried out a series of coordinated attacks across Paris—at the Stade de France, Bataclan theater, and various cafés—killing 130. Even if the scope was limited to Western liberals, the aftermath of the attacks revealed a striking lack of consensus on a host of issues, including the limits of free speech, the treatment of religions versus racial groups, and the centrality of secularism to the liberal idea. Turns out, we are not all one.

French schoolteachers were reportedly dumbfounded that (some) Muslim students refused to stand up for a moment of silence after the *Charlie Hebdo* attacks.[1] But this is where confusion seeped into the debate. Within France, there was *not* a cultural divide on the killings at *Charlie Hebdo*. To even suspect that a significant number of French Muslims might support the slaughter of innocents is troubling. However, beyond the killings themselves, there is, in fact, a cultural divide—one that shines light on some of the most problematic aspects of how we in the West talk about Islam, values, and violence.

For example, French Muslims are more likely than non-Muslims to view blasphemy as unacceptable. They are more likely to think that attacks on the Prophet Mohamed and the Quran should be criminalized as hate speech and incitement, much like denial of the Holocaust is. It was problematic, then, to view condemnation of the Paris killings and affirming the right to blaspheme as two sides of the same coin. For many Muslims, they weren't. To treat them as a package deal was not only odd—after all, opposing murder and opposing blasphemy are quite different things—but also dangerous.

Polling data offers additional insight into what European Muslims think about the role of religion in private and public life. (I'll focus here on French and British Muslims, two of the largest Muslim populations in Europe.) For starters, the baseline of religious observance varies considerably. According to the 2009 Gallup Coexist Index, 58 percent of French Muslims either "very strongly" or "extremely strongly" identify with their religion, compared with only 23 percent of the French public.[2] The numbers for Britain are even starker: 75 percent versus 23 percent. Talk of a "clash of civilizations" is as unwise as it is imprecise, but there does appear to be a clash of values. Somewhat remarkably, 0 percent—yes, 0 percent—of British Muslims apparently believe homosexuality is morally acceptable. Among French Muslims, the proportion is much higher, at 35 percent, but that is still more than forty percentage points lower than the 78 percent of French people who say that homosexuality is morally acceptable.[3]

What about blasphemy? According to a 2006 Pew poll, 79 percent of French Muslims blamed the 2005 cartoon controversy—in which a Danish newspaper published various images of the Prophet Mohamed—on Western nations' "disrespect for the Islamic religion," while 67 percent of the general population blamed "Muslims' intolerance."[4] Needless to say, this is a massive gap in perception.

Britain, meanwhile, has had a spirited debate over the role of communal sharia courts in adjudicating family law. In a controversial 2008 address, the Archbishop of Canterbury Rowan Williams argued that civil and religious law need not be mutually exclusive.[5] In this sense, the question of sharia in the United Kingdom is not a theoretical one. According to a 2007 Policy Exchange survey, 28 percent of British Muslims said they would "prefer to live under sharia law." The number shoots up to 37 percent among 16- to 24-year-olds.[6] The question's phrasing isn't wholly satisfying since many Muslims might prefer a third alternative—a dualistic mix of secular and religious law—but, in any case, 28 percent is still a rather sizable minority. On a number of other issues, including female veiling, polygamy, apostasy, and whether Muslim women can marry non-Muslim men, the 16-to-24 category consistently emerges as the most enamored by strict interpretations of Islamic law. Apparently, youth and tolerant, liberal attitudes do not go hand in hand.

The implication is that people who spent their formative years in Britain are more religiously conservative than their elders, despite being immersed in the British educational system rather than, say, the Pakistani or Egyptian ones.

SOMETHING IS HAPPENING, and as frightening and foreign as it may be, it isn't necessarily a mystery. We live in an age of resurgent ideology, whether in Israel, where right-wing radicals increasingly hold sway, or in India, the world's largest democracy, where Hindu nationalists claimed a landslide victory in the 2014 elections and, with it, the opportunity to govern alone for the first time in the history of the Indian republic. In the heart of Western democracy, meanwhile, unapologetically anti-Muslim forces—who seem intent on echoing Europe's tragic past—gain ground, with their calls for an exclusivist nativism based on the imagined glories of better days. With the apparent weaknesses of neoliberalism and social democracy alike, many are searching for more meaningful politics beyond unfettered individualism. And seeking a deeper sense of belonging in one's own community—whether that's a sect, tribe, or nation—often means casting out those who aren't quite the same.

This longing, if we can call it that, tends to take a different form in the Middle East and other Muslim-majority contexts. For societies that have suffered one tragedy after another, nostalgia offers an opportunity for escape. The memory of the last caliphate lingers. The citizens of countries such as Egypt, Jordan, and Pakistan are deeply conservative, with sizable majorities supporting the implementation of Islamic law to varying degrees.[7] This, though, isn't about religion in the narrow sense. Here, for better or worse, the call to Islam, and an idealized notion of sharia, evokes a more just, equitable order—something that has been in short supply for much of the modern era.

While it certainly helps, one doesn't need to be a card-carrying Islamist to favor Islamist policies. There can be

Islamism without Islamists. In Egypt, the brutally *anti*-Islamist regime of strongman Abdel Fattah al-Sissi employed "vice squads" in a national campaign against moral "perversions."[8] In Malaysia, an ostensibly secular government repeatedly upheld bans on non-Muslims using the word "Allah."[9] In short, even non-Islamists, if they want to win elections or strike up a populist pose, need to be responsive to the public mood, and that mood is often conservative. Meanwhile, countries such as Turkey and Tunisia that took a different path and tried to reengineer their societies in an explicitly secular mold could only muster fleeting success—at the high cost of subverting democracy for decades.

One of the main arguments of this book has been straightforward enough, although its implications are more messy and complex: Islam, for a variety of cultural, historical, and theological reasons, is distinctive in how it relates to politics. In chapter 2, we saw how analogues to the Reformation are symptoms of wishful thinking—and historically imprecise to boot. Not all peoples, cultures, and religions follow the same path to the same end point. We *aren't* all the same, and why should we be?

With the implosion of the Middle East, the rise of the Islamic State, and the alienation of Muslim minority communities in Europe, many in the West have come to view the Middle East—and even Muslims more generally—as more trouble than they're worth. The subtext of a great deal of post–Arab Spring commentary is not really about Islam and violence as much as it is about a deeper philosophical divergence. Impatience and exhaustion have replaced the euphoria of those faded days of Arab springtime, which have grown increasingly difficult to remember with any real clarity. For many, particularly in the more secular corners of Europe, there is a desire, and sometimes a demand, for Muslims to embrace liberalism and an anger that they simply won't. *Why can't they just get their act together?*

The conversations taking place about Muslims—much of the time without actual Muslims present—are variations on a distinctly post-9/11 narrative. With the Middle East's intensifying violence, however, the discussions have managed to become even more problematic and paternalistic. The "Islamism is the problem" and "Islam needs a reformation" themes have become something of an epidemic, more often than not featuring an inability, or unwillingness, to understand how and why religion, in the broadest sense of the word, matters in the way that it does to so many in the Middle East.

After the attacks of September 11, 2001, the author Christopher Hitchens, essayist and critic Paul Berman, and others framed the war on terrorism as an existential struggle. They were enlisting their readers in a fight about something bigger—a fight over ideals and ideas. This wasn't just about terrorism. It was about reasserting faith in Western liberalism and defending it against Islamist totalitarianism. The prose was romantic, too, befitting a new ideological struggle that would be waged on an epic scale. In reading the great political theorist Michael Walzer's February 2015 meditation on Islamism and the left in the age of the Islamic State, I was reminded of Berman's 2003 book *Terror and Liberalism*. I remember its stark, white cover. Even the title suggested a certain clarity. Walzer's essay is a continuation of this sort of polemic, ending appropriately with a call to arms. "My friends and neighbors are not ready to enlist; many of them won't acknowledge the dangers posed by Islamist zealotry," he writes. "But there are dangers and the secular left needs defenders. So here I am, a writer, not a fighter, and the most helpful thing I can do is to join the ideological wars."[10]

To the extent that there is such a war to be fought, it is one that we in the West can't hope to win. (Perhaps polemics are needed, except that real people "don't live polemically."[11]) In the wake of the attacks on *Charlie Hebdo*, the French prime minister, Manuel Valls, declared war on "radical Islamism," a difficult war to fight without a working definition of either "radical" or "Islamism."[12] Like Valls, Walzer never really defines Islamism, instead using the term rather expansively to include not just violent extremism but any kind of religious "zealotry." He includes the Muslim Brotherhood founder Hassan al-Banna in his list of zealots, which suggests he considers the Brotherhood part of the same Islamist camp—including the likes of al-Qaeda and the Islamic State—that must be fought and defeated. On closer examination, it becomes clear that advocates of the "Islamism is the problem" line aren't just opposing Islamists but the very idea of intertwining religion and politics, an idea that enjoys widespread appeal that goes well beyond Islamists. Even if Walzer's struggle is right and just, it is almost ludicrously detached from Middle East realities. Forcing people to be liberal or secular, particularly when they don't want to be, doesn't tend to work well.

There are those who will view such arguments as culturally relativist—as examples of Western liberals reneging yet again on their liberalism. Walzer writes that "individual liberty, democracy, gender equality, and religious pluralism aren't really Western values; they are universal values that first appeared in strong, modern versions in Western Europe and the Americas."[13] This is fine as far as it goes, but it raises a question: Why aren't some "universal" values universally held? And, if they aren't universally held, is it enough to insist that they should be?

The Persistence of Foundational Divides

One can hope that somehow—despite what I have argued in this book—Islam in decades or perhaps centuries will succumb, like other religions before it, to the appeals of secularization. My argument here is not that such an outcome is impossible but, rather, that it is *improbable* and extremely unlikely in the near to medium term.

The struggle for the postcaliphate order has persisted, in one form or another, since at least 1924. A resolution of the role of religion and state has proved elusive. But to say that Islam has not changed or adapted would be inaccurate. The idea of Islamism—a product of both modernity and secularism—would make little sense to early Muslims (why would Islam need an "ism" at the end of it anyway?). Islamists hoped to "modernize" Islam so that Islam could be made safe for the state and the state safe for Islam.

Frustratingly, however, the gap between Islamists and their opponents has not only persisted but also widened. The attempts to find some kind of modus vivendi have so far fallen short, in different ways and for different reasons. Islam—a religion and, for many, a way of life—and the nation-state have proved more difficult to reconcile than the early Islamic modernists we met earlier in the book would have ever imagined. It is not a heartening thought: This is what foundational divides look like *after* repeated efforts to address and even resolve them.

There is simply no reason to think that such foundational divides will dissipate on their own. They reflect, after all, fundamental differences over the most existential of questions—the role of religion, the nature of political allegiance (to a state or to a religious community), and the meaning of the nation. In Europe, these divides reached their final and definitive resolution as Christianity's hold over Europeans weakened, giving way to something resembling a secular consensus. To be sure, conservative and evangelical Christians continued to advocate for religious values in public life. In Europe, they were a tiny, dwindling minority. In the United States, they were a larger minority, but one with a built-in ceiling of influence, and, in any case, they did not put forward—and, as I argued in chapter 2, *could not* put forward—a comprehensive legal-social project anchored in religion.

WHETHER THE ISLAMIST project—reconciling the premodern Islamic tradition with the modern tradition of the nation-state—can succeed remains an open question. The scholar of Islamic law Wael Hallaq takes issue with Islamists for precisely this reason, arguing that they have become obsessed with the modern state, to the extent of "taking [it] for granted and, in effect, as a timeless phenomenon."[14] A growing number of foreign-policy hands, including Henry Kissinger and Dennis Ross, have made the opposite case, arguing that Islamism, despite its versatility, is essentially incompatible with the Westphalian order. Ross, who served as a diplomat and advisor in the administrations of George H. W. Bush, Bill Clinton, and Barack Obama, writes that "what the Islamists all have in common is that they subordinate national identities to an Islamic identity."[15] To say that Egyptian national identity and "Islamic identity" can somehow be separated would be news, for one, to Egypt's Sissi, a supposed "Islamic reformer" who has become an unlikely darling for what we might call "stability firsters." Sissi, for instance, wrote in his U.S. Army War College thesis that "democracy cannot be understood in the Middle East without an understanding of the concept of El Kalafa [the caliphate]." The early caliphate, he went on, is "considered the ideal form of government and [is] widely recognized as the goal for any new form of government."[16] Eight years later, during his campaign for the presidency, Sissi claimed that a head of state's job included "presenting God [correctly]."[17] Meanwhile, other "moderate" U.S. allies, such as the Moroccan and Jordanian monarchies, are constitutionally endowed with religious legitimacy (the Moroccan king is *amir al-mumineen*, or "leader of the faithful").

More problematically, though, Ross and Kissinger appear unaware of, or perhaps indifferent to, the state centrism of mainstream Islamists. (This can lead to broad and sometimes bizarre brushstrokes, as when Kissinger, in *World Order*, manages to lump together al-Qaeda, Hamas, Hezbollah, the Taliban, Iran, the Islamic State, and Hizb ut-Tahrir, all in the same sentence.[18]) Islamism, of the mainstream rather than extremist variety, has attempted to make peace with the state, hoping to reform and redirect it instead of destroying it in favor of some pan-Islamic caliphal fantasy. The Brotherhood never did revolution well for precisely this reason. It did slow, plodding gradualism. Even when it flirted with revolutionary action in the 1940s, a young, ambitious Gamal Abdel Nasser, who gave the oath of allegiance (*baya'a*) to Hassan al-Banna, quickly grew disillusioned with the Brotherhood for prioritizing its own interests over that of the revolution.

These considerations make the movement to cast all Islamists as the problem—and to argue for constraining their political participation or even excluding them altogether—particularly dangerous. The demonization and marginalization of Islamists who have attempted to work within existing state structures threatens to radicalize them not so much toward terrorism but, rather, toward revolution against the state. This process has already begun and will only intensify in the absence of viable alternatives.

Across the region, the state, as it is currently imagined, is at the heart of the problem. The Arab world suffers from weak, failing, and failed states. But it also suffers from strong or "over-developed" states, to use Yezid Sayigh's apt description.[19] More than that, the Arab regional order suffers from the "exaltation" of the state—something most obvious, and frightening, in the case of Egypt, where President Sissi has enthusiastically promoted the sacralization of state power. This is the democrat's dilemma: Security and stability would seem to depend on strong states, particularly in the short term, but the demands of pluralism and at least a semblance of democracy require ultimately constraining, and even weakening, those same states.

Islamism, Liberalism, and the State

To the extent that one accepts the nation-state as the only realistic option for political organization, mainstream Islamism's state centrism is generally a good thing. Yet even if the Brotherhood and other Islamists are, or were, amenable to the Westphalian order, that didn't necessarily mean the Westphalian order was amenable to them.

This leaves us at an impasse. The state-centric order in the Arab world, for all of its artificiality and arbitrariness, is preferable to ungoverned chaos and permanently contested borders. For the Westphalian system to survive in the region, Islam, and even Islamism, may be needed to legitimate it. To drive even the more participatory variants of Islamism out of the state system is to doom weak states and strong, brittle ones alike to a long, destructive cycle of civil conflict.

Since the demise of the Ottoman caliphate, the Middle East can claim more than ninety years of accumulated experience. Yet efforts to establish inclusive and consensual states and "normalize" the role of religion have all fallen short. Even in Turkey, with its more than sixty years of off-and-on democratic experience, the problem of religion and state persists, threatening to derail the country and its politics off course.

In the post–Arab Spring era, regimes, instead of working to minimize ideological polarization, refocused their efforts on marginalizing Islamist parties. Arab autocrats convinced themselves that past failures to crush Islamists were a result of not enough force, rather than too much. From a moral standpoint, trying to eradicate mass movements that are deeply entrenched in society is problematic, to put it mildly. But even if one were willing to put moral considerations completely to the side—as, sadly, too many have—it would still be a fool's errand. After all, you can try to kill an organization, but killing an idea is a different matter. Decades of rather vigorous attempts should have made this more than apparent. In Tunisia, Libya, and Syria, Islamist organizational structures ceased to exist in any real sense after years, if not decades, of eradicationist policies. (In Hafez al-Assad's Syria, mere membership in the Brotherhood was punishable by death.) With the democratic openings of 2011, however, Islamist movements reemerged as powerful, even dominant actors in all three countries.

IN AUGUST 2014, a young British Muslim named Faheem Hussain posted an 8,500-word essay on his blog, the modestly titled *Some Thoughts*.[20] As a graduate student in philosophy, he seemed more interested in writing for himself and finding a space to tease out challenging philosophical dilemmas.

His essay, entitled "Egypt's Liberal Coup," was, more than anything else, a thought experiment. Hussain was interested in how ideas could have an almost autonomous power. Ideas, in this sense, were dangerous. No one, of course, would argue that ideas didn't matter, but what about when they not only shaped but predetermined political outcomes, making political violence all but inevitable? In the piece, he questions whether Western liberals, in a mode of knowing self-righteousness, were right to condemn Egyptian liberals for their enthusiastic support of a coup against Egypt's first democratically elected government. "What will concern us is to scrutinize philosophically whether a liberal justification for a military coup can be provided," Hussain writes. In his search for answers, he travels the canon of Western liberal thought, from John Locke to John Rawls.

The tensions between liberalism and democracy are at the heart of Hussain's inquiry. As I explored in my previous book, democracy and liberalism have generally gone hand in hand in the Western experience, to the extent that the two concepts became inseparable in the public imagination.[21] This has led to quite a bit of analytic confusion. Liberalism is about a set of rights and liberties, including freedom of speech, conscience, and religion, with the ostensible aim of expanding individual autonomy and agency. The protection of such freedoms depends on the rule of law, drawing from constitutional principles that enshrine nonnegotiable rights.[22]

The word "nonnegotiable" points to the inherent tensions between constitutional liberalism and democracy. With certain rights built into the system from the very start, clear limits are imposed on what elected majorities can hope to do. In what are today the world's most successful democracies, the foundations of constitutional liberalism preceded democracy, allowing the latter to flourish. As the scholars Richard Rose and Doh Chull Shin write, "Countries in the first wave [of democracy], such as Britain and Sweden, initially became modern states, establishing the rule of law, institutions of civil society and horizontal accountability to aristocratic parliaments."[23] Democracy, in the sense of political equality and universal suffrage, only came later, and even then only gradually.

There will always be a small minority, particularly in countries with stark class divisions, which argues that voting should be restricted to those who are literate and educated, just as various poll tests and taxes were used centuries ago to screen out the poor, blacks, and even Catholics.[24] But there is little risk of such restrictions being imposed. Even otherwise autocratic countries pay lip service to "democracy" and hold regular elections (even if the Great Leader wins 98 percent of the vote). With democracy having become such an uncontested normative good, the sequencing of the past—liberalism first, democracy later—is simply not replicable. Imagine telling a Tunisian or an Egyptian, just after unseating a dictator of thirty years, that they needed to be patient and to work on establishing the foundations of constitutional liberalism before they could vote in a new president. The fact that citizens, at least in the early glow of revolution, demand—and expect—new elections is undoubtedly a good thing, but, like all good things, it comes at a cost. Getting democracy "backward" has led to the rise of "illiberal democracies," a notion that has long been both implicit and explicit in centuries of political theory and that was popularized by Fareed Zakaria in his 2003 book *The Future of Freedom: Illiberal Democracy at Home and Abroad.*

Democracy and liberalism are both inherent goods, as most Americans would argue. In recent American history, we run into cases where democracy (as expressed through the results of elections) and liberalism (as constitutionally guaranteed rights) come into conflict. What if a state legislature votes to restrict the right of two men or two women to express their love for each other in the way that they see fit? Should state institutions be compelled to provide abortion services for women who freely make the choice, with their own bodies, to end a pregnancy after a certain period of time has passed? In some European countries, the tensions are even starker. In France, for example, that the state actively blocks women from wearing a piece of clothing—and denying them employment if they refuse—would seem to be a particularly blatant violation of individual autonomy and free expression. It is also a violation of freedom of religion and conscience. Most of these women are wearing the head scarf not on a whim but because they believe it to be an obligation commanded by God. Yet this is what the French people, as expressed through their representatives, have voted for, and because the French constitution enshrines a militant secularism, no superior court—and France already features weaker judicial review than the United States—is likely to overturn such a law.

I have chosen somewhat loaded language in phrasing these dilemmas of law and choice, because that is precisely what they are—dilemmas. When two goods come into conflict, one has to make a choice. In established democracies, where citizens reach some level of consensus over shared norms, the stakes are high but usually not *too* high. In a fragile country in transition— and one already deeply polarized over questions of stateness— the very existence of democracy is called into question, provoking wholesale repression, mass killings, and perhaps even civil war. This is what happened in Egypt. Democracy is always a good thing in theory but not necessarily in practice, and it is Egyptians, and not anyone else, who have to live with the consequences of large numbers of people exercising their right to vote.

The Islamists who won five consecutive elections—two referenda, two parliamentary contests, and one presidential poll—were not radicals bent on imposing some entirely new social order (if they had been, they probably wouldn't have kept on winning). There are numerous reasons why many Egyptians grew tired with the Muslim Brotherhood—a deteriorating economy and perceptions of growing insecurity and "chaos"—but, for secular elites and even not-so-secular elites such as Sissi and other top military brass, the overriding, existential concern revolved around the nature of the Egyptian state.

A FEW DAYS AFTER the first post-Mubarak parliamentary elections concluded in January 2012, I remember visiting my great aunt in her extravagant flat, tucked off to the side of the presidential palace in the tree-lined streets of the Cairo suburb of Heliopolis. Her place of residence—her life, really—felt a bit surreal against the backdrop of a dirty, chaotic city that always seemed on the verge of imploding in a cacophony of noise and fury. The apartment, which I had fond memories of from when I was young, was brimming with antique furniture, fine art, and the smell of something delicious being cooked up by a flurry of servants.

This time around, she was in a state of shock and confusion. She wanted to hear what I thought. It was one thing for the Brotherhood to win close to 40 percent, but how could 28 percent of her countrymen vote for ultraconservative Salafi parties? Like most Egyptians, she personally knew Brotherhood members even if she didn't quite like them, but she hadn't had much experience with Salafis and seemed totally unaware that, in the final years of the Mubarak era, they had extended their reach deep into Egyptian society. She might as well have been in mourning—and, in a way, she was. She mourned not only for what she feared Egypt might become, but for a country that she could no longer recognize, a country that was no longer really hers.

It raised the question: Was it worth it? For liberals like my great aunt, it apparently wasn't. It was easy, after the military reassumed control of the country, to dismiss people like her as liberals in name only. In a powerful, prescient piece after the July 2013 coup, the then literary editor of *The New Republic*, Leon Wieseltier, wrote that Cairo, once "the capital of Arab hope," had become "the capital of Arab despair." Perhaps more interestingly, he wrote that it was "time to stop calling these people liberals."[25] How could real liberals support a military dictator, enthusiastically joining his personality cult no less? A fair question. But, as Faheem Hussain points out, there is a long history of liberals striking Faustian bargains to protect hard-won liberties from the uncouth, and presumably all too pious, masses. "Enlightenment philosophes," writes Hussain, "were prepared to make a spoken or unspoken agreement with authoritarian interests, promising obedience and loyalty as long as core liberal values such as freedom of expression over private beliefs were maintained, at least those opinions that wouldn't trouble the security of the state." It makes sense, then, to compare Arab liberals not to Western liberals today but to liberals during a comparable period in Western history, when the choice between liberal values and mass democracy was starker. Hussain goes on, "As the philosophes did before them, Egyptian liberals find themselves within societies that have religious majorities who view liberal ideas as at best religiously problematic, or at worst foreign or infidel."[26]

Yet, as much as liberals might fear Islamist rule, this doesn't necessarily mean that they are secular. Most wouldn't identify as such, particularly in a country like Egypt where "secularism" is associated with lack of religious commitment and even atheism (for similar reasons, some liberals avoid self-identifying as liberals).[27] All the major liberal parties support—or at least say they support—article 2 of the constitution, which states that the principles of sharia are the primary source of legislation. This would, of course, be anathema to American and European liberals, but, again, it makes little sense to understand Egyptian liberals in anything but their own religious and social context.

Western liberals in the early Enlightenment were products of *their* own context. Published in 1689, John Locke's *A Letter Concerning Toleration* is a classic of the Western Enlightenment canon, and it certainly counted as "liberal," even radically so, in its own time and place. But, as might be expected of anyone who came of age in the seventeenth century, Locke's toleration had its limits. He viewed atheists and Catholics (if they refused to renounce papal authority) as dangerously subversive. Since they did not share the same loyalties to God and country, they were to be cast outside the fold of political community. As he saw it, the trust deficit was simply too large. No ruler can tolerate a church whose followers "*ipso facto* deliver themselves up to the protection and service of another prince." Atheists, meanwhile, were simply beyond the pale. "Those are not at all to be tolerated who deny the being of a God," Locke writes. "Promises, covenants, and others, which are the bonds of human society, can have no hold upon an atheist."[28]

Similarly, James Madison—one of the "founding fathers" and lead drafter of the Bill of Rights—wouldn't be considered a liberal by today's standards, considering that he owned hundreds of slaves over the course of his life. Unlike many of his contemporaries, Madison never freed any of his slaves, even upon his death.[29] Yet as Hussain writes, "to reject his liberal credentials for this would be absurd as Madison is acknowledged as one of the preeminent liberal theorists, just as absurd as it would be to deny that owning another person as 'property' thereby denying them 'inalienable rights' could be considered anything other than illiberal."[30]

One might also consider different versions of the same person and how his or her views evolve over time. If, for instance, we judged the President Obama of 2008 according to today's standards of mainstream liberalism on, say, gay marriage, then his liberal credentials would be very much in doubt. This, however, would have limited utility, since at that time the vast majority of Democrats did not yet support gay marriage. To put it differently, holding (some) illiberal views does not necessarily disqualify someone from being a liberal. Again, one must take context—time and place—into account.

With this in mind, it would be fair to call at least some Egyptian liberals "liberals," however much we might abhor their reneging on prior democratic commitments. Moreover, from the standpoint of rational self-interest, their decision to side with the military rather than let the democratic process play out is understandable and even justifiable on liberal terms. It was the most sensitive period of the transition, that early phase when decisions over elections, constitution drafting, and institution building take on outsized meaning and have lasting consequences. This is the problem of "path dependence"—the notion that the longer a certain path is followed the more difficult it becomes to change course. That the Muslim Brotherhood and Salafi parties successfully pushed for a transitional process that played to their strengths made their future entrenchment more likely. The incredibly lopsided results of the first parliamentary elections—with Islamists winning nearly three-quarters of the seats and the two major liberal parties winning only around 9 percent each—drove home the reality that liberals were at a severe disadvantage in any electoral competition. For groups that lack a clear ideology and preexisting social networks and organizational structures, building viable political parties is no easy task, taking years or even decades. Who knew how dominant the Brotherhood—and God forbid, the Salafis—would be by then? The state was the prize, and it was a prize that the Islamists would "win" if given the chance—if someone didn't stop them. The worst-case scenario, which, as many liberals saw it, was also the most likely, was that Egypt—as a state, an identity, and a nation—would be altered irrevocably. The changes would be permanent and, as Hussain puts it, the dream of "a potentially liberal Egypt" would be doomed, perhaps for a lifetime and possibly longer.[31]

For the few willing to suspend their alarmism, the best-case scenario wasn't nearly as bad, but it wasn't exactly great, either. Even if Islamists started losing, the very fact of democratization would still be a problem. To the extent that Egyptians were illiberal, any elected government was likely to reflect that illiberalism to at least some degree. Even liberal parties would have to learn the language of religion if they wanted to win outside major urban centers. Democratization, then, does something very simple—it closes the gap between government and mass sentiment, and in a center-right country this effectively skews the entire political system rightward. Islamism, in this sense, doesn't necessarily require Islamists (whereas liberalism generally requires liberals).

As the only case where Islamists have won consecutive elections (and managed to stay in power), Turkey's recent experience with democracy looms large. There was a time when the AKP seemed like a model for a kinder, gentler Islamism that liberals could learn to live with. But in the light of Erdogan's illiberal turn, Arab liberals look at Turkey and see their fears vindicated. With secular parties weak, disorganized, and lacking anything resembling a coherent message, it becomes difficult to envision how the AKP could lose an election anytime soon. Even in the June 2015 parliamentary elections, the AKP—after alienating everyone but its own base, grappling with Erdogan's authoritarian tendencies, and presiding over a sputtering economy, as well as epic foreign policy failures— still managed to win 47 percent of the seats. (The party was able to essentially win back what it lost in snap elections just five months later.)

Turkey's shift toward illiberalism reinforced secularist

fears, including in Tunisia, over Islamists' ultimate intentions. Regardless of what Islamists do, and even if they demonstrate "good" behavior, there will be a significant subsection of society that will see them as existential threats. That they may seem "moderate" today only makes them more threatening, because they are hiding who they *really* are. In this vein, liberals feared Morsi and the Brotherhood not necessarily for what they had done, but for what they might do in the future. Needless to say, it is difficult to have a rational debate about something that hasn't actually happened yet.

Even when Islamists aren't the problem, they *are* the problem. Even when they make historic compromises, as in Tunisia, they still provoke antidemocratic behavior on the part of a powerful array of domestic, regional, and international actors. The goal, then, must be to build in guarantees for those who wish to derail democracy out of fear of what it might bring. In other words, it is the region's most antidemocratic actors—who contrary to popular belief aren't Islamists but secularists—who must be catered to and reassured. Admittedly, this shifts the burden onto Islamist parties, which might sound like the political equivalent of blaming the victim. But politics isn't a morality play, and it certainly isn't fair. For at least the short to medium term, Islamists will need to temper their ambitions and restrain themselves in the quest for power. But that can only take you so far. The only long-term solution is to find a place for Islam, in its varied political forms, within the democratic process.

IT IS DIFFICULT TO imagine it now, but continental Europe struggled with foundational divides—with periodic warnings of civil war—as recently as the 1950s. Belgium, Switzerland, Austria, and the Netherlands were divided into ideologically opposed subcultures, sometimes called "spiritual families" or "pillars." These countries became models of "consensual democracy," where the subcultures agreed to share power through creative political arrangements.

If we have learned anything, though, it is that lessons learned in Europe are not easily applied to the Middle East. Consensual democracy works best when there are multiple centers of power in society, none of which is strong enough to dominate on its own. While this more or less holds true in Lebanon, and even then precariously, it is not applicable in much of the region. In the countries we've focused on—Egypt, Turkey, and to a lesser extent Tunisia—the perception that Islamists are too strong and secularists too weak makes polarization significantly worse than it might otherwise be.

In continental Europe, the lines were also drawn more clearly. In Belgium, for instance, there were distinct groups of Flemish and Walloon that could be plainly identified. Our three country cases, however, are relatively homogenous. More homogeneity is almost always viewed as a positive factor in forging national identity, but it can also have its drawbacks. Islamists and non-Islamists are different, but not different enough. They live in the same cities, go to the same schools, visit each other on holidays, and sit together at family dinners. This can make it better. It can also make it worse.

Despite this surface-level homogeneity, the underlying principles of consensual democracy—that power should be shared, dispersed, and restrained—can still be useful. A "pure" parliamentary system with only a ceremonial president could have helped alter Egypt's course. But this is not what Egypt had. From independence onward, the Egyptian president had always been a towering figure in the country's politics, casting a shadow on everything else. As the first elected civilian president, Morsi was, in fact, weaker than all of his predecessors, yet he still enjoyed disproportionate powers in Egypt's centralized, top-heavy system. Not surprisingly, then, he became a lightning rod for the opposition. The fact that presidential contests are all or nothing—only one person, after all, can win—further heightened the existential tenor of political competition. These dynamics allowed the military to capitalize on the anger that had coalesced around the person of President Morsi.

A parliamentary system, on the other hand, would have put power in the hands of a strong prime minister, who could have much more easily been replaced—without necessitating a rejection of the democratic process Egyptians had agreed to less than a year earlier. Early elections and no-confidence votes are regular features of parliamentary democracy.[32] Presidents, however, are generally difficult to impeach, requiring voters to wait four years or longer to express their buyers' remorse. Despite their claims to the contrary, presidents invariably represent one party—their own. A prime minister, on the other hand, is more likely to govern in coalition with other parties, making him accountable to a larger number of stakeholders. All other things being equal, parliamentary systems also make coups against elected leaders less likely. Of course, coups can and will still happen, but, even when they do, parliamentarism offers a clearer way out. Ousted parties can more easily reconstitute themselves in parliamentary systems, as Turkey's recurring cycle of military intervention followed by Islamist success suggests.

Political design can only take you so far, however. At some point, parties and politicians must work in good faith to lower the political stakes. There are any number of creative possibilities. Parties, for example, can agree to "postpone" debates on the divisive issues that are likely to fracture the unsteady, diverse coalitions that toppled the authoritarian regimes in the first place. This, though, is anathema to how we like to think of democracy's development. After thirty years of Hosni Mubarak's rule, it was only natural to expect Egyptians to want to debate anything and everything among themselves; discussions over the role of religion had been suppressed for far too long. But by instituting an "interim period" before contending with the most divisive issues, democratic competition could be regularized—both sides could, potentially, gain enough trust in each other. Of course, the ideological polarization—over perennial touchstones like alcohol consumption, sex segregation, women's rights, and educational curricula—would inevitably come. It was only a question of whether, when it did, Egyptians would be better equipped to work through the polarization peacefully, without recourse to violence. Here, as ever, the rule of thumb is *not* to assume the end of ideology or some kind of natural moderation process. Rather, we should assume foundational divides as a constant, then work around them to limit their negative effects.

The Liberal Veto and Its Limits

One way to address foundational divides is to build "liberal vetoes" into the political system from the beginning. The most effective way to do this is through permanent guarantees in a constitution. The U.S. Bill of Rights is, in this sense, a towering achievement, imposing clear limits on the desires of the majority. If members of Congress wanted to issue legislation prohibiting Muslims from holding cabinet positions, for instance, they wouldn't be able to, however large their majority. The constitution wouldn't allow it. But this raises its own set of difficult questions. After a revolution, who gets to write the constitution?

There are three possibilities. Historically, elite commissions and committees often drafted constitutions, the most notable example being the United States in 1787. The postwar Japanese constitution, meanwhile, was commissioned by General Douglas MacArthur and drafted by "approximately two dozen Americans during Japan's postwar occupation, with relatively minor revisions made by Japanese government officials and virtually no public consultation," writes Alicia Bannon.[33] When Corazon Aquino led the Philippines' democratic transition in the 1980s, she appointed a fifty-member commission that drafted a constitution that continues to govern the Philippines to this day. Such top-down approaches have generally fallen out of favor.

Today, the most common approach, adopted by both Tunisia and Egypt in 2011, is to do it democratically. Tunisia directly elected a parliament that doubled as a constituent assembly, while in Egypt, the elected parliament selected the hundred men and women whose sole job was to draft a new constitution. This is the most obvious—and, I would argue, fair—approach. To the extent that societies should be able to chart their own course, why shouldn't the population have a say on the basic framework of their political system-to-be? To shut ordinary citizens out is to undermine the legitimacy of any constitutional document, particularly in polarized societies where one group is likely to dominate any appointed body to the exclusion of others. There is simply no way to achieve "fair" representation except through some kind of democratic selection process (which is precisely why we have democracy in the first place). To appoint, rather than elect, a committee also raises the question of who, exactly, is doing the appointing. If a constitutional committee is largely made up of old-regime elites, for example, it can taint the process from the very beginning.

Tunisia's and Egypt's constitution-drafting processes reflected the international consensus around the need for popular participation and buy in. A democratic constitution, writes Vivien Hart, an expert on how constitutions transform conflict, "is no longer simply one that establishes democratic governance." Rather, "it is also a constitution that is made in a democratic process."[34] Hart concludes that "participatory constitution making is backed by an international norm and an emerging legal right," based on an increasingly expansive understanding of the United Nation's Declaration of Human Rights.[35]

The democratic approach to constitution drafting, however, is problematic for the same reasons that democracy is problematic—it can lead to illiberal outcomes in societies where large numbers of citizens, perhaps even a majority of the population, espouse illiberal beliefs and attitudes. If Egypt had directly elected its constituent assembly, close to 75 percent of the members would have been Islamist. As it turned out, "only" 50 percent were—nearly 25 percent less than their actual electoral weight would have suggested. But while Islamists may have seen this as a concession, liberals, rightly, saw the constituent assembly as what it still was: an Islamist-dominated body.

In her study of Kenya's constitution-drafting process in the early 2000s, Bannon labels the presumed need for broad participation "the participation myth"—certain conditions can, in fact, "make broad participation either helpful or undesirable in light of an individual country's circumstances."[36] While also citing negative experiences in Nicaragua and Chad, Bannon argues that the broadly participatory process in Kenya was not only expensive, in terms of "expense, time, and opportunity cost," but also divisive, leading to "ethnic pandering and polarization."[37]

Lastly, instituting a democratic selection process while, at the same time, agreeing on a limited number of "supraconstitutional principles" is a third path. Islamists and secularists, however, are unlikely to agree on nonnegotiables. (If they could, then the ideological divide wouldn't be nearly as large as it currently is.) In the end, something—or someone—has to give. Either Islamists voluntarily concede some of their preferences, agreeing for example to include only mild Islamic language, or a supreme body, perhaps one where Islamists are underrepresented, must formulate something resembling a "bill of rights" binding on all participants.

This third way would loosely mirror the constitution-drafting process in postapartheid South Africa. Nelson Mandela's African National Congress initially wanted to elect a constituent assembly to draft the constitution but gave in to the concerns of F. W. de Klerk's National Party, which feared a new constitution would not adequately protect the white population. In 1993, twenty-six parties negotiated a set of supraconstitutional principles, similar to the U.S. Bill of Rights, before directly electing a constituent assembly.[38] Mandela and de Klerk soon shared the Nobel Peace Prize.

Practicality aside, the South African model—in part because we know, after the fact, that it was successful—sounds appealing. I should include a major caveat here, however. As a "small-d" democrat, I am deeply uncomfortable with nondemocratic solutions that circumscribe self-determination. Democracy is about representing and reflecting the popular will, and to limit or subvert that on something as fundamental as a constitution sets a troubling precedent. Why shouldn't Egyptians, Jordanians, or Turks have the right to try out an alternative ideological project outside the confines of liberal democracy, however much we might disagree with it? That should be their choice, not anyone else's. However, that conversation is moot if democracy fails to take hold in the first place. A democratic approach to constitution drafting in Egypt ended up fueling polarization and pushed liberals to consider extralegal regime change. If we wish to prioritize the survival of democracy in hostile conditions, then some things, at least in the short term, will need to be prioritized over others. These are necessary evils.

This means that, during any constitution-drafting process, Islamists will have to exhibit self-restraint and agree to postpone ideological objectives. If they are unwilling to do so, liberal supraconstitutional principles, per the South African model, will need to be enacted—imposed, really—before the drafting process begins. Islamists would no doubt protest any such arrangement as "unfair," and they would be right. Liberalism is only neutral to those who are already liberals.[39] As the literary theorist and legal scholar Stanley Fish argues, "It cannot be a criticism of a political theory or of the regime it entails that it is unfair. Of course it is. The only real question is whether the unfairness is the one we want."[40]

But if a liberal veto is an evil, however necessary, it need not be permanent. Even robust liberal vetoes can be overridden, so there will still be opportunities in the future—after a democratic transition passes through its most vulnerable phase—for countries to experiment with more explicitly religious policies, if enough citizens decide that's what they would like to do. This basic premise applies even in the world's liberal democracies, which are not necessarily immune to bouts of illiberalism. It is only really a question of how high the majoritarian bar is. In the United States, two-thirds of Congress and 75 percent of the states can amend or repeal provisions in the Bill of Rights. For example, they could theoretically pass a constitutional amendment banning abortion. In countries like Egypt, Tunisia, and Turkey, where alcohol is currently legal and relatively easy to find, the issue of alcohol consumption is a touchstone for endless "what if" questions. Yet Prohibition happened in the United States, with large majorities in the Senate and House of Representatives as well as forty-six of forty-eight states backing the Eighteenth Amendment (of course, banning alcohol in the United States wasn't justified on primarily religious grounds, while in Muslim-majority countries, prohibition is seen as fulfilling an explicitly Quranic directive).

As the votes on Prohibition demonstrate, the majority, if it's large enough, can supersede the liberal veto. In this sense, built-in constraints and constitutional guarantees aren't enough, on their own, to limit illiberal outcomes. American liberalism depends, more fundamentally, on the electoral distribution of the population. There simply aren't enough far-right Christian evangelicals to change the nature of the state, assuming they would even want to. The vast majority of Americans are liberals (in the classical sense), and basic liberal norms are deeply entrenched in American political culture. Liberalism, then, needs liberals to survive and prosper. What, though, about countries where the electoral distribution of the population is lopsided in the other direction?

. . .

THE FOUNDATIONAL DIVIDES that I have focused on over the course of this book are as real and organic as they could possibly be. They are genuine, deeply felt, and revolve around "big" issues. But they are also new and manufactured. It is possible to be both at the same time. Polarization is inevitable when Islam ceases to be, as it once was, a source of unity and solidarity and becomes instead the province of one particular party. Parties compete for state power, and when the state is strong and overdeveloped, it raises the stakes considerably, fueling an endless cycle of polarization.

The three mainstream "models" of reconciling religion and state—the traditional Brotherhood model, the AKP model in Turkey, and the Ennahda model in Tunisia—all have their drawbacks, as we have seen. Turkey, at least from an Islamist perspective, has been the most successful of the three, insofar as Islamists have been able to fend off coup attempts and stay in power for a significant period of time. Turkey had advantages, however, that most Arab countries lack. As a NATO power and regional leader in its own right, Turkey was less susceptible to outside attempts to derail the democratic process. Turkey benefitted tremendously from the prospect of EU accession, which provided a major constraint on antidemocratic domestic actors such as the military. Yet Turkey also confirms what many already suspected: Islamist participation in the democratic process, even in the best of circumstances, is inherently polarizing and destabilizing.

It is ironic that we've come to this. For decades, Western observers encouraged Islamists to embrace the democratic process. This meant deemphasizing their strictly religious origins and practicing politics through newly established political parties. The goal, after all, was to transform a religious movement into something more "normal"—something that could better fit the contest for power inherent to the modern nation-state.

At first, Islamists were reluctant, but they were quick learners, realizing soon enough that as the largest movements in their respective countries, they, by the sheer force of numbers, would be the primary beneficiaries of the expansion of electoral democracy. Across the region, they formed political arms, establishing some degree of functional separation between movement and party. They not only came to terms with elections; they came to see elections as a necessary—sometimes the only—means of large-scale political change. In this sense, Islamists, like nearly everyone else, were products of a post–Cold War euphoria, and rightfully so. For all its faults, this *was* the best way to push for gradual political change. There weren't any viable alternatives. Or, to put it differently, Islamists had lost the ability to think beyond the very things—namely party, state, and democracy—that they had initially doubted.

The gap between Islam and democracy, and even Islamism and democracy, appeared to be closing. This was the promise of a new era, where anything could be resolved through peaceful participation and democratic commitment, just as long as there was enough of it. But with the advent of the Arab Spring, a few things became clear: Islamists didn't go well together with democracy, not so much because of what they did, but because of the fears they provoked and the polarization they fueled. Even in the best of circumstances—when they made one compromise after another—the divisiveness remained. The problem was that the polarizing effects of participation were built in to the Islamist project. Religion—the metaphysical rather than the material—was the fault line at the very heart of the new Middle East.

It is possible to hope, and to wait. But even if the arc of history bends, it doesn't necessarily bend in the right direction, whatever that may be. It doesn't necessarily bend toward liberalism or toward some imagined end of ideology where parties decide to content themselves with fights over the intricacies of economic platforms.

In Europe, the conclusion of the continent's wars of religion only truly came after Christianity's slow drift into the shadows of politics. There was nothing left to fight for, because there weren't enough people willing to fight for it. In this sense, secularization offered a solution for weary European nations: It diminished the stakes, making politics less fraught and dangerous. When substantive divides did reemerge—with the rise of communists or, later, far-right populists and neofascists—the democracy that had been forged over decades was strong enough to withstand the pressure.

If Islam is, in fact, distinctive in how it relates to politics and if a reformation is not in the cards—or if it's already happened—then the foundational divides that have torn the Middle East apart will persist, and for a long time to come. People dislike, fear, and even hate each other for legitimate reasons. As we have seen, the problem of religion and state has no easy resolution. It has been nearly a century since the demise of the last caliphate, yet the struggle has only intensified. The very project—political Islam—that proposed a resolution to the divide has only exacerbated it. They did what they were supposed to do, but perhaps too well. The more Islamists came to terms with democracy, political parties, and the nation-state, the more they found themselves rejected and repressed. It might as well be the region's motto: Be careful what you wish for.

The hope, then, might need to be modest. Egyptians, Tunisians, and Turks—and many others—will continue to see the world in fundamentally different ways and want fundamentally different things, and that's fine as far as it goes. But they will need to agree, however reluctantly, to do so through the untidy, inconclusive give-and-take of politics. This will, at least initially, prove both messy and destabilizing. But the postcaliphate order will have only truly begun when something inclusive, legitimate, and lasting takes root. For that to happen, the democratic process must play out for a long enough period so that Islam, Islamism, and democracy can evolve in a natural, uncontrived fashion.

Islamist movements, for their part, may need to unlearn some of the last several decades of checkered democratic experience. Elections are a means, not an end. And in the West, we've generally gotten it backward; the problem with most Islamists isn't their opposition to the modern nation-state but, rather, their obsession with it. That obsession has worked against them, producing the opposite of what they intended—even more instability and division and over powerful states ripe for authoritarian capture. There was a time when Islamists saw society, rather than the state, as the engine of social transformation. The legacy of a failed Arab Spring and a new "caliphate" called the Islamic State will likely be this: forcing them, and perhaps us as well, to reimagine the nature of political change.

NOTES

1: "TO TAKE JOY IN A MASSACRE"

1. Human Rights Watch, "UN Human Rights Council: Adoption of the UPR Report on Egypt," March 20, 2015, http://www.hrw.org/news /2015/03/20/un-human-rights-council-adoption-upr-report-egypt; see also Human Rights Watch, "Egypt: Security Forces Used Excessive Lethal Force," August 19, 2013, http://www.hrw.org/news/2013/08/19 /egypt-security-forces-used-excessive-lethal-force.
2. Philip Gourevitch, *We Wish to Inform You That Tomorrow We Will Be Killed with Our Families: Stories from Rwanda* (New York: Picador, 1998), p. 7.
3. James Piscatori, "Imagining Pan-Islam: Religious Activism and Political Utopias," *Proceedings of the British Academy* 131 (Oxford: Oxford University Press, 2004), p. 425; for more on the historical development of the caliphate, see Reza Pankhurst, *The Inevitable Caliphate? A History of the Struggle for Global Islamic Union, 1924 to the Present* (London: Hurst, 2013).
4. Mark Lilla, "The Politics of God," *New York Times Magazine*, August 19, 2007, http://www.nytimes.com/2007/08/19/magazine/19Religion-t .html?ref=magazine&pagewanted=all.

5. "A New Statement by IS Spokesman Abu Muhammad al-'Adnani ash-Shami, Dated September 22, 2014," September 25, 2015, https://pietervanostaeyen.wordpress.com/2014/09/25/abu-muhammad-al-adnani-ash-shami-indeed-your-lord-is-ever-watchful/.
6. Interview with author, Muslim Brotherhood member, August 9, 2010.
7. Robert Kagan, "Why the U.S. Wants to Avoid Conflict," *Wall Street Journal*, http://www.wsj.com/articles/robert-kagan-why-the-u-s-wants-to-avoid-conflict-1409942201.
8. Francis Fukuyama, "The End of History," *National Interest*, Summer 1989, p. 18.
9. *Muslim Public Opinion on US Policy, Attacks on Civilians and al Qaeda*, Program on International Policy Attitudes at the University of Maryland, April 24, 2007, http://www.worldpublicopinion.org/pipa/pdf/apr07/START_Apr07_rpt.pdf.
10. Douglas M. McLeod, "Support for the Caliphate and Radical Mobilization," START *Research Brief*, January 2008, http://www.start.umd.edu/sites/default/files/files/publications/research_briefs/20080131_Caliphate_and_Radicalization.pdf.
11. Scott Atran, "ISIS Is a Revolution," *Aeon*, December 15, 2015, https://aeon.co/essays/why-isis-has-the-potential-to-be-a-world-altering-revolution.
12. Michael Cook, *Ancient Religions, Modern Politics: The Islamic Case in Historical Perspective* (Princeton: Princeton University Press, 2014), pp. 299–300.
13. Pew Research Center, "The World's Muslims: Religion, Politics and Society," April 30, 2013, http://www.pewforum.org/files/2013/04/worlds-muslims-religionpolitics-society-full-report.pdf.
14. For more on the applicability and purposes of the *hudud* punishments, see Khaled Abou El Fadl, "Life in the Light of God: Islamic Law, Ethical Obligation and the Problem of Punishment," *ABC Religion and Ethics*, September 30, 2014, http://www.abc.net.au/religion/articles/2014/09/30/4097456.htm.
15. YouGov UK Siraj, "Survey Results: Egypt Poll," April 2011, http://today.yougov.co.uk/sites/today.yougov.co.uk/files/ygs-archives-yougovsiraj-egypt-200411.pdf.
16. "Arab Barometer: Jordan Country Report," University of Jordan, August 2011, p. 23, http://www.arabbarometer.org/sites/default/files/countyreportjordan2_0.pdf.
17. Elie Kedouri, *Democracy and Arab Political Culture* (Washington, D.C.: Washington Institute for Near East Policy, 1992), p. 1.
18. Mark Landler, "Obama Seeks Reset in Arab World," *New York Times*, May 11, 2011, http://www.nytimes.com/2011/05/12/us/politics/12prexy.html?_r=0.
19. Reuters Africa, "TEXT-President Mubarak's Speech After Mass Protest," February 7, 2011, af.reuters.com/article/idAFLDE7102JP20110201.
20. Fukuyama, "End of History," p. 18.

21. Shadi Hamid, *Temptations of Power: Islamists and Illiberal Democracy in a New Middle East* (Oxford: Oxford University Press, 2014).
22. Interview with author, Rached Ghannouchi, February 13, 2015.
23. Interview with author, Gehad al-Haddad, August 14, 2013.
24. "Aspen Ideas Festival, July 2014," *The Atlantic*, http://www.theatlantic .com/live/events/aspen-ideas-festival/2014/.
25. Alasdair MacIntyre, *After Virtue: A Study in Moral Theory* (Indiana: University of Notre Dame Press, 2007), p. 253.
26. Ibid., p. 236.
27. Sheri Berman, "The Continuing Promise of the Arab Spring," *Foreign Affairs*, July 7, 2013, https://www.foreignaffairs.com/articles/middle -east/2013-07-17/continuing-promise-arab-spring.
28. Tarek Osman, "Imagining a New Arab Order," *Cairo Review of Global Affairs*, December 3, 2014, http://www.aucegypt.edu/gapp/cairoreview /pages/articledetails.aspx?aid=712.
29. Koert Debeuf, "Islamism. It's Losing Currency," *Free Arabs*, December 15, 2014, http://www.freearabs.com/index.php/ideas/102-stories /1924-jb-span-trend-jb-span-islamism-is-losing-currency.
30. Patrick Kingsley, "Egypt's Atheists Number 866—Precisely," *Guardian*, December 12, 2014, http://www.theguardian.com/world/2014/dec/12 /egypt-highest-number-atheists-arab-world-866.
31. Henry Kissinger, *World Order* (New York: Penguin, 2014), p. 2.
32. Noah Feldman, *The Fall and Rise of the Islamic State* (Princeton: Princeton University Press, 2008), pp. 6–7.
33. Osman, "Imagining a New Arab Order."
34. Barack Obama, CNN interview with Fareed Zakaria, February 1, 2015, http://cnnpressroom.blogs.cnn.com/2015/02/01/pres-obama-on -fareed-zakaria-gps-cnn-exclusive/.
35. "President Obama Delivers a Statement on the Murder of James Foley," August 20, 2014, www.whitehouse.gov.
36. Plato, *The Republic*, trans. B. Jowett (New York: Random House, 1974), p. 189.
37. Atran, "ISIS Is a Revolution."
38. Francis Fukuyama, *The Origins of Political Order* (New York: Farrar, Straus and Giroux, 2012), p. 29.
39. Noah Feldman turns the modernization paradigm on its head when he argues that "if one notices that, for thirteen hundred years, Islam provided the dominant language of politics in the Middle East, and if one treats the twentieth century as a brief aberration . . . then the reemergence of Islam looks like a return to the norm, and the rise of a secular nationalism looks like the historical phenomenon in need of special explanation," Feldman, *The Fall and Rise*, p. 20.
40. Fukuyama, *The Origins of Political Order*, p. 38.
41. For a discussion of the meaning of *asabiyah*, see Bruce Lawrence, introduction to Ibn Khaldun, *The Muqaddimah* (Princeton: Princeton University Press, 2015), pp. xiv–xv.

42. Joseph Liow, "The Arab Spring and Islamist Activism in Southeast Asia: Much Ado about Nothing?" Working Paper, Brookings Institution, Rethinking Political Islam Series, August 2015, http://www.brookings.edu /~/media/Research/Files/Reports/2015/07/rethinking-political-islam /Final-Working-Papers/Southeast-Asia_Liow_FINALv.pdf?la=en.

43. Robin Bush, "Regional Syari'ah Regulations: Anomaly or Symptom?" *Expressing Islam: Religious Life and Politics in Indonesia*, ed. Greg Fealy and Sally White (Singapore: Institute of Southeast Asian Studies, 2008), pp. 3–4, 11, https://asiafoundation.org/resources/pdfs/ShariaRegula tions08RobinBush.pdf.

44. Ibid., p. 7.

45. Liow, "Arab Spring," p. 7.

46. "The World's Muslims: Unity and Diversity," Pew Research Center, Forum on Religion and Public Life, August 9, 2012, p. 131, http://www .pewforum.org/Muslim/the-worlds-muslims-unity-and-diversity.aspx.

47. Ibid., p. 201.

48. *Qahira al-Youm* [*Cairo Today*], November 27, 2014; see @shadihamid, Twitter, https://twitter.com/shadihamid/status/538086175169589248.

49. Arend Lijphart, "Consociational Democracy," *World Politics* 21 (1969), p. 219.

50. Ibid.

2: IS ISLAM "EXCEPTIONAL"?

1. Wael B. Hallaq, *The Impossible State: Islam, Politics, and Modernity's Moral Predicament* (New York: Columbia University Press, 2013), p. ix.

2. Fouad Ajami, *The Arab Predicament: Arab Political Thought and Practice Since 1967* (Cambridge: Cambridge University Press, 1981), p. 55.

3. Mahmoud Mohamed Taha, *The Second Message of Islam* (Syracuse: Syracuse University Press, 1996).

4. Michael Walzer, "Introduction: The Jewish Political Tradition," in *Jewish Political Tradition*, volume 1, *Authority*, ed. Michael Walzer, Menachem Lorberbaum, and Noam J. Zohar (New Haven: Yale University Press, 2000), p. xxii.

5. Walzer, Lorberbaum, and Zohar, "The Gentile State," in *Jewish Political Tradition*, pp. 433–34.

6. David Ben-Gurion, "The Eternity of Israel," in *Authority*, ed. Walzer, Lorberbaum, and Zohar, p. 491.

7. Natan Sachs, e-mail message to the author, September 7, 2015.

8. Reza Aslan, *Zealot: The Life and Times of Jesus of Nazareth* (New York: Random House, 2013), p. xxix.

9. Brad Gregory, *The Unintended Reformation: How a Religious Revolution Secularized Society* (Cambridge: Belknap Press of Harvard University Press, 2012), p. 134.

10. Aslan, *Zealot*, p. xxviii.
11. Sahih Muslim, Book 36, Hadith 199, Sunnah.com, http://sunnah.com /muslim/36/199. See also http://sunnah.com/search/?q=pumpkin +soup.
12. Joshua Ralston, *Law and the Rule of God: A Christian-Muslim Exchange* (Ph.D. dissertation, Emory University, 2015), p. 132.
13. Ibid., p. 139.
14. Ibid., p. 111.
15. "Chicago Statement on Biblical Inerrancy," International Council on Biblical Inerrancy, http://library.dts.edu/Pages/TL/Special/ICBI_1.pdf.
16. John Renard, *Islam and Christianity: Theological Themes in Comparative Perspective* (Berkeley: University of California Press, 2011), p. 30.
17. Maurice Borrmans, *Guidelines for Dialogue between Christians and Muslims* (New York: Paulist Press, 1990), p. 104.
18. Daniel A. Madigan, "People of the Word: Reading John's Prologue with a Muslim," *Review and Expositor* 104 (2007), p. 93.
19. Michael Cook, *Ancient Religions, Modern Politics: The Islamic Case in Historical Perspective* (Princeton: Princeton University Press, 2014), p. xv.
20. Shahab Ahmed, *What Is Islam? The Importance of Being Islamic* (Princeton: Princeton University Press, 2016), p. 6.
21. Ibid., p. 223.
22. David D. Kirkpatrick, "Egypt's New Strongman, Sisi Knows Best," *New York Times*, May 24, 2014, http://www.nytimes.com/2014/05/25 /world/middleeast/egypts-new-autocrat-sisi-knows-best.html.
23. Cook, *Ancient Politics*, p. 213.
24. Max Weber famously argued that capitalism evolved in northern Europe because of the Protestant, and more specifically, Calvinist work ethic.
25. Gregory, *Unintended Reformation*, p. 136.
26. Peter Brown, quoted in Gregory, ibid.
27. John Witte, Jr., "Facts and Fictions about the History of Separation of Church and State," *Journal of Church and State* 48 (2006), pp. 18–19.
28. Ibid., p. 18.
29. Philip Benedict, *Christ's Churches Purely Reformed: A Social History of Calvinism* (New Haven: Yale University Press, 2002), p. 11.
30. Diarmaid MacCulluch, *Christianity: The First Three Thousand Years* (London: Penguin Books, 2010), p. 597.
31. Brad Gregory, *The Unintended Reformation: How a Religious Revolution Secularized Society* (Cambridge: Belknap Press of Harvard University Press, 2012), p. 45.
32. John Witte, Jr., *Law and Protestantism: The Legal Teachings of the Lutheran Reformation* (Cambridge: Cambridge University Press, 2002), p. 2.
33. MacCulloch, *Christianity*, p. 621.
34. Gregory, *Unintended Reformation*, p. 109.

35. Witte, "Facts and Fictions," p. 21. See also Benedict, *Christ's Churches*, p. 424.
36. Laurence R. Iannaccone, "Why Strict Churches Are Strong," *American Journal of Sociology* (March 1994), p. 1181.
37. See also Gregory, *Unintended Reformation*, p. 160.
38. Benedict, *Christ's Churches*, p. 7.
39. Ibid., p. 25.
40. Ibid., p. 98.
41. Cook, *Ancient Religions*, p. 351.
42. MacCulloch, *Christianity*, p. 608.
43. This refers to the groups' names as rendered in English. In other languages, including German, other names were sometimes used.
44. Cook, *Ancient Religions*, pp. 299–300.
45. Els Witte, *Political History of Belgium: From 1830 Onwards* (Brussels: Academic and Scientific Publishers, 2009), p. 74.
46. Ibid., p. 74.
47. Ibid., p. 83.
48. Ibid., p. 88.
49. For a discussion of Qutb, Attas, and other Muslim thinkers' views on Christianity, see Ralston, *Law and the Rule of God*, pp. 97–111.
50. Youssef M. Choueiri, *Islamic Fundamentalism* (Boston: Twayne Publishers, 1990), p. 32.
51. Nikki R. Keddie, *Sayyid Jamal Ad-Din "Al-Afghani": A Political Biography* (Berkeley: University of California Press, 1972), pp. 391–92. For more on Afghani's religious and political thought, see also Albert Hourani, *Arabic Thought in the Liberal Age*, pp. 103–29.

3: ISLAM'S REFORMATION

1. Selcuk Aksin Somel, "Ottoman Islamic Education in the Balkans in the Nineteenth Century," *Islamic Studies* 36 (1997), p. 439.
2. Simon A. Wood, *Christian Criticisms, Islamic Proofs: Rashid Rida's Modernist Defense of Islam* (Oxford: Oneworld, 2008), p. 17.
3. For more on Rida's life and thought, see Emad Eldin Shahin, *Through Muslim Eyes: M. Rashid Rida and the West* (Herndon: International Institute of Islamic Thought, 1992).
4. Jonathan A. C. Brown, *Misquoting Muhammad: The Challenge and Choices of Interpreting the Prophet's Legacy* (London: Oneworld, 2014), p. 79
5. Rashid Rida, "Criticisms of the Christians and the Proofs of Islam," in Simon A. Wood, *Christian Criticisms, Islamic Proofs* (Oxford: Oneworld, 2008), p. 69.
6. Ibid., p. 98.
7. Ibid., p. 117.
8. Ibid., p. 144.

9. Rashid Rida, *The Muhammadan Revelation* (Alexandria: Al-Saadawi Publications, 1996), p. 107.
10. Albert Hourani, "Rashid Rida and the Sufi Orders: A Footnote to Laoust," *Bulletin d'Etudes Orientales* (1977), p. 235.
11. Ibid., p. 33.
12. Rashid Rida, "Criticisms of the Christians and the Proofs of Islam," p. 98.
13. Ibid., p. 189.
14. Ibid., pp. 171–72.
15. Brown, *Misquoting Muhammad*, pp. 122–23.
16. Mohamed Fadel, "Modernist Islamic Political Thought and the Egyptian and Tunisian Revolutions of 2011," *Middle East Law and Governance* 3 (2011), p. 96.
17. Ibid., pp. 100–01.
18. Noah Feldman, *The Fall and Rise of the Islamic State* (Princeton: Princeton University Press, 2008).
19. Reza Pankhurst, *The Inevitable Caliphate? A History of the Struggle for Global Islamic Union, 1924 to the Present* (London: Hurst, 2013), p. 19. Pankhurst writes, "This point of Islamic law is confirmed in practically every single book written on Islamic governance up until the twentieth century, all of which narrate an agreement on the obligation to establish the caliphate which goes beyond that even of orthodox scholarship, and also includes practically all of the minority sects" (18).
20. Albert Hourani, *Arabic Thought in the Liberal Age: 1798–1939* (Cambridge: Cambridge University Press, 1983), p. 161.
21. For more on the founding of the Brotherhood and Hassan al-Banna's intellectual and political thought, see Richard P. Mitchell, *The Society of the Muslim Brothers* (New York: Oxford University Press, 1993), and Gudrun Kramer, *Hasan al-Banna* (Oxford: Oneworld, 2010).
22. Khalil al-Anani, "The Power of the Jama'a: The Role of Hasan Al-Banna in Constructing the Muslim Brotherhood's Collective Identity," *Sociology of Islam* 1 (2013), p. 48.
23. Hassan al-Banna, *Memoirs of Hasan al-Banna Shaheed* (Karachi: International Islamic Publishers, 1981), p. 127.
24. Hassan al-Banna, "Our Message," *Collection of Epistles*, p. 5, available at http://www.masmn.org/Books/Hasan_Al_Banna/Rasail/index.htm.
25. Ibid., p. 4.
26. For a discussion of the broader meanings and expressions of sharia, see Wael B. Hallaq, *Shari'a: Theory, Practice, Transformation* (Cambridge: Cambridge University Press, 2009), pp. 1–3.
27. Hallaq, *The Impossible State*, p. 11.
28. For a discussion of wine drinking in Islamic history, see Shahab Ahmed, *What Is Islam? The Importance of Being Islamic* (Princeton: Princeton University Press, 2016), pp. 57–71.
29. Brown, *Misquoting Muhammad*, p. 77.
30. Interview with author, Hamdi Hassan, November 26, 2010.

31. Human Rights Watch, "UN Human Rights Council: Adoption of the UPR Report on Egypt," March 20, 2015, http://www.hrw.org/news /2015/03/20/un-human-rights-council-adoption-upr-report-egypt.
32. John Gray, "The Truth about Evil," *Guardian*, October 21, 2014, http:// www.theguardian.com/news/2014/oct/21/-sp-the-truth-about-evil -john-gray.
33. Rida, "Criticisms of the Christians and the Proofs of Islam," p. 98.
34. Banna, "The Message of the Teachings," *Collection of Epistles*, p. 127.
35. Banna, "The Message of the Fifth Conference," *Collection of Epistles*, p. 88.
36. Richard P. Mitchell, *The Society of the Muslim Brothers* (New York: Oxford University Press, 1993), pp. 130–32.
37. Khaled Moheiddin, *Memories of a Revolution: Egypt 1952* (Cairo: The American University in Cairo Press, 1995), p. 22.
38. Anwar el-Sadat, *In Search of Identity* (New York: Harper and Row, 1977), p. 22.
39. Anwar el-Sadat, *Revolt on the Nile* (New York: John Day, 1957), p. 29.
40. Michael Willis, *Power and Politics in the Maghreb: Algeria, Tunisia, and Morocco from Independence to the Arab Spring* (New York: Columbia University Press, 2012), p. 172.
41. Anani, "Power of the Jama'a," p. 60.
42. Banna, "To What Do We Invite Humanity," *Collection of Epistles*, p. 33.
43. Banna, "Our Message," p. 5.
44. Simon A. Wood, *Christian Criticisms, Islamic Proofs* (Oxford: Oneworld, 2008), p. 39.
45. Fernando Henrique Cardoso, "Associated-Dependent Development and Democratic Theory," in *Democratizing Brazil: Problems of Transition and Consolidation*, ed. Alfred Stepan (New York: Oxford University Press, 1989), p. 307.
46. Hassan al-Banna, "Peace in Islam," *Collection of Epistles*, p. 164.

4: THE MUSLIM BROTHERHOOD

1. Interview with author, senior advisor to President Mohamed Morsi, April 8, 2013.
2. Abdel Fattah al-Sissi, "Democracy in the Middle East," U.S. Army War College, March 15, 2006, reprinted in David D. Kirkpatrick, "Sisi's Thesis on Democracy in the Middle East," *New York Times*, May 24, 2014, http://www.nytimes.com/interactive/2014/05/24/world/middleeast /sisi-doc.html.
3. Ibid., p. 6.
4. Interview with author, senior advisor to President Morsi, April 8, 2013.
5. Interview with author, Morsi administration official, February 17, 2015.
6. Interview with author, senior advisor to President Morsi, January 10, 2014.

7. "#3896: Egyptian Opposition Activist Loses His Cool Following President Morsi's Speech," from *Sada al-Balad* (Egypt), posted on MEMRI, July 2, 2013, www.memritv.org/clip/en/3896.htm.

8. Interview with author, Wael Haddara, January 25, 2014.

9. "Leaked Recordings between Sissi and Journalist Yasser Rizk," YouTube, December 11, 2013, https://www.youtube.com/watch?v=dhhmR2LB4 pA&feature=youtube.

10. Ibid. See also David D. Kirkpatrick, "Egypt's New Strongman, Sisi Knows Best," *New York Times*, May 24, 2014, http://www.nytimes.com/2014 /05/25/world/middleeast/egypts-new-autocrat-sisi-knows-best.html.

11. Ibid.

12. Kirkpatrick, "Egypt's New Strongman."

13. Ghada Sharif, "Ya Sissi . . . Inta Taghmaz bi 'Ainak Bas!" [Oh Sissi . . . all it would take is just one wink!]," *Al-Masri Al-Youm*, July 25, 2013, http://www.almasryalyoum.com/news/details/198680#f6fc5af 502e019.

14. "Women's 'Sisi Pajamas' Hit the Egyptian Market," *Al Arabiya*, November 29, 2013, http://english.alarabiya.net/en/variety/2013/11/30/Women -s-Sisi-pajamas-hit-the-Egyptian-market.html.

15. Interview with author, Islamist journalist, January 14, 2014.

16. "In translation: Belal Fadl on Egypt becoming a 'Nation of Snitches,'" *Arabist*, November 11, 2014, http://arabist.net/blog/2014/11/9/in -translation-belal-fadl-on-egypt-becoming-a-nation-of-snitches; original Arabic article, Belal Fadl, *Mada Masr*, November 2, 2014, http://bit.ly /1GCJbU3.

17. Sara Khorshid, "Egypt's New Police State," *New York Times*, November 16, 2014, http://www.nytimes.com/2014/11/17/opinion/egypts -new-police-state.html.

18. Interview with author, prominent Islamist activist, February 1, 2015.

19. Interview with author, former parliamentary candidate, August 3, 2013.

20. Steven Brooke, "The Muslim Brotherhood's Social Outreach after the Egyptian Coup," Brookings Institution working paper, Rethinking Political Islam series, August 2015, p. 2, http://www.brookings.edu/~ /media/Research/Files/Reports/2015/07/rethinking-political-islam /Final-Working-Papers/Egypt_Brooke_FINALv.pdf?la=en.

21. Ibid., p. 4-5.

22. Interview with author, senior Muslim Brotherhood official, November 17, 2013.

23. Michelle Dunne and Scott Williamson, "Egypt's Unprecedented Instability by the Numbers," Carnegie Endowment for International Peace, March 24, 2014, http://carnegieendowment.org/2014/03/24/egypt-s -unprecedented-instability-by-numbers/h5j3.

24. Human Rights Watch, "UN Human Rights Council: Adoption of the UPR Report on Egypt," March 20, 2015, http://www.hrw.org/news /2015/03/20/un-human-rights-council-adoption-upr-report-egypt.

25. David D. Kirkpatrick, "Hundreds of Egyptians Sentenced to Death

in Killing of a Police Officer," *New York Times*, March 24, 2014, http://
www.nytimes.com/2014/03/25/world/middleeast/529-egyptians
-sentenced-to-death-in-killing-of-a-police-officer.html.

26. Emad Shahin, "Sentenced to Death in Egypt," *Atlantic*, May 19, 2015,
http://www.theatlantic.com/international/archive/2015/05/death
-sentence-egypt-emad-shahin/393590/.

27. Steven Brooke, "Egypt's Crackdown on Islamist Charities," *Foreign Policy*, December 27, 2013, http://foreignpolicy.com/2013/12/27/egypts
-crackdown-on-islamist-charities/.

28. Leila Fadel, "Egypt's Crackdown on Islamists Spreads to Mosques,
Charities," NPR, October 18, 2013, http://www.npr.org/blogs/parallels
/2013/10/18/236256570/egypts-crackdown-on-islamists-spreads-to
-mosques-charities.

29. Brooke, "Muslim Brotherhood's Social Outreach," p. 8.

30. Nathan J. Brown and Michele Dunne, "Egypt's Judges Join In," *Foreign
Affairs*, April 1, 2014, https://www.foreignaffairs.com/articles/middle
-east/2014-04-01/egypts-judges-join.

31. Interview with author, Morsi administration official, February 17, 2015.

32. Zogby Research Services, "After Tahrir: Egyptians Assess Their Government, Their Institutions, and Their Future," June 2013, p. 11, http://
static1.squarespace.com/static/52750dd3e4b08c252c723404/t
/52928b8de4b070ad8eec181e/1385335693242/Egypt+June+2013
+FINAL.pdf.

33. Nathan J. Brown, "Post-Revolutionary al-Azhar," Carnegie Endowment
for International Peace, September 2011, http://carnegieendowment.org
/files/al_azhar.pdf.

34. Ahmed Morsy and Nathan J. Brown, "Egypt's al-Azhar Steps Forward," Carnegie Endowment for International Peace, November 7,
2013, http://carnegieendowment.org/2013/11/07/egypt-s-al-azhar
-steps-forward.

35. For a more extensive documentation of the role of clerics in justifying
the use of violence against Sissi's political opponents, see Mohamad Elmasry, "The Rabaa Massacre and Egyptian Propaganda," *Middle East Eye*,
August 13, 2015, http://www.middleeasteye.net/columns/rabaa-massacre
-and-egyptian-propaganda-131958993.

36. David D. Kirkpatrick and Mayy El Sheikh, "Egypt Military Enlists Religion to Quell Ranks," *New York Times*, August 25, 2013, http://www
.nytimes.com/2013/08/26/world/middleeast/egypt.html.

37. See for example Amr Osman, "Ali Gomaa: Kill Them, They Stink,"
Middle East Monitor, November 21, 2013, https://www.middleeast-
monitor.com/articles/africa/8421-ali-gomaa-kill-them-they-stink,
although I have made some slight changes to the English translation
for accuracy.

38. "Al-fideo al-kamil li fatwa al-doktor Ali Gomaa bi jawaz quatl hamal li
man al-saleh min al-khawarij alladhi tamma 'ardahu li-dhubat wa al-

junud," YouTube, posted by Dr. Ali Gomaa, August 25, 2013, https://www.youtube.com/watch?v=u9WE_zBV-fw. See also Elmasry, "Rabaa Massacre."

39. Brooke, "Muslim Brotherhood's Social Outreach," p. 5.

40. Steven Brooke, "Brotherhood Activisms and Regime Consolidation in Egypt," *Washington Post*, January 29, 2015, http://www.washingtonpost.com/blogs/monkey-cage/wp/2015/01/29/brotherhood-activism-and-regime-consolidation-in-egypt/.

41. Abigail Hauslohner, "Egypt's Muslim Brotherhood Finds Havens Abroad," *Washington Post*, November 6, 2013, http://www.washingtonpost.com/world/middle_east/egypts-muslim-brotherhood-finds-havens-abroad/2013/11/05/438f2dfe-463a-11e3-95a9-3f15b5618ba8_story.html.

42. Interview with author, Hamza Zawba, January 11, 2014.

43. Interview with author, Asmaa Shokr, February 22, 2015.

44. See Hamid, *Temptations of Power*, pp. 89, 96–97, 128.

45. Interview with author, Ammar el-Beltagy, February 18, 2015.

46. Interview with author, Amr Darrag, February 19, 2015.

47. Hassan al-Banna, "On Jihad," *Collection of Epistles*, p. 117, http://www.masmn.org/Books/Hasan_Al_Banna/Rasail/index.htm.

48. Ibid., p. 119.

49. John Calvert, *Sayyid Qutb and the Origins of Radical Islamism* (New York: Columbia University Press, 2010), p. 198.

50. Ibid, p. 202.

51. For an overview of the arguments in *Preachers, Not Judges*, see Barbara Zollner, *The Muslim Brotherhood: Hasan al-Hudaybi and Ideology* (New York: Routledge, 2008).

52. Human Rights Watch, "All According to Plan: The Raba'a Massacre and Mass Killings of Protesters in Egypt," August 2014, http://www.hrw.org/sites/default/files/reports/egypt0814web_0.pdf, pp. 7–8.

53. Human Rights Watch, pp. 8, 10, 34.

54. Mike Hanna, "Egypt's Government Crosses a Red Line," *Al Jazeera*, August 20, 2013, http://blogs.aljazeera.com/blog/middle-east/egypts-government-crosses-red-line.

55. For more on the efficacy of violence in contexts of civil war, see Stathis N. Kalyvas, *The Logic of Violence in Civil War* (Cambridge: Cambridge University Press, 2006).

56. Maria Stephan and Erica Chenoweth, "Why Civil Resistance Works: The Strategic Logic of Nonviolent Conflict," *International Security* 33 (2008), p. 12.

57. Ibid., p. 15.

58. I explore these arguments in more detail in Shadi Hamid, "Islamists and the Failure of Nonviolent Action," in *Civilian Jihad: Popular Struggle, Democratization, and Governance in the Middle East*, ed. Maria J. Stephan (New York: Palgrave, 2009).

59. Interview with author, Asmaa Shokr, February 22, 2015.
60. Karim's comments here and below are from interview with author, February 24, 2015.
61. Waleed Abdulrahman, "Sheikh Ashoush Provocative in Debate: Morsi Is Not Ruling by Sharia," *Al Arabiya*, November 14, 2012, http://www.alarabiya.net/articles/2012/11/14/249473.html.
62. David D. Kirkpatrick, "Online, American Helps Fuel Attacks in Egypt," *New York Times*, February 27, 2015, http://www.nytimes.com/2015/02/28/world/american-agitator-helps-fuel-attacks-in-egypt.html?_r=0.
63. Shahid Bolsen, "Un-Capitalist Capitalism," September 19, 2014, https://shahidkingbolsen.wordpress.com/2014/09/19/34/.
64. Kirkpatrick, "Online, American Helps Fuel Attacks in Egypt."
65. Shahid Bolsen, Facebook post, November 29, 2014, https://www.facebook.com/shahid.bolsen/posts/1529217370654547.
66. Shahid Bolsen, Facebook post, January 31, 2015, https://www.facebook.com/shahid.bolsen/posts/1554417704801180.
67. Shahid Bolsen, Facebook post, November 30, 2014, https://www.facebook.com/shahid.bolsen/posts/1529553183954299.
68. Shahid Bolsen, Facebook post, January 25, 2015, https://www.facebook.com/permalink.php?story_fbid=797404066980539&id=791212564266356.
69. See also Mokhtar Awad and Samuel Tadros, "Allah versus KFC," *Foreign Policy*, February 27, 2015, http://foreignpolicy.com/2015/02/27/allah-versus-kfc-egypt-arab-spring-terrorism.
70. Shahid Bolsen, Facebook post, January 22, 2014, https://www.facebook.com/shahid.bolsen/posts/1414750988767853.
71. Hallaq, *The Impossible State: Islam, Politics, and Modernity's Moral Predicament*, p. x.
72. Shahab Ahmed, *What Is Islam? The Importance of Being Islamic* (Princeton: Princeton University Press, 2016), p. 125.
73. "They Shall By No Means Harm You but with a Slight Evil," *Al Furqan Media*, August 2013, https://azelin.files.wordpress.com/2013/07/shaykh-abc5ab-mue1b8a5ammad-al-e28098adnc481nc4ab-al-shc481mc4ab-22they-will-not-harm-you-except-for-some-annoyance22-en.pdf.
74. Aaron Zelin, "The Islamic State of Iraq and Syria Has a Consumer Protection Office," *Atlantic*, June 13, 2014, http://www.theatlantic.com/international/archive/2014/06/the-isis-guide-to-building-an-islamic-state/372769/.
75. "ISIS Punishes Cleric Who Objected to Pilot's Killing," February 6, 2015, http://english.alarabiya.net/en/News/middle-east/2015/02/06/ISIS-punishes-cleric-who-objected-to-pilot-s-killing.html.
76. Interview with author, Abdullah El-Haddad, January 31, 2015.
77. Interview with author, Amr Darrag, February 19, 2015.
78. For the definitive treatment of the final days of diplomacy before the massacre, see David D. Kirkpatrick, Peter Baker, and Michael R. Gordon,

"How American Hopes for a Deal in Egypt Were Undercut," *New York Times*, August 17, 2013, http://www.nytimes.com/2013/08/18/world /middleeast/pressure-by-us-failed-to-sway-egypts-leaders.html.

5: THE TURKISH MODEL

1. "Erdogan's Vast New Palace to Cost over $600 Million," Agence France-Presse, November 4, 2014, http://news.yahoo.com/erdogans-vast-palace -cost-over-600-million-202016685.html.
2. Turkey Constitutional Court, March 7, 1989, basis no. 1989/1, decision no. 1989/12, *Official Gazette of the Republic of Turkey* 1989, no. 20216.
3. Ibid.
4. Human Rights Watch, "Memorandum to the Turkish Government on Human Rights Watch's Concerns with Regard to Academic Freedom in Higher Education, and Access to Higher Education for Women Who Wear the Headscarf," June 29, 2004, http://www.hrw.org/sites/default /files/related_material/headscarf_memo.pdf.
5. See Banu Eligür, *The Mobilization of Political Islam in Turkey* (New York: Cambridge University Press, 2010), pp. 67–74.
6. Jenny White, *Muslim Nationalism and the New Turks* (Princeton: Princeton University Press, 2013), p. 39.
7. Stephen Kinzer, "Turks' High Court Orders Disbanding of Islamic Party," *New York Times*, January 17, 1998, http://www.nytimes.com /1998/01/17/world/turks-high-court-orders-disbanding-of-islamic -party.html.
8. When the AKP took power in 2002, Erdogan was still formally barred from running for parliament. As a result, Erdogan did not become prime minister until 2003, when, after the AKP amended the article of the constitution on eligibility for office, he was able to run for a seat in Siirt.
9. Deborah Sontag, "The Erdogan Experiment," *New York Times Magazine*, May 11, 2003, http://www.nytimes.com/2003/05/11/magazine /the=erdogan=experiment.html?pagewanted=all.
10. Hale Yilmaz, *Becoming Turkish: Nationalist Reforms and Cultural Negotiations in Early Republican Turkey, 1923–1945* (Syracuse: Syracuse University Press, 2013), p. 147.
11. Stanford J. Shaw, "The Nineteenth Century Ottoman Tax Reforms and Revenue System," *International Journal of Middle East Studies* 6 (1975), p. 425.
12. David Lepeska, "Turkey Cast the Diyanet," *Foreign Affairs*, May 17, 2015, https://www.foreignaffairs.com/articles/turkey/2015-05-17/turkey -casts-diyanet.
13. James Gibbon, "God Is Great, God Is Good: Teaching God Concepts in Turkish Islamic Sermons," *Poetics* 38 (2008), p. 400.

14. "Basic Principles and Objectives," Presidency of Religious Affairs, http:// www.diyanet.gov.tr/en/category/basic-principles-and-objectives/23.

15. See Hamid, *Temptations of Power*, especially chapters 2-4.

16. Stephen Kinzer, "Turkish Leader Wins a Key Vote to Limit Religious Education," *New York Times*, August 17, 1997, http://www.nytimes.com /1997/08/17/world/turkish-leader-wins-a-key-vote-to-limit-religious -education.html.

17. Deborah Sontag, "The Erdogan Experiment," *New York Times Magazine*, May 11, 2003, http://www.nytimes.com/2003/05/11/magazine /the-erdogan-experiment.html?pagewanted=all.

18. For a discussion of "positive conditionality," see Shadi Hamid and Peter Mandaville, "Bringing the United States Back into the Middle East," *Washington Quarterly*, Fall 2013, https://csis.org/files/publication/TWQ _13Winter_Hamid-Mandaville.pdf.

19. Sebnem Arsu, "Premier of Turkey Seeks Limits on Abortions," *New York Times*, May 29, 2012, http://www.nytimes.com/2012/05/30/world /europe/turkish-premier-calls-for-more-abortion-restrictions.html.

20. Interview with author, senior AKP official, February 20, 2015.

21. Orhan Kemal Cengiz, "Erdogan's Reforms Meant to Education 'Pious Generation,'" *Al-Monitor*, June 26, 2014.

22. Ahmet T. Kuru, "Reinterpretation of Secularism in Turkey: The Case of the Justice and Development Party," in *The Emergence of a New Turkey: Democracy and the AK Parti*, ed. M. Hakan Yavuz (Salt Lake City: University of Utah Press, 2006), p. 145.

23. Ibid., p. 146.

24. Uğur Akinci, "Turkey and the US in 1997: Different Voices, Same Chord," *Hurriyet Daily News*, January 18, 1998, http://www.hurri yetdailynews.com/turkey-and-the-us-in-1997different-voices-same -chord.aspx.

25. See E. P. Licursi, "The Ergenekon Case and Turkey's Democratic Aspirations," Freedom House, February 7, 2012, https://freedomhouse.org /blog/ergenekon-case-and-turkey%E2%80%99s-democratic -aspirations#.VUvU7NpViko; "Retired Gen. Çevik Bir Jailed in Postmodern Coup Case," *Today's Zaman*, April 16, 2012, http://www.today szaman.com/latest-news_retired-gen-cevik-bir-jailed-in-postmodern -coup-case_277588.html.

26. Jenny B. White, "The Turkish Complex," *American Interest*, February 20, 2015, http://www.the-american-interest.com/2015/02/02/the -turkish-complex/.

27. Quotations from Mazhar Bagli, here and below, are from interview with author, February 20, 2015.

28. Ihsan Dagi, "Postmodern Authoritarianism in Action," *Today's Zaman*, November 10, 2013, http://www.todayszaman.com/columnists_post modern-authoritarianism-in-action_331058.html.

29. Howard Eissenstat, "Stunted Democracy: Erdogan, the AKP, and Tur-

key's Slide into Authoritarianism," Project on Middle East Democracy, January 29, 2015, http://pomed.org/pomed-publications/eissenstat2015/.

30. "Freedom in the World 2015: Turkey," Freedom House, 2015, https://freedomhouse.org/report/freedom-world/2015/turkey#.VXRdI2RViko.

31. Claire Sadar, "Power, Paternalism and Fate in Soma," May 19, 2014, https://ataturksrepublic.wordpress.com/2014/05/19/power-paternalism-and-fate-in-soma/.

32. White, "Turkish Complex."

33. Ibid.

34. See, for example, Semih Idiz, "Qatar's Egypt Reconciliation Embarrasses Erdogan," *Al-Monitor*, December 23, 2014, http://www.al-monitor.com/pulse/originals/2014/12/turkey-qatar-syria-erdogan-difficult-situation.html; Semih Idiz, "Erdogan Continues to Consolidate Power," *Al-Monitor*, December 16, 2014, http://www.al-monitor.com/pulse/originals/2014/12/turkey-erdogan-consolidate-his-power-gulen-movement.html.

35. Kadri Gursel, "The Davutoglu Charm Offensive," *Al-Monitor*, November 24, 2013, http://www.al-monitor.com/pulse/originals/2013/11/davutoglu-turkey-foreign-policy-isolation-middle-east.html.

36. Interview with author, Ibrahim Kalin, February 20, 2015.

37. Mustafa Akyol, "How Not to Win Friends and Influence the Turkish People," *Foreign Policy*, June 3, 2013, http://foreignpolicy.com/2013/06/03/how-not-to-win-friends-and-influence-the-turkish-people/.

38. Serkan Demirtas, "Erdogan More Conservative Than Democrat Ahead of 2014 Polls," *Hurriyet Daily News*, May 29, 2013, http://www.hurriyetdailynews.com/erdogan-more-conservative-than-democrat-ahead-of-2014-polls-.aspx?pageID=449&nID=47779&NewsCatID=429.

39. Interview with author, advisor to senior AKP officials, February 17, 2015.

40. Quotations from Yasar Yakis, here and below, are from interview with author, February 20, 2015.

41. Quotations from senior advisor to Ahmet Davutoglu, here and below, are from interview with author, February 20, 2015.

42. Interview with author, AKP parliamentary candidate, February 24, 2015.

43. Interview with author, senior aide to President Abdullah Gul, February 17, 2015.

44. Interview with author, advisor to senior AKP officials, February 17, 2015.

45. "Erdogan Explains His Vision for New Turkey," *Daily Sabah*, April 10, 2015, http://www.dailysabah.com/politics/2015/04/10/erdogan-explains-his-vision-for-new-turkey.

46. Mustafa Akyol, "Will Erdogan Be Turkey's Next Ataturk," *Al-Monitor*, July 9, 2014, http://www.al-monitor.com/pulse/ar/originals/2014/07/akyol-ataturk-erdogan-president-akp-power-methods-illiberal.html#; Mustafa Akyol, "Erdogan's Great Patriotic War," *Al-Monitor*, March 20,

2014, http://www.al-monitor.com/pulse/fr/originals/2014/03/erdogan
-nationalist-propaganda-video.html#.

47. "The World's Muslims: Unity and Diversity," Pew Research Center, August 9, 2012, http://www.pewforum.org/2012/08/09/the-worlds
-muslims-unity-and-diversity-2-religious-commitment/.

48. Ali Carkoglu and Binnaz Toprak, *Religion, Society and Politics in a Changing Turkey*, trans. Cigdem Aksoy Fromm, ed. Jenny Sanders (Istanbul: Turkish Economic and Social Studies Foundation [TESEV], 2007), pp. 33, 43.

49. "World's Muslims: Unity and Diversity."

6: TUNISIA

1. Alexander Christie-Miller, "Erdogan Launches Sunni Islamist Revival in Turkish Schools," *Newsweek*, December 16, 2014, http://www.news
week.com/2014/12/26/erdogan-launches-sunni-islamist-revival-turkish
-schools-292237.html.

2. "Turks Divided on Erdogan and the Country's Direction," Pew Research Center, July 30, 2014, http://www.pewglobal.org/2014/07/30/turks
-divided-on-erdogan-and-the-countrys-direction/; "Turks Downbeat about Their Institutions," Pew Research Center, September 7, 2010, http://www.pewresearch.org/2010/09/07/turks-downbeat-about
-their-institutions/.

3. "World DataBank: World Development Indicators," World Bank, http://
databank.worldbank.org/data/views/reports/tableview.aspx.

4. Interview with author, Sayida Ounissi, February 6, 2015.

5. Monica Marks, "Tunisia Opts for an Inclusive New Government," *Washington Post*, February 3, 2015, http://www.washingtonpost.com/blogs
/monkey-cage/wp/2015/02/03/tunisia-opts-for-an-inclusive-new
-government/.

6. Nissaf Slama, "'Irhal' Campaign Attempts to Oust Ennahda Officials," *Tunisia Live*, August 14, 2013, http://www.tunisia-live.net/2013/08/14
/erhal-campaignattempts-to-oust-enahdha-officials/.

7. For more on how Ennahda reacted to the Egyptian coup, see Monica Marks, "Tunisia's Ennahda: Rethinking Islamism in the Context of ISIS and the Egyptian Coup," working paper, Brookings Institution, Rethinking Political Islam series, August 2015, http://www.brookings
.edu/~/media/Research/Files/Reports/2015/07/rethinking-political
-islam/Final-Working-Papers/Tunisia_Marks_FINALv.pdf?la=en.

8. Interview with author, Rached Ghannouchi, February 13, 2015.

9. Interview with author, Meherzia Laabidi, February 6, 2015.

10. Interview with author, Imen Ben Mohamed, February 9, 2015.

11. See Shadi Hamid, "Arab Islamist Parties: Losing on Purpose?" *Journal of Democracy* 22 (2011), pp. 68–80.

12. Interview with author, senior Ennahda official, February 7, 2015.

13. Anthony Shadid, "Islamists' Ideas on Democracy and Faith Face Test in Tunisia," *New York Times*, February 17, 2012, http://www.nytimes.com/2012/02/18/world/africa/tunisia-islamists-test-ideas-decades-in-the-making.html.
14. Ibid.
15. Interview with author, Said Ferjani, February 7, 2015.
16. Interview with author, Ennahda campaign organizer, February 12, 2015.
17. Anne Wolf, "Can Secular Parties Lead the New Tunisia?" Carnegie Endowment for International Peace, April 30, 2014, http://carnegieendowment.org/2014/04/30/can-secular-parties-lead-new-tunisia.
18. Pew Research Center, spring 2014 survey, topline results, http://www.pewglobal.org/files/2014/10/Pew-Research-Center-Tunisia-Report-TOPLINE-October-15-2014.pdf, p. 17.
19. "Tunisian Confidence in Democracy Wanes," Pew Research Center, October 15, 2014, http://www.pewglobal.org/2014/10/15/tunisian-confidence-in-democracy-wanes/.
20. "The World's Muslims: Religion, Politics and Society," Pew Research Center, April 30, 2013.
21. Interview with author, Noureddine Arbaoui, February 11, 2015.
22. Interview with author, Rached Ghannouchi, February 13, 2015.
23. Ibid.
24. Monica Marks, "Convince, Coerce, or Compromise? Ennahda's Approach to Tunisia's Constitution," Brookings Doha Center Analysis Paper, February 10, 2014, http://www.brookings.edu/research/papers/2014/02/10-ennahda-tunisia-constitution-marks.
25. Duncan Pickard, "The Current Status of Constitution Making in Tunisia," Carnegie Endowment for International Peace, April 19, 2012, http://carnegieendowment.org/2012/04/19/current-status-of-constitution-making-in-tunisia.
26. "Tunisian Confidence."
27. Interview with author, Riadh Chaibi, February 10, 2015.
28. Human Rights Watch, "Tunisia: Sweeping Political Exclusion Law," June 15, 2013, http://www.hrw.org/news/2013/06/15/tunisia-sweeping-political-exclusion-law.
29. Interview with author, civil-society activist, February 6, 2015.
30. Ursula Lindsey, "Tunisia's Rachid Ghannouchi on Blasphemy, Homosexuality, Equality," *Arabist*, April 6, 2015, http://arabist.net/blog/2015/4/6/tunisias-rachid-ghannouchi-on-blasphemy-homosexuality-equality.
31. Interview with author, Habib Ellouze, February 14, 2013.
32. Interview with author, Habib Ellouze, February 10, 2015.
33. Interview with author, Azzam Tamimi, February 2, 2015.
34. See Abdel Moneim Abul Futouh, interview, February 5, 2012, YouTube, http://www.youtube.com/watch?v=hgWJRuVOyDc&list=UUQpLme0GRI0L8MRC_d2aSrA&index=9&feature=plcp&fb_source=message.

35. Unlike some other Ennahda figures, Rached Ghannouchi doesn't disassociate himself from the terms "Islamism" or "Islamists" and sees himself as a figure within the broader "Islamic movement."
36. Interview with author, Riadh Chaibi, February 10, 2015.
37. Interview with author, Noureddine Arbaoui, February 11, 2015.
38. Seymour Lipset and Stein Rokkan, *Party Systems and Voter Alignments: Cross-National Perspectives* (London: Free Press, 1967).
39. Nick Sitter, "Cleavages, Party Strategy and Party System Change in Europe, East and West," *Perspectives on European Politics and Society*, volume 3 (2002), p. 448.
40. Ibid.

7: ISIS

1. Christopher M. Blanchard, Carla E. Humud, Kenneth Katzman, and Matthew C. Weed, "The 'Islamic State' Crisis and U.S. Policy," Congressional Research Service, May 27, 2015, https://fas.org/sgp/crs /mideast/R43612.pdf, p. 2.
2. "Tunisia Blocks More Than 12,000 Would-Be Jihadists: Minister," *Agence France-Presse*, April 17, 2015, http://news.yahoo.com/tunisia-blocks -more-12-000-jihadists-minister-202230331.html.
3. Yassine's comments, here and below, are from interview with author, February 12, 2015.
4. Jessica Stern, "Response to Marc Sageman's 'The Stagnation in Terrorism Research,'" *Terrorism and Political Violence* 26 (2014), p. 607.
5. For an in-depth look at the split between Jabhat al-Nusra and the Islamic State of Iraq and how it affected the world of jihad, see Daniel Byman and Jennifer Williams, "ISIS vs. Al Qaeda: Jihadism's Global Civil War," *National Interest*, February 24, 2015, http://nationalinterest.org/feature /isis-vs-al-qaeda-jihadism%E2%80%99s-global-civil-war-12304.
6. Vera Mironova, Loubna Mrie, and Sam Whitt, "Islamists at a Glance: Why Do Syria's Rebel Fighters Join Islamist Groups? (The Reasons May Have Less to Do with Religiosity Than You Might Think)," *Political Violence @ a Glance*, August 13, 2014, http://politicalviolenceataglance.org /2014/08/13/islamists-at-a-glance-why-do-syrias-rebel-fighters-join -islamist-groups-the-reasons-may-have-less-to-do-with-religiosity-than -you-might-think/; see also Vera Mironova, Loubna Mrie, and Sam Whitt, *Fight or Flight in Civil War? Evidence from Rebel-Controlled Syria* (August 11, 2014), http://ssrn.com/abstract=2478682.
7. Thomas Hegghammer, "Why Terrorists Weep: The Socio-Cultural Practices of Jihadi Militants," Paul Wilkinson Memorial Lecture, University of St. Andrews, April 16, 2015, http://hegghammer.com/_files /Hegghammer_-_Wilkinson_Memorial_Lecture.pdf.
8. Samuel Huntington, *Political Order in Changing Societies* (New Haven: Yale University Press, 1968), p. 269.

9. Michael Weiss and Hassan Hassan, *ISIS: Inside the Army of Terror* (New York: Regan Arts, 2015), p. 163.

10. Shadi Hamid and Steven Brooke, "Promoting Democracy to Stop Terror, Revisited," *Policy Review*, February/March 2010, http://www.hoover.org /research/promoting-democracy-stop-terror-revisited.

11. See, for example, Edward D. Mansfield and Jack Snyder, *Electing to Fight: Why Emerging Democracies Go to War* (Cambridge: MIT Press, 2007).

12. Interview with author, DJ Costa, February 14, 2015.

13. Interview with author, Tunisian filmmaker, February 14, 2015.

14. Marc Lynch, "Islam Divided between *Salafi-jihad* and the *Ikhwan*," *Studies in Conflict and Terrorism* 33 (2010), p. 483.

15. Fabio Merone and Francesco Cavatorta, "The Emergence of Salafism in Tunisia," *Jadiliyya*, August 17, 2012, http://www.jadaliyya.com/pages /index/6934/the-emergence-of-salafism-in-tunisia.

16. "Khateer jiddan al-fidio Rached al-Ghannouchi ra'is harakat al-Nahda," YouTube, October 10, 2012, https://www.youtube.com /watch?v=5aFECUkDyug.

17. For more on the religious-secular binary, see Shahab Ahmed, *What Is Islam? The Importance of Being Islamic* (Princeton: Princeton University Press, 2016), especially pp. 157–216.

18. Interview with author, Muslim Brotherhood activist, February 22, 2015.

19. William McCants, *The ISIS Apocalypse: The History, Strategy, and Doomsday Vision of the Islamic State* (New York: St. Martin's Press, 2015), p. 57.

20. Ibid., p. 58.

21. Ibid., p. 61.

22. Graeme Wood, "What ISIS Really Wants," *Atlantic*, March 2015, http:// www.theatlantic.com/features/archive/2015/02/what-isis-really-wants /384980/.

23. Jamie Tarabey, "To Its Citizens, ISIS also Shows a Softer Side," *Voactiv*, March 20, 2015, http://www.vocativ.com/world/isis-2/to-its-citizens -isis-also-shows-a-softer-side/.

24. Skinner, quoted in ibid.

25. Abu Bakr Naji, in *The Management of Savagery: The Most Critical Stage through Which the Islamic Nation Will Pass*, trans. William McCants, 2006, https://azelin.files.wordpress.com/2010/08/abu-bakr-naji-the -management-of-savagery-the-most-critical-stage-through-which -the-umma-will-pass.pdf.

26. "The Media of al-Furat Province Presents: The Harvesting of Spies," Isdarat, May 2, 2015, https://isdarat.org/15917.

27. Aymenn al-Tamimi, "Islamic State 'Euphrates Province' Statement: Translation and Analysis," September 10, 2014, http://www.aymennjawad .org/2014/09/islamic-state-euphrates-province-statement.

28. Naji, *Management of Savagery*, p. 5.

29. William McCants, "Why Islamic State Really Wants to Conquer Baghdad," Brookings Institution, November 12, 2014, http://www.brookings .edu/blogs/markaz/posts/2014/11/12-baghdad-of-al-rashid-mccants.

30. Ibid.
31. Yasir Qadhi, "Experts Weigh In (Part 5): Is Quietist Salafism the Alternative to ISIS?" Brookings Institution, April 1, 2015, http://www.brookings.edu/blogs/markaz/posts/2015/04/01-yasir-qadi-quietist-salafism-experts-weigh-in.
32. William McCants, e-mail message to the author, September 27, 2015.
33. Martin Chulov, "ISIS Kills Hundreds of Iraqi Sunnis from Albu Nimr Tribe in Anbar Province," *Guardian*, October 30, 2014, http://www.theguardian.com/world/2014/oct/30/mass-graves-hundreds-iraqi-sunnis-killed-isis-albu-nimr; "Hundreds of Iraqi Tribesmen Opposed to Islamic State Found in Mass Graves," Reuters, October 30, 2014, http://www.reuters.com/article/2014/10/30/us-mideast-crisis-iraq-grave-idUSKBN0IJ1DI20141030.
34. Naji, *Management of Savagery*, p. 72.
35. "Drone Wars: Pakistan: Friday, October 31, 2008," New America Foundation, http://securitydata.newamerica.net/drones/pakistan/leaders-killed.html; see also, Lawrence Wright, "The Master Plan," *New Yorker*, September 11, 2006, http://www.newyorker.com/magazine/2006/09/11/the-master-plan.
36. Naji, *Management of Savagery*, p. 74.
37. Ziya Meral, "The Question of Theodicy and Jihad," *War on the Rocks*, February 26, 2015, http://warontherocks.com/2015/02/the-question-of-theodicy-and-jihad/.
38. Quoted in Elias Groll, "I'm Back! Baghdadi Appeals to Muslims to Sign Up with Islamic State," *Foreign Policy*, May 14, 2015, http://foreignpolicy.com/2015/05/14/im-back-baghdadi-appeals-to-muslims-to-sign-up-with-islamic-state/.
39. Meral, "Question of Theodicy."
40. Abu Mohammed al-Adnani, "The Scout Doesn't Lie to His People," *Al-Furqan Media*, January 2014, p. 5, Jihadology, https://azelin.files.wordpress.com/2014/01/shaykh-abc5ab-mue1b8a5ammad-al-adnc481nc4ab-22the-scout-doesnt-lie-to-his-people22-en.pdf.
41. Andrew W. March and Mara Revkin, "Caliphate of the Law: ISIS' Ground Rules," *Foreign Affairs*, April 15, 2015, https://www.foreignaffairs.com/articles/syria/2015-04-15/caliphate-law.
42. Ibid.
43. Charles C. Caris and Samuel Reynolds, "ISIS State Governance in Syria," Middle East Security Report 22, Institute for the Study of War, July 24, pg. 27, http://www.understandingwar.org/sites/default/files/ISIS_Governance.pdf.
44. Ibid.
45. "Al-Furqan Media Presents a New Video Message from the Islamic State of Iraq and al-Sham: 'The Best Ummah,'" Jihadology, May 28, 2014, http://jihadology.net/2014/05/28/al-furqan-media-presents-a-new-video-message-from-the-islamic-state-of-iraq-and-al-sham-for-the-good-of-the-ummah/.

46. Caris and Reynolds, "ISIS Governance in Syria," p. 27.
47. "Non-Syrian ISIL Court Judge Speaks about the Supremacy of Islamic Courts in Syria," YouTube, posted by Eretz Zen, November 23, 2013, https://www.youtube.com/watch?v=76_K9zwNBuw.
48. Ibid.
49. "Manbij and the Islamic State's Public Administration," Goha's Nail, August 22, 2014, https://gohasnail.wordpress.com/2014/08/22/manbij -and-the-islamic-states-public-administration/.
50. Ibid.
51. Weiss and Hassan, *ISIS: Inside the Army of Terror*, p. 165.
52. Mara Revkin, e-mail message to the author, August 14, 2015.
53. Aymenn al-Tamimi, "Critical Analysis of the Islamic State's Health Department," August 27, 2015, http://jihadology.net/2015/08/27 /the-archivist-critical-analysis-of-the-islamic-states-health -department.
54. Mara Revkin, "Experts Weigh in (Part 5): How Does ISIS Approach Islamic Scripture?" Brookings Institution, May 13, 2015, http://www .brookings.edu/blogs/markaz/posts/2015/05/12-isis-approach-to -scripture-revkin.
55. March and Revkin, "Caliphate of Law."
56. "Su'al: Ma hakam taqlid ba'd al-markat al-almiya wa aridaha fi al-souq bi nafs ism al-marka?" April 3, 2015, https://justpaste.it/imitation- brandsfatwa.
57. For more on the dynamics of local support for ISIS in its Iraqi and Syrian territory, see Mara Revkin, "Experts Weigh In: Is ISIS State Good at Governing?" Brookings Institution, November 20, 2015, http://www .brookings.edu/blogs/markaz/posts/2015/11/20-experts-weigh-in-isis -governance-revkin-mccants.
58. Nour Malas, "Iraqi City of Mosul Transformed a Year after Islamic State Capture," *Wall Street Journal*, June 9, 2015, http://www.wsj.com /articles/iraqi-city-of-mosul-transformed-a-year-after-islamic-state -capture-1433888626.
59. Revkin, "Experts Weigh In: Is ISIS Good at Governing?"
60. Mohammad Fadel, "Experts Weigh In (Part 4): How Does ISIS Approach Islamic Scripture?" *Markaz*, Brookings Institution, May 7, 2015, http://www.brookings.edu/blogs/markaz/posts/2015/05/07-fadel-isis -approach-to-scripture.
61. "The Fading of the Grayzone," *Dabiq*, October 2014, p. 44, http://media .clarionproject.org/files/islamic-state/islamic-state-isis-magazine -Issue-4-the-failed-crusade.pdf.
62. "A New Audio Message from Abu Bakr al-Baghdadi ~ March Forth Whether Light or Heavy," May 14, 2015, https://pietervanostaeyen .wordpress.com/2015/05/14/a-new-audio-message-by-abu-bakr-al -baghdadi-march-forth-whether-light-or-heavy/.
63. Andrew March, "Experts Weigh In (Part 3): How Does ISIS Approach Islamic Scripture?" *Markaz*, Brookings Institution, May 5, 2015, http://

www.brookings.edu/blogs/markaz/posts/2015/05/04-isis-scripture
-march-dhimma.

64. Graeme Wood, "What ISIS's Leader Really Wants," *New Republic*,
September 1, 2014, http://www.newrepublic.com/article/119259
/isis-history-islamic-states-new-caliphate-syria-and-iraq.

65. I discuss the complex relationship between the Islamic State and Islam in greater depth in "Does ISIS Really Have Nothing to Do with
Islam?" *The Washington Post*, November 18, 2015, https://www
.washingtonpost.com/news/acts-of-faith/wp/2015/11/18/does-isis
-really-have-nothing-to-do-with-islam-islamic-apologetics-carry
-serious-risks/.

66. Erika Solomon, Guy Chazan, and Sam Jones, "ISIS Inc: How Oil Fuels
the Jihadi Terrorists," *Financial Times*, October 14, 2015, http://
www.ft.com/intl/cms/s/2/b8234932-719b-11e5-ad6d-f4ed
76f0900a.html#axzz3ofUahGsh. For more on ISIS sources of funding, see Charles Lister, "Profiling the Islamic State," Brookings Doha
Center, November 2014, http://www.brookings.edu/~/media/Rese
arch/Files/Reports/2014/11/profiling%20islamic%20state%20lister
/en_web_lister.pdf.

67. Heather Pringle, "ISIS Cashing in on Looted Antiquities to Fuel
Iraq Insurgency," *National Geographic*, June 27, 2014, http://news
.nationalgeographic.com/news/2014/06/140626-isis-insurgents-syria
-iraq-looting-antiquities-archaeology/.

68. Thanassis Cambanis, "The Surprising Appeal of ISIS," *Boston Globe*,
June 29, 2014, http://www.bostonglobe.com/ideas/2014/06/28/the
-surprising-appeal-isis/l9YwC0GVPQ3i4eBXt1o0hI/story.html.

69. Revkin, "Experts Weigh In: Is ISIS Good at Governing?"

70. March, "Experts Weigh In (Part 3)."

71. Fadel, "Experts Weigh In (Part 4)."

72. For an overview of the scholarly tradition on the question of war and
jihad, see Khaled Abou El Fadl, "The Rules of Killing at War: An Inquiry into Classical Sources," *The Muslim World* 89 (April 1999).

73. I thank Will McCants for underscoring this point.

74. George Orwell, "Review of *Mein Kampf* by Adolf Hitler," *New English
Weekly*, March 1940, https://docs.google.com/file/d/0BzmBhYakPbY
tT3k5cDd4Sm1SRUE/edit.

8: ISLAM, LIBERALISM, AND THE STATE

1. Maia de la Baume, "Paris Announces Plan to Promote Secular Values,"
New York Times, January 22, 2015, http://www.nytimes.com/2015/01
/23/world/europe/charlie-hebdo-attack-leads-to-changes-in-french
-schools.html; Dov Alfon, "The Cracks in French Unity Are Already
Appearing," *Haaretz*, January 12, 2015, p. 19, http://www.haaretz.com
/news/world/.premium-1.636480.

2. Dalia Mogahed, "The Gallup Coexist Index 2009: A Global Study of Interfaith Relations," Gallup, 2009, http://www.olir.it/areetematiche/pagine/documents/News_2150_Gallup2009.pdf.

3. Ibid., p. 31.

4. Pew Research Center, "Pew Global Attitudes Project: Spring 2006 Survey," 2006, p. 59, http://www.pewglobal.org/files/pdf/253topline.pdf.

5. Rowan Williams, "Archbishop's Lecture—Civil and Religious Law in England: A Religious Perspective," February 7, 2008, http://rowanwilliams.archbishopofcanterbury.org/articles.php/1137/archbishops-lecture-civil-and-religious-law-in-england-a-religious-perspective.

6. Munira Mirza, Abi Senthilkumaran, and Zein Ja'far, "Living Apart Together: British Muslims and the Paradox of Multiculturalism," Policy Exchange, 2007, http://www.policyexchange.org.uk/images/publications/living%20apart%20together%20-%20jan%2007.pdf.

7. See Hamid, *Temptations of Power*, pp. 57–58.

8. Jannis Grimm, "Sisi's Moralism," *Sada*, December 19, 2014, http://carnegieendowment.org/sada/2014/12/19/sisi-s-moralism/hxo3.

9. Thomas Fuller, "The Right to Say God Divides a Diverse Nation," *New York Times*, November 3, 2014, http://www.nytimes.com/2014/11/04/world/asia/in-malaysia-allah-is-reserved-for-muslims-only.html.

10. Michael Walzer, "Islamism and the Left," *Dissent Magazine*, Winter 2015, http://www.dissentmagazine.org/article/islamism-and-the-left.

11. Decca Aitkenhead, "Johann Hari: I Failed Badly. When You Harm People, You Should Shut Up, Go Away, and Reflect on What Happened," *Guardian*, January 2, 2015, http://www.theguardian.com/media/2015/jan/02/johann-hari-interview-drugs-book-independent.

12. Krishnadev Calamur, "France 'At War with Jihadism and Radical Islamism,' Prime Minister Says," NPR, January 13, 2015, http://www.npr.org/sections/thetwo-way/2015/01/13/377020079/france-at-war-with-jihadism-and-radical-islamism-prime-minister-says.

13. Walzer, "Islamism."

14. Hallaq, *The Impossible State* (New York: Columbia University Press, 2013), p. x.

15. Dennis B. Ross, "Islamists Are Not Our Friends," *New York Times*, September 11, 2014, http://www.nytimes.com/2014/09/12/opinion/islamists-are-not-our-friends.html. See also Henry Kissinger, *World Order* (New York: Penguin, 2014).

16. Abdel Fattah al-Sissi, "Democracy in the Middle East," U.S. Army War College, March 15, 2006, reprinted in David D. Kirkpatrick, "Sisi's Thesis on Democracy in the Middle East," *New York Times*, May 24, 2014, http://www.nytimes.com/interactive/2014/05/24/world/middleeast/sisi-doc.html.

17. David D. Kirkpatrick, "Sisi's Thesis on Democracy in the Middle East," *New York Times*, May 24, 2014, http://www.nytimes.com/2014/05/25/world/middleeast/egypts-new-autocrat-sisi-knows-best.html.

18. Kissinger, *World Order*, pp. 121–22.

19. Yezid Sayigh, "The Arab Region at Tipping Point," Carnegie Endowment for Middle East Peace, August 21, 2014, http://carnegie-mec.org/2014/08/21/arab-region-at-tipping-point.

20. Faheem Hussain, "Egypt's Liberal Coup," August 13, 2014, https://faheemabdmominhussain.wordpress.com/2014/08/13/egypts-liberal-coup/. A shorter version was published on the Web Site *Open Democracy*: https://www.opendemocracy.net/arab-awakening/faheem-hussain/egypt%27s-liberal-coup.

21. Hamid, *Temptations of Power*.

22. See also Fareed Zakaria, *The Future of Freedom: Illiberal Democracy at Home and Abroad*. (New York: W. W. Norton, 2003).

23. Richard Rose and Doh Chull Shin, "Democratization Backwards: The Problem of Third-Wave Democracies," *British Journal of Political Science* 31 (2001), pp. 331–54, 332.

24. See, for example, Alaa Aswany, Twitter, December 8, 2012, https://twitter.com/AlaaAswany/status/277509957308514304, and Mohamed Elmenshawy, "The Dilemma of Egypt's Future Elections," *Foreign Policy*, August 13, 2013, http://foreignpolicy.com/2013/08/13/the-dilemma-of-egypts-future-elections/.

25. Leon Wieseltier, "Its Name Is Facism,'" *New Republic*, August 15, 2013, http://www.newrepublic.com/article/114328/obamas-inaction-egypt-diminishing-americas-power.

26. Hussain, "Egypt's Liberal Coup."

27. As Mustafa al-Naggar, founder of the Justice Party, explained it to me: "None of us are using the word 'liberalism' because for the Egyptian street 'liberalism' equals disbelief" (Hamid, *Temptations of Power*, p. 17).

28. John Locke, *A Letter Concerning Toleration* (The Hague: Martinus Nijhoff, 1963), available online at http://press-pubs.uchicago.edu/founders/documents/amendI_religions10.html.

29. Ibid.

30. "Madison and Slavery," James Madison's Montpelier, http://www.montpelier.org/research-and-collections/people/african-americans/madison-slavery.

31. Hussain, "Egypt's Liberal Coup."

32. For more on the advantages of parliamentary systems, see Juan J. Linz, "The Perils of Presidentialism," *Journal of Democracy* 1 (1990), Juan J. Linz and Arturo Valenzuela, *The Failure of Presidential Democracy: Comparative Perspectives*, volume 1 (Baltimore: Johns Hopkins University Press, 1994). For more on the advantages of *consensual* parliamentary systems, see Arend Lijphart, *Thinking about Democracy: Power Sharing and Majority Rule in Theory and Practice* (New York: Routledge, 2008). For other perspectives, including on different kinds of presidential regimes, see Scott Mainwaring and Matthew Soberg Shugart, *Presidentialism and Democracy in Latin America* (Cambridge: Cambridge University Press, 1997).

33. Alicia L. Bannon, "Designing a Constitution-Drafting Process: Lessons from Kenya," *Yale Law Journal* 116 (2007).
34. Vivien Hart, "Democratic Constitution Making," United States Institute of Peace, July 2003, pp. 2–3, 3, http://www.usip.org/sites/default /files/resources/sr107.pdf.
35. Ibid., pp. 5, 12.
36. Bannon, "Designing a Constitution-Drafting Process," p. 1842.
37. Ibid., p. 1846, 1848.
38. Jamal Benomar, "Constitution-Making after Conflict: Lessons for Iraq," *Journal of Democracy* 15 (2004), p. 88; "A Bill of Rights for a New South Africa," African National Congress, February 1993, http://www.anc.org .za/show.php?id=231.
39. For a discussion of liberalism's nonneutrality, see Stanley Fish, "Mission Impossible: Settling the Just Bounds between Church and State," *Columbia Law Review* 97 (1997), p. 2266, and Lenn Goodman, "The Road to Kazanistan," *American Philosophical Quarterly* 45 (2008), p. 85.
40. Fish, "Mission Impossible," p. 2256.

INDEX